Katherine Mansfield and the
Origins of Modernist Fiction

By the same author:

*Feminine Consciousness in the Modern British Novel*

# Katherine Mansfield and the Origins of Modernist Fiction

*Sydney Janet Kaplan

*Cornell University Press*

Ithaca and London

Copyright © 1991 by Cornell University

All rights reserved. Except for brief quotations in a review, this book, or parts thereof, must not be reproduced in any form without permission in writing from the publisher. For information, address Cornell University Press, 124 Roberts Place, Ithaca, New York 14850.

First published 1991 by Cornell University Press


International Standard Book Number 0-8014-2328-7 (cloth)
International Standard Book Number 0-8014-9915-1 (paper)
Library of Congress Catalog Card Number 90-45880
Printed in the United States of America
*Librarians: Library of Congress cataloging information*
*appears on the last page of the book.*


⊛The paper in this book meets the minimum requirements
of the American National Standard for Information Sciences—
Permanence of Paper for Printed Library Materials, ANSI Z39.48-1984.

*For Linda Bierds*

# Contents

# Acknowledgments

**B**rief portions of this book have appeared in different versions in *Women's Language and Style: Studies in Contemporary Language* 1 (1978), ed. Edmund L. Epstein and Douglas R. Butturff; *The Cream City Review* 13 (Winter 1989); and *The Women's Review of Books* 5 (July 1988). Chapter 5, "'A Gigantic Mother': Mansfield and the City," appeared in a different form in *Women Writers and the City*, ed. Susan M. Squier, copyright © 1984 by the University of Tennessee Press; used by permission.

I am grateful also to the following: Oxford University Press (New Zealand) for permission to quote from *Poems of Katherine Mansfield*, ed. Vincent O'Sullivan, and from *The Urewera Notebook*, ed. Ian Gordon; J. E. Traue, Chief Librarian at the Alexander Turnbull Library in Wellington, New Zealand, for permission to quote passages from Mansfield's manuscripts published in *The Turnbull Library Record*; Alfred A. Knopf, Inc., for permission to reprint portions of *The Short Stories of Katherine Mansfield*, *The Journal of Katherine Mansfield*, *Katherine Mansfield's Letters to John Middleton Murry*, *The Letters of Katherine Mansfield*, and *Novels and Novelists* by Katherine Mansfield; Oxford University Press for permission to quote from *The Collected Letters of Katherine Mansfield*, vols. I–II, ed. Vincent O'Sullivan and Margaret Scott, 1984, 1987, and from *Katherine Mansfield: Selected Letters*, ed. Vincent O'Sullivan, 1989; The Hogarth Press, Ltd., for permission to quote from *The Diary of Virginia Woolf*, vol. I; *The Letters of Virginia Woolf*, vol. II; *The Common Reader, First Series; Contemporary Writers;* and *Mrs. Dalloway;* Harcourt Brace Jovanovich, Inc., for permission to quote from

# Acknowledgments

the following: *The Diary of Virginia Woolf, vol. I, 1915–1919*, ed. Anne Olivier Bell, copyright © 1977 by Quentin Bell and Angelica Garnett; *The Letters of Virginia Woolf, vol. II, 1912–1922*, ed. Nigel Nicolson and Joanne Trautmann, copyright © 1976 by Quentin Bell and Angelica Garnett; *Mrs. Dalloway*, by Virginia Woolf, copyright 1925 by Harcourt Brace Jovanovich, Inc., and renewed 1953 by Leonard Woolf; *Contemporary Writers* by Virginia Woolf, copyright 1965 by Leonard Woolf; *The Common Reader* by Virginia Woolf, copyright 1925 by Harcourt Brace Jovanovich, Inc., and renewed 1953 by Leonard Woolf.

I thank the University of Washington for two professional leaves for the research and writing of this book; the University of Washington Graduate School Research Fund for a grant to study the Mansfield papers at the Alexander Turnbull Library in Wellington, New Zealand; and the staff of the Alexander Turnbull Library for their friendly assistance. I am especially indebted to Margaret Scott and Vincent O'Sullivan for their kindness to me when I was in New Zealand. I will always remember their taking me on a delightful drive around Wellington, Karori, and Days Bay to see the locations of Mansfield's stories.

I also thank Bernhard Kendler, my editor at Cornell University Press, for his interest in and support of this project; Elizabeth Holmes and Kay Scheuer for copy editing; Beverly Wessel for her help with many of the details of manuscript preparation; the staff of the University of Washington Library—in particular, David Fraley and Cynthia Fugate; Molly Hite for her encouragement and for her wit; Sara van den Berg for her knowledge of Freudian theory; and my colleagues in the Women Studies Program and the Feminist Colloquium for providing an ongoing forum for discussion of feminist theory, which led, indirectly, to my investigation of several topics in this book. Finally, I owe special thanks to Linda Bierds, to whom this book is dedicated, for her research assistance in New Zealand and for the astute editorial suggestions that arose from her own poetic sensibility; and to my son, Frederick Kaplan, for his repeated urging that I complete this book. During the course of its development, he grew from boy to man.

S. J. K.

*Seattle, Washington*

Katherine Mansfield and the
Origins of Modernist Fiction

# ও I

# Introduction

T his book explores the role of Katherine Mansfield (1888–1923) in the development of British modernism. Through her critical writings as well as her brilliant innovations in fiction, she influenced, reflected, and conveyed modernist aesthetic principles. Although not a systematic theorist, Katherine Mansfield belongs with Virginia Woolf at the very core of British modernism. In terms of her influence on the development of modernist fiction, Mansfield's transformative effect has been as decisive as that of any modernist writer of prose. As Ian Gordon once remarked: "She had the same kind of directive influence on the art of the short story as Joyce had on the novel. After Joyce and Katherine Mansfield neither the novel nor the short story can ever be quite the same again."[1]

To insist on Mansfield's significance to the development of modernist fiction might surprise some of the current revisionary critics of modernism, who have nearly erased her from the history of the movement, but it would not have surprised critics during the 1920s or 1930s, when Mansfield was widely imitated, discussed, and revered.[2] In 1934, for example, T. S. Eliot selected Mansfield's "Bliss"

[1]Ian A. Gordon, *Katherine Mansfield*, British Writers and Their Work, no. 3 (Lincoln: University of Nebraska Press, 1964), p. 105.

[2]The recent burgeoning of studies on the evolution of modernism reflects considerable concern over defining the movement's boundaries, philosophical and political antecedents, and canonized adherents. The following are only a few examples of the many such books on modernism from which the contributions of Katherine Mansfield are excluded: Michael Levenson, *A Genealogy of Modernism: A Study of English Literary Doctrine 1908–1922* (Cambridge: Cambridge University Press,

as an illustration of the dominant experimental tendency of contemporary fiction,[3] and two years later Willa Cather praised her capacity "to throw a luminous streak out into the shadowy realm of personal relationships."[4]

Although feminist criticism has produced a vast number of studies about the life and work of Virginia Woolf, it has devoted far less attention to Katherine Mansfield.[5] Mansfield's contributions to the

---

1984); Louis Menand, *Discovering Modernism: T. S. Eliot and His Context* (New York: Oxford University Press, 1987); Ricardo J. Quinones, *Mapping Literary Modernism: Time and Development* (Princeton: Princeton University Press, 1985); and Sanford Schwartz, *The Matrix of Modernism: Pound, Eliot, and Early Twentieth-Century Thought* (Princeton: Princeton University Press, 1985). Hugh Kenner briefly mentions her only to undercut her significance by criticizing John Middleton Murry's devotion to her career and by choosing to quote only from critics who were "shrewd about her limitations." See *A Sinking Island: The Modern English Writers* (London: Barrie & Jenkins, 1988), pp. 158–59.

[3]Eliot's appreciation of Mansfield is ambivalent, however. Although he discusses "three contemporary short stories, all of very great merit," linking Mansfield's "Bliss" to Lawrence's "The Shadow in the Rose Garden" and Joyce's "The Dead," he notes that "the moral implication [of "Bliss"] is negligible. . . . We are given neither comment nor suggestion of any moral issue of good and evil, and within the setting this is quite right. The story is limited to this sudden change of feeling, and the moral and social ramifications are outside of the terms of reference. As the material is limited in this way—and indeed our satisfaction recognises the skill with which the author has handled perfectly the *minimum* material—it is what I believe would be called feminine." T. S. Eliot, *After Strange Gods* (New York: Harcourt, Brace, 1934), p. 38.

[4]Willa Cather, *Not under Forty* (New York: Knopf, 1936), p. 135. Mansfield's transformation of the short-story genre influenced the work of many twentieth-century writers, including Elizabeth Bowen, Conrad Aiken, Dorothy Parker, Eudora Welty, and Carson McCullers. See for example, Katherine Anne Porter, "The Art of Katherine Mansfield" (1937), in *The Days Before* (New York: Harcourt, Brace, 1952), pp. 82–87.

[5]The only book-length critical study of Mansfield from a declaredly feminist perspective is Kate Fullbrook, *Katherine Mansfield* (Bloomington: Indiana University Press, 1986). Mansfield receives only limited attention in Sandra M. Gilbert and Susan Gubar's *No Man's Land: The Place of the Woman Writer in the Twentieth Century, vol. I: The War of the Words; vol. II: Sexchanges* (New Haven: Yale University Press, 1988, 1989). She is not included (except in passing) among the authors discussed in the essays collected in *The Female Imagination and the Modernist Aesthetic*, ed. Sandra M. Gilbert and Susan Gubar (New York: Gordon and Breach, 1986); or in Gillian Hanscombe and Virginia L. Smyers, *Writing for Their Lives: The Modernist Women 1910–1940* (London: The Women's Press, 1987). I was surprised to discover her absence from *Women's Writing in Exile*, ed. Mary Lynn Broe and Angela Ingram (Chapel Hill: University of North Carolina Press, 1989), which considers a large number of other female modernists such as H. D., Rhys, Stein, and Barnes in terms of the experience of exile or expatriation, a subject about which Mansfield knew as much as anyone. Since Mansfield's "exile" took place in England rather than France,

development of modern fiction have been largely taken for granted. Her innovations in the short-fiction genre (especially the "plotless" story, the incorporation of the "stream of consciousness" into the content of fiction, and the emphasis on the psychological "moment") preceded Virginia Woolf's use of them, and they have been absorbed and assimilated—often unconsciously—by writers and readers of the short story. Mansfield never became one of the "lost" or "neglected" women writers needing rehabilitation by feminist critics. Unlike some of the female modernists who are currently being reclaimed by feminist scholars—writers whose highly experimental work was published by small presses and avant-garde journals and never reached a large public readership—Mansfield developed a huge following, which began to take on the features of a cult by the 1930s.[6] Although this mass popularity subsided, even during the '40s and '50s she retained a "respectable" critical reputation. Her stories were included in most college anthologies of fiction; if anything, Mansfield was the anthologist's "token" woman. Her frequent use of irony and her insistence on organic unity in fiction made her writing especially amenable to the methods of the New Critics. That scrutiny ensured the continuity of her reputation, but also guaranteed that her work would be treated in isolation from its social, political, and historical contexts.

The initial problem for feminist criticism was to rescue Mansfield from everyone's assumed familiarity with her. She needed also to be rescued from years of popular legend: the well-known portrait of the artist as Camille. This latter problem was compounded by her husband's role in creating that legend. After her death John Middleton Murry began to devote a large part of his own career to the editing of her work. He brought out unfinished stories she had never intended for publication; he organized her letters; and he created the document that had the greatest critical influence: *Journal of Katherine Mansfield*.[7] Murry also wrote many articles—actually

---

she is not discussed in Shari Benstock's revisionary study of modernist women: *Women of the Left Bank: Paris, 1900–1940* (Austin: University of Texas Press, 1986).

[6]Mansfield was especially admired by French readers. See Christiane Mortelier, "The Genesis and Development of the Katherine Mansfield Legend in France," *Journal of the Australasian Universities Language and Literature Associations* 34 (November 1970), 252–63.

[7]John Middleton Murry, ed., *Journal of Katherine Mansfield* (London: Constable, 1954); hereafter cited in the text as *Journal*. Murry first published the journal in 1927;

testimonials—about their relationship, and allowed these to become sentimental, maudlin, and finally untrustworthy as portraits of a real woman.[8] Claire Tomalin pointedly remarks that "unable to control her while she lived, Murry could not resist manipulating her after her death to fit the pattern he preferred."[9]

The publication at the end of the 1970s of two fully researched biographies of Mansfield by Antony Alpers and Jeffrey Meyers altered Murry's portrait of her, revealing her complex and avant-garde life-style, her nonconforming sexuality, and the difficulties in her relationship with Murry.[10] These books changed the popular conception of Mansfield, but their interpretations of many details of her life seemed to call out for feminist analysis. Claire Tomalin's more recent biography is a start in the right direction. Although Tomalin does not articulate her analysis of Katherine Mansfield's life in terms of feminist theory, she does center it in her own identification with Mansfield as a woman, and draws attention to the changes in women's status at the time of Mansfield's entry into the literary world.

Katherine Mansfield was born on October 14, 1888, in Wellington, New Zealand. As the third daughter in a family of four girls and one boy, Kathleen Mansfield Beauchamp (who later altered that name to create her pen name) had a comfortable, privileged childhood. Her father was a powerful figure in Wellington, a self-made man who left school at fourteen and eventually became the director of the Bank of New Zealand. Her parents had the foresight—even if it was mainly for social rather than philosophical reasons—to ensure

---

the 1954 edition is what he called the "definitive edition," although a comparison with the original notebooks in the Alexander Turnbull Library in Wellington makes it clear how much he left out or rearranged. For discussions of Murry's editing of Mansfield's papers, see Gordon, pp. 117–20; and Philip Waldron, "Katherine Mansfield's *Journal*," *Twentieth Century Literature* 20 (January 1974), 11–18.

[8]Jeffrey Meyers, one of Mansfield's biographers, believes that "Murry's guilt about his selfish and irresponsible treatment of Katherine led directly to the egoistic enshrinement of his wife." See "Murry's Cult of Mansfield," *Journal of Modern Literature* 7 (February 1979), 16.

[9]Claire Tomalin, *Katherine Mansfield: A Secret Life* (New York: Knopf, 1988), p. 242.

[10]Jeffrey Meyers, *Katherine Mansfield: A Biography* (New York: New Directions, 1978); Antony Alpers, *The Life of Katherine Mansfield* (New York: Viking, 1980). Alpers's book is a complete revision of his earlier study, *Katherine Mansfield: A Biography* (New York: Knopf, 1954).

that their daughters were properly educated. Kathleen and her two older sisters were sent to London in 1903 to attend Queen's College, an advanced institution for the education of young women. After three years in London, the Beauchamp sisters returned to New Zealand, but Kathleen was determined to escape from the restrictions of family, colonial life, and bourgeois social conventions. She wanted an artistic career and knew that she needed to be in London to achieve it. She returned to London in 1908, setting out with a small allowance from her father, to attempt to establish herself as a writer. She had some early successes—stories published in the leading journal, *The New Age*, and her first book, *In a German Pension*, in 1911—and then two later collections, *Bliss and Other Stories* (1920) and *The Garden Party and Other Stories* (1922). Other collections of stories, her letters, and the *Journal of Katherine Mansfield* were published posthumously. After a turbulent period of experimentation and upheaval in her personal life, Mansfield settled into a long relationship with the critic John Middleton Murry. They married in 1918. Their relationship was intense and filled with conflict, and they spent long periods apart, especially in the last years when Mansfield went abroad in search of a climate that would not exacerbate her advancing illness. Katherine Mansfield's life was productive, eventful, and short—tragically short. She died of tuberculosis in 1923, when she was only thirty-four years old.

I do not intend here to write another biography of Mansfield, although I do consider her intellectual and sexual development, especially the ways in which her own personal evolution relates to more general experiences of women writers of her time. Although biography can reveal how the impetus for her own innovations came out of a desperate attempt to understand, sort out, and make manageable socially unacceptable impulses and desires, psychoanalytic interpretations by themselves are not enough to account for that impetus.[11] Neither should we assume that Mansfield's innovations are attributable primarily to literary influence. Many of the most revolutionary innovations employed in her short fiction occurred even earlier than in the works of her contemporaries. It is _ necessary to demonstrate how her stylistic evolution ultimately de-

[11]For a perceptive, well-grounded psychoanalytic reading of Mansfield's work see C. A. Hankin, *Katherine Mansfield and Her Confessional Stories* (London: Macmillan, 1983).

rived from a social change in which she found herself at the very center: the rise in women's expectations and the alterations in their roles in society during the first decades of the twentieth century.

It has long been my view that the traditional definitions of modernism are flawed because they cancel out the significant efforts of women.[12] I believe that contrary to traditional definitions of the period, women are at the center rather than the margins of British modernism, and this is no less the case with Katherine Mansfield than it is with Virginia Woolf. Seen through the lenses of women's experiences, the very shape of this period's concerns must change. Women's attempts to discover new methods for conveying their reality coincided with men's attempts to discover new methods for conveying their own unease over crumbling certainties of gender roles.

The attempt to define modernism continues to occupy theorists; and articles, books, and MLA papers on the subject abound. Some of the definitions are contradictory, some enlarge or contract the movement's chronology or its geography, yet it is possible to highlight several developments in the late nineteenth century which affected almost all the writers of this period—either as ideological issues to be incorporated into their work or as social factors to which they needed to respond. Although this is not the place to retell in detail the story of the development of modernism—that combination of revolt against Victorian fathers, recognition of the artist's alienation, pursuit of the contemporary in language, psychology and behavior, creation of dynamic original forms in which to contain a newly awakened sense of present reality—it is still necessary to restate the fact that until recently the academic critical tradition generally ignored the presence, let alone the overwhelming significance, of women writers—*as women*—in the creation of the movement.[13] The crucial, the vital link

[12]My interest in Katherine Mansfield follows from my investigation of the roles of women writers during the modernist period which I began in *Feminine Consciousness in the Modern British Novel* (Urbana: University of Illinois Press, 1975).

[13]The neglect of women writers in nonfeminist books on modernism continues, unfortunately, as Daniel Pearlman notes in his review of new books on modernism in *Contemporary Literature* 28 (Fall 1987), 403: "I find it worth mentioning that there is little consideration given to the role of women in the development of modernism in any of these works except the reasonable amount of attention bestowed on Virginia Woolf by Quinones and Karl. Not even the vast scope of Karl's work, however, finds room for much more than footnoted acknowledgment of contributions by other female moderns—e.g. Gertrude Stein, Isadora Duncan, Frida Kahlo. One suspects that such figures had a larger influence than is suggested."

between experimentation and the need to express a definite sense of *women's* reality either went unnoticed or was patronizingly trivialized—or even willfully denied—by such critics. Fortunately, since about 1970 feminist critics have begun to understand how determinedly, how often painfully, these writers worked at inventing new ways of shaping language or structuring reality in order to communicate experiences and feelings their inherited masculine culture would neither accept nor allow.[14] A number of critics have started to delineate the shape of what some of them call "female modernism," a project larger than the one I have undertaken here, and one with its own inherent problems, but of obvious relevance to my work on Katherine Mansfield.[15]

The distortion of our understanding of the modernist period has been intensified further by the long-standing critical tendency to look at the period as if it were all of a piece, and to equate modernism itself with its later, conservative, antidemocratic formulations. Michael Levenson's book *A Genealogy of Modernism* is very helpful in correcting that tendency by its careful delineation of the chronology of the movement—or rather, one strand of the movement. (He does not mention Mansfield in his book, which focuses entirely on the line of modernism descending from Conrad, Hulme, and Ford to Pound and Eliot.) Levenson insists that "modernism was individualist before it was anti-individualist, anti-traditional before it was traditional, inclined to anarchism before it was inclined to authoritarianism."[16] Mansfield's development shares many features of the early formulation without its hidden seeds of reaction.

[14]The relationship between modernist experimentation and women writers' specific use of it for the deconstruction of dominant ideologies of gender is the subject of Rachel Blau DuPlessis, *Writing beyond the Ending: Narrative Strategies of Twentieth-Century Women Writers* (Bloomington: Indiana University Press, 1985).

[15]On some of the difficulties of defining a female modernism, see Shari Benstock, "Beyond the Reaches of Feminist Criticism: A Letter from Paris," *Tulsa Studies in Women's Literature* 3 (Spring–Fall 1984), 5–27. Benstock questions the possible emergence of "a hierarchy of women authors" in the attempt to establish a canon of female modernists. Celeste M. Schenck, in Broe and Ingram, *Women's Writing in Exile,* cautions that in the attempt to undo the marginalization of women in modernism, feminist critics "may inadvertently erect a complementary Modernist canon to the one already in place" ("Exiled by Genre: Modernism, Canonicity, and the Politics of Exclusion," p. 245). As an indication of the diverse interest in the subject of women and modernism, see the issue "Toward a Gendered Modernity," *Tulsa Studies in Women's Literature* 8 (Spring 1989), particularly Marianne DeKoven, "Gendered Doubleness and the 'Origins' of Modernist Form," pp. 19–42.

[16]Levenson, p. 79.

Levenson says that "English modernism achieved its decisive formulation in the early twenties—not only because of legitimizing masterworks such as *Ulysses* or *The Waste Land* but because there developed a rhetorically effective doctrine to explain and justify that body of work. For this rhetoric and doctrine Eliot was in large measure responsible."[17] My argument is that the "rhetoric and doctrine" of the Eliot formulation (traced by Levenson through interactions with Ford, Hulme, and Pound) produced the hegemonic definition of modernism, whereas the submerged voice in this formulation is the female, which achieves "its decisive formulation in the [mid- to late] twenties—not only because of legitimizing masterworks such as [*Pilgrimage*, "Prelude," or *To the Lighthouse*] but because there developed a rhetorically effective doctrine to explain and justify that body of work. For this rhetoric and doctrine [Woolf] was in large measure responsible."

If the names are changed in this way, the reading of modernism shifts dramatically.[18] Emerging out of a caldron of nineteenth-century problems, influences, and arguments, as Woolf remarked in "Modern Fiction," "the accent falls differently from of old."[19] Although some of the influential characters in the story are the same (Pater, Symons, Bergson, the James brothers), others make a greater impact on the women than on the men: George Eliot, the Brontës, Olive Schreiner, the '90s writers of *The Yellow Book*, as well as theorists and activists of the women's movement. Instead of Ford, Hulme, Pound, and Eliot, we can talk about May Sinclair, Dorothy Richardson, Katherine Mansfield, and Virginia Woolf.

But there is a disparity in these two strands of development, and it conforms to Elaine Showalter's description of how "women's cul-

[17]Ibid., p. 219.

[18]I should mention here that my rewording of Levenson's outline of modernist development is a rhetorical strategy only, and not an attempt to construct an alternative female modernist canon that would encapsulate hierarchical principles of ordering. My emphasis on Woolf's consolidation of the discoveries of her predecessors and contemporaries is due to her dominant influence in the later emergence of an Anglo-American feminist literary project grounded in the insights of *A Room of One's Own*, which, as Jane Marcus has suggested, "is the first modern text of feminist criticism, the model in both theory and practice, of a specifically socialist feminist criticism" ("Still Practice, A/Wrested Alphabet: Toward a Feminist Aesthetic," *Tulsa Studies in Women's Literature* 3 [Spring/Fall 1984], 79).

[19]Virginia Woolf, "Modern Fiction," *The Common Reader: First Series* (New York: Harcourt, Brace & World, 1925), p. 154.

ture forms a collective experience within the cultural whole."[20] Her use of Edwin Ardener's model of dominant and muted groups is especially illuminating when applied to the condition of middle-class women in the early twentieth century. While the modernist women writers shared in the knowledge of the men's line of intel-lectual development (reading, in general, many of the same works that reflected the nineteenth-century critical heritage), they also ex-perienced their own immersion in a submerged area, a tradition of women's writings and an experience of a "women's culture" apart from as well as simultaneous with the one shared with men. But as in any supposedly binary opposition, the two worlds cannot be said to be really parallel. Because of the dominance of the patriarchy, the women acknowledge their inheritance from the fathers, but speak among themselves about their inheritance from the mothers; the men acknowledge only their inheritance from the fathers. Mothers represent what must be escaped from. (The reader should note that Levenson's "genealogy" is strictly that of the male line. It is as if there were *no* mothers.[21]) Consequently, I want to argue that the modernism emerging from the women's line is fuller, more com-plex than the male modernism and now, in retrospect, more rele-vant to our own cultural predicament in this last part of that same century they entered with awakening consciousness.

Undoubtedly, any attempt to analyze Mansfield's significance must be grounded in theoretical considerations of gender and re-sponsive to the question of the meaning of sexuality itself in her writings. Her attempts to experiment with sexuality in her own life and the creative results of such experimentation need to be explored in relation to theories about the construction of gender and about sexuality as an organizing principle in the unconscious aesthetics that structured her works.

[20]Elaine Showalter, "Feminist Criticism in the Wilderness," *Critical Inquiry* 8 (Winter 1981), 197.

[21]For a discussion of the rejection of the mother in modernist fiction (a discussion noteworthy for its absence of any acknowledgment of feminist theories on this subject), see Quinones, pp. 54–57. Quinones remarks that "rather than needing to liberate themselves from their fathers—an all-too-easy task, in most cases—the real problem for many of the Modernists was to achieve freedom from the mother" (p. 55) because "the mother has become for Modernism the voice of submission to that which is conventionally social, to the larger general processes of life, foremost among which, for her, is the procreative" (p. 56).

I find that missing from most of the canonical studies of modernism are not only discussions of the roles of women, but also an awareness of how sexual practices and their encodings mark the structure and texture of modernist writing as a whole.[22] Anxiety over definitions of acceptable sexuality permeates the literature of the period, from Eliot's Tiresias figure, to Hemingway's exaggerated codes of masculinity, to the emphasis on the nonorganic, hard, geometric art forms admired by Hulme, and so on. Oscar Wilde's cultural dominance in the late nineteenth century and the symbolic links among decadence, the figure of the dandy, and homosexual practices are rejected in various ways by male modernist writers. Lawrence's emphasis on a new version of male bonding also opposes that Wildean view of experience and artistic creation.[23] But Wilde's effect on Mansfield was far-reaching and profound, as I suggest in the next chapter.

Although a good part of Katherine Mansfield's impetus toward a new genre of short fiction reflects a need to express a specifically female vision that could not be incorporated into the traditional structure she had inherited, it would be a mistake to consider it an entirely conscious program on her part. If anything, she strove to separate herself from any definition as a feminist theorist. Except for brief periods in late adolescence and during her involvement in her early twenties with *The New Age*, she neither allied herself with the suffrage movement nor studied the ideology of feminism. In fact, unlike those of Virginia Woolf, Mansfield's critical essays and personal letters curiously lack much discussion of women's role in literature, although she reviews many books by women. She would never proceed like Dorothy Richardson, for example, who insisted on creating what she called "a feminine equivalent for the current masculine realism."[24] Nor would she ever go as far as Virginia Woolf with theories about women and fiction such as those in *A Room of One's Own*. Nevertheless, it is clear to me that Mansfield's personal struggles, as well as her insights into the lives of women,

---

[22]Gilbert and Gubar take up this question in considerable detail in *No Man's Land*.

[23]A fascinating study of the dynamics of men's relationships in the literature preceding the modernist period is that of Eve Kosofsky Sedgwick, *Between Men: English Literature and Male Homosocial Desire* (New York: Columbia University Press, 1985).

[24]Dorothy M. Richardson, "Foreword" to *Pilgrimage*, vol. 1 (New York: Knopf, 1967), p. 9.

were the efforts of an emerging feminist consciousness no matter what terms of definition for her own awareness she might have chosen. As Kate Fullbrook suggests, "Katherine Mansfield's feminism came as a matter of course, so much so that overt discussion of it as a political principle is absent from her writing while its underlying presence is everywhere."[25]

Although the "rhetoric and doctrine" of a women's line of British modernism may have been consolidated by Woolf, Mansfield's contribution to the literary revolution Woolf articulated should not be underestimated. Although she was six years younger than Woolf, Mansfield was, if anything, the more innovative writer at the beginning of their friendship. In a letter in August 1917, Katherine Mansfield wrote: "We have got the same job, Virginia, & it is really very curious & thrilling that we should both, quite apart from each other, be after so very nearly the same thing. We are, you know; there's no denying it."[26] Unfortunately, we don't know Woolf's answer as it seems that most of her letters to Mansfield have not survived,[27] but clearly the dialogue continued, for three years later Mansfield wrote to Woolf: "You are the only woman with whom I long to talk *work*. There will never be another."[28] What these and other letters suggest is a continuing discussion about writing and women, about the struggle to discover new methods, to discard old certainties.

While Mansfield was less programmatic than Woolf or Richardson, she was, nonetheless, experimenting with techniques for probing "feminine consciousness" earlier than either of them. (In fact, of the female modernists, only Gertrude Stein was writing experimental fiction before Katherine Mansfield.) By 1908 in "The Tiredness of Rosabel," Mansfield was working with states of consciousness as a way of giving shape and depth to a short story. That story, centered in Rosabel's mind, moves back and forth in time through Rosabel's own fantasies and reflections, but what is most significant

[25]Fullbrook, p. 22.

[26]Vincent O'Sullivan and Margaret Scott, eds., *The Collected Letters of Katherine Mansfield*, vol. I (Oxford: Clarendon, 1984), p. 327; this book and vol. 2 (1987) hereafter cited in text as *Letters* I or II.

[27]Nigel Nicolson and Joanne Trautmann, eds., *The Letters of Virginia Woolf*, vol. II (New York: Harcourt Brace Jovanovich, 1976), p. 449. The editors include the one available letter of Woolf to Mansfield, and mention in a footnote that only one other letter is known to survive.

[28]"Fifteen Letters from Katherine Mansfield to Virginia Woolf," *Adam International Review* nos. 370–75 (1972–73), 24.

about that earliest story told completely from "within" is its attempt to describe a *woman's* consciousness. Mansfield's comment to Woolf after reading a draft of *Kew Gardens,* that they were "after so very nearly the same thing," reflects her awareness that Woolf was now ready to attempt a similar plunge into experimentation.

Although Mansfield and Woolf were drawn together by their mutual interest in writing and in women, their feminism had developed along separate lines because of significant differences in experience, education, and class. From the beginning of her career Mansfield chose to ally herself with other writers excluded from the establishment. Her association with A. R. Orage, Beatrice Hastings, and the rest of the iconoclastic group who produced *The New Age*, beginning in 1909, situated her entry into the literary world with that of other newcomers to the intelligentsia. Wallace Martin mentions how *The New Age* attracted those who were brought into the reading public by increased access to education, but who became "aware of the disparity between their abilities and their opportunities, and painfully conscious of the necessity to increase their knowledge if they wished to improve their status and, more important, change the society that had produced it."[29] Although Mansfield's break with her bourgeois, colonial background was not total, years of living on the edge financially would effectively link her with many of the attitudes and values of bohemia—by necessity if not always by conviction. She was attracted to the sense of security she noted in the lives of Virginia Woolf and other members of Bloomsbury, but she remained always an outsider to a considerable extent. Her satirical portraits of well-to-do pseudo-bohemians (such as Bertha and her friends in "Bliss," the group of artist-parasites around Isabel in "Marriage à la Mode," the parents and party guests in "Sun and Moon," and the "literary gentleman" in "Life of Ma Parker") all reflect her persistent awareness of exclusion.

Her own background—an upwardly mobile, newly rich colonial family—gave her no prestige among the English intellectuals. She could not claim connections with the comfortable world of the academic and artistic establishment; neither could she gain admiring, if condescending, praise from the left-wing bourgeoisie, who might

[29]Wallace Martin, *The New Age under Orage: Chapters in English Cultural History* (New York: Barnes & Noble, 1967), p. 7.

have adored her if she had risen from the working classes. (Lawrence had the advantage here.) Mansfield's background was thus tainted with "money" and "trade," while her revolt against it left her without money and without "connections."

Her long-term alliance with John Middleton Murry, then, can be seen in relation to class as well as to artistic revolt. Murry was born into an impoverished—but notably, an unglamorously impoverished—family. His father was a poor clerk (perhaps similar to Leonard Bast in Forster's *Howards End*) who had struggled to enter the middle class. Murry's own revolt against family was to resist pressures to finish his education at Oxford (secured by his own relentless hard work since early childhood, paid for by scholarships and his father's overwork). His decision to quit Oxford shortly before he would have taken his degree in order to pursue a literary career—the substitution of art for academic respectability—came about largely through the influence of Mansfield, who urged him to reject security in the name of personal integrity. The resulting Mansfield-Murry collaboration on the production of the new journal *Rhythm* ultimately brought them into intimate contact with D. H. Lawrence, an artist significantly alienated from the English establishment.

In a certain respect, Mansfield's own "modernity" began in childhood. Unlike Woolf, who was cloistered in her parents' Victorian household, educated by tutors or her parents, not exposed to the complex social/pedagogical flavor of the classroom, Mansfield had an upbringing more familiar to late-twentieth-century readers, especially to white, middle-class Americans. In spite of a gloss of newly arrived wealth, the Beauchamp family was organized around rather typical conventions of bourgeois family life. The children were not raised by servants; they attended, at least for a while, a local school (which provided the details of social hierarchy on a small scale that make the late story "The Doll's House" [1921] so devastating, with its revelation of children's cruelty toward outsiders).

Narrow and self-satisfied as Mansfield assumed New Zealand to be, it afforded her some advantages that Woolf had never enjoyed. Suffrage for women was already achieved in New Zealand by 1893; thus Mansfield spent her youth in an environment in which it was assumed that women might participate in the political process. The intensity of the feminist debate as Woolf would have known it was missing from her adolescent experience.[30] As a pioneer society, New Zealand was less bound to tradition in important respects. I say "less bound," for European concepts of cultural superiority certainly remained dominant. As a self-made man, Mansfield's father, Harold Beauchamp, was representative of a new class of people who were moving rapidly up the scale toward wealth and an affected gentility. The family's snobbery (best illustrated by such stories as "The Doll's House" and "The Garden-Party") reveals the thinness of its social veneer; a status so recently achieved had to be differentiated by innumerable material markers.

One determining factor for Mansfield was her family's belief in the value of women's education. Perhaps it was her parents' understanding that so steep a rise in social prominence as their own would no longer be possible for their descendants in a more settled society. Education was equated with social refinement, with being "modern," and being modern was useful to a developing economy. Mansfield attended several schools, including a girls' school and later, as we have seen, a famous college for women in London, where she was educated by intelligent women who struggled to instill in their pupils a belief in the value of education.[31] Consequently, her formal education (which introduced her to late nineteenth-century avant-garde literature in addition to the traditional canon) propelled her toward modernism more rapidly than Woolf's, and it also gave her a more secure sense of women's intellectual achievements and possibilities.

The differences between Mansfield's "Prelude" and Woolf's *To the Lighthouse* are instructive in this respect. Stanley Burnell, patterned after Harold Beauchamp, is not Mr. Ramsay (patterned after Leslie Stephen), in spite of their authority as the heads of their

---

[30]Not that genuine equality had been achieved in New Zealand as a result of the awarding of suffrage, rather that the concentrated focus on the single issue of the vote was eliminated.

[31]In 1899, at the year's end prize-giving ceremony at school, the Chief Justice of New Zealand, Sir Robert Stout, gave an address called "Higher Education for Women." It impressed Harold Beauchamp and certainly had no little effect on his willingness to send his daughters abroad to complete their education. See Alpers, *The Life of Katherine Mansfield,* p. 18. See also the description of Stout's address in Ruth Elvish Mantz and J. Middleton Murry, *The Life of Katherine Mansfield* (London: Constable, 1933), p. 137.

families. The businessman is quite another figure than the establishment scholar, the philosopher ensconced in tradition. The weight of
the phallocentric intellectual tradition` represented by Leslie Ste-
phen's authority and knowledge (symbolized by his extensive library, which provided Woolf with the major part of her education)
was totally unknown to Katherine Mansfield. If anything, she—and
I mean by that, a very young "she" indeed—was the sole representative of cultural tradition in her family. Woolf had to spend
years overcoming the ways the patriarchal inheritance limited her
self-confidence. She was at times overburdened by her awareness of
women's exclusion from that tradition, and felt divided by her need
to be both included and separate from it.

Mansfield, on the contrary, believed that she had no intellectual
equals in her family or in their social circle. This belief may account
for the self-confidence visible throughout her letters and notebooks.
She could make fun of her parents' philistinism and enjoy her own
sense of superiority. Her poorly educated parents recognized the
value of education for their children in terms of social prestige and
refinement, if pragmatically with an eye to finding them "good"
husbands. Mansfield never had to feel intellectually inadequate beside her father. There are definite advantages for a writer who is not
threatened by the authority of tradition. Mansfield did not have to
undo Victorian conventions about the passivity of women as em-
bodiments of spirit rather than mind, even if she needed to fight
against Victorian bourgeois conceptions of women as wives and
mothers foremost. Moreover, that image of women in a pioneer
society veered more toward the practical, the *active*: women as hard-
working, organizing, overseeing managers of households. Linda
Burnell's retreat into passivity in "Prelude" is perceived by others in
the family as aberrant, a symptom of illness.

Mansfield's reaction to the bourgeois spirit represented by her
family was to turn toward an avant-garde European response to the
very capitalist hegemony she recognized in her own father and his
power in society. For her, the pursuit of art was the means to reject
his materialist values; she did not have to reject his *intellectual*
achievements at the same time. Moreover, her heritage from this
newer, less constricted individualistic pursuit of success (as crass as it
may have ŝeemed) was productive in its own way. It spoke for
individualism, assertiveness, innovation—qualities suspect among

upholders of class-bound, hierarchical concepts of order. Of course, like the Americans of her generation who were seeking "culture," she too came to London in search of the imagined depth and richness of a tradition she had had only limited and watered-down versions of, at home. But that tradition in its power and coerciveness was not in her bones, as it was in Virginia Woolf's. For Mansfield it was something to try on, to learn about, to experiment with. Experimentation for her would never have the sense of being a transgression, an assault on the father. How could she transgress, intellectually, against a father who left school at age fourteen? Her own transgressions would be more overtly sexual, and they would be more overtly material as well. She would try to reject the monetary basis of value that obsessed the world of her parents.[32] Yet that obsession with money contained along with it a submerged respect for achievement in any field. Mansfield received encouragement—even if inconsistently—to write and in fact to publish her first attempts at fiction. Her father, in particular, as a businessman without cultural pretensions, still saw some value in "product," no matter what its source.

In some ways we can speak of Katherine Mansfield as a prototype of the "modern" woman in a time of rapid transition. She was more independent than the average woman and her life-style was closer to that of the men in her circle, yet she was punished as a woman for following that very life-style. In her fiction, one can find a feminist critique of women's historical situation. Her fiction also reveals anxiety over changing views of women's sexuality (that is, the loss of more "innocent" notions of romantic friendships, the increasing tendency to interpret sexual identity in medical and/or psychological terms). She did not connect her understanding of alienation and victimization with either a Marxist or a feminist political analysis. (Of course Woolf did not do so either until years after Mansfield's

[32]Mansfield's journal contains evidence of her growing disassociation from her parents' materialist values. For example: "Damn my family! O Heavens, what bores they are! I detest them all heartily. . . . Even when I am alone in my room, they come outside and call to each other, discuss the butcher's orders or the soiled linen and—I feel—wreck my life" (*Journal*, p. 21). In her unpublished novel "Juliet," written when she was seventeen, the father is described as "thoroughly commonplace and commercial" and as having an "undeniable *trade* atmosphere." "The Unpublished Manuscripts of Katherine Mansfield: 'Juliet,'" ed. Margaret Scott, *The Turnbull Library Record* 3 (n.s.) (March 1970), 8.

death.) Mansfield died too early and after undergoing too much personal suffering. She went only so far as to link her own suffering to human suffering in general, although it is no accident that most of the victims in her stories are members of an underclass, whether in terms of economics or in terms of their relative positions within the family structure. She did not articulate her social critique of human suffering in recognizably political terms.

As the title of this book suggests, I see Katherine Mansfield as a writer who articulated a particular kind of modernist aesthetics of fiction and created a dramatically new structure for fiction. I emphasize the word "origins" because I want to explore the initiating moments, the recognitions that exploded previous conceptions of fictional possibilities. Mansfield's emergence as a modernist began in late adolescence, and by her early twenties her style was refined and perfected, reflecting a merging of experimental techniques (symbolism, impressionism, internal monologue, stream of consciousness, cinematic visual effects, etc.) with feminist insights, protest, and self-assertion.

This book is not a chronological study of Mansfield's writing, however, nor is it a "reading" of her major stories.[33] Instead, in the chapters following, I consider Mansfield in relation to a number of issues that seem to me important in discerning the particular nature of women's participation in modernism. These issues range from the question of influence, the problematics of genre, and the encoding of sexuality to the critical debate over impersonality and the struggle for technique. My emphasis throughout is on Mansfield's writing process, on her emergence as a writer. I recognize that in so doing I may be accused of valorizing concepts held suspect by some postmodernists: "personality," "talent," "genius," "individuality." But I refuse to relinquish the significance of "authorship," because

[33]I refer readers to several recent books on Mansfield for developmental and evaluative studies: Fullbrook, *Katherine Mansfield;* C. A. Hankin, *Katherine Mansfield and Her Confessional Stories*; Gillian Boddy, *Katherine Mansfield: The Woman and the Writer* (New York: Penguin, 1988); and Clare Hanson and Andrew Gurr, *Katherine Mansfield* (London: Macmillan, 1981). An earlier study, considered the standard before the Mansfield papers were available, is still useful: Sylvia Berkman, *Katherine Mansfield: A Critical Study* (New Haven: Yale University Press, 1951). Other books on Mansfield include: Saralyn R. Daly, *Katherine Mansfield* (New York: Twayne, 1965); Marvin Magalaner, *The Fiction of Katherine Mansfield* (Carbondale: Southern Illinois University Press, 1971); and Rhoda B. Nathan, *Katherine Mansfield* (New York: Continuum, 1988).

that relinquishment ensures that the voices of women—as women—will be silenced again. I am also suspicious of literary theory
that ignores the reality of writing as process, focusing instead on the
finality of structure, symbol, or silence. I seek evidence of development, change, resistance, disagreement, disavowal, reconsideration.
Unpublished writings, letters, drafts, sketches, diaries are often as
illuminating in these respects as final products, because questions of
professionalism and the material considerations of publishing and
surviving affect what later becomes known as "text." Such refusal
to abide by traditional definitions of what constitutes the object of
critical attention is a function of the feminist effort to subvert the
patriarchal authority inherent in the canonization of "texts." Such
refusal provides also the imaginative force, the vitality of the writing of women modernists, especially of the fiction of Katherine
Mansfield.

# 2

## Katherine Mansfield and
## the Problem of Oscar Wilde

In 1906–7, Katherine Mansfield copied these quotations from *The Picture of Dorian Gray* into her notebook along with numerous other passages from the works of Wilde:

> "All influence is immoral—immoral from the scientific point of view." (*Journal*, p. 12)

> "To realise one's nature perfectly—that is what each of us is here for." (p. 4)

While the first quotation might lead us to believe that she was quoting Wilde in order to insist that she was not influenced by him, the second (copied several months earlier) more clearly exposes her attraction to the Wildean aesthetic mystique. Mansfield even interspersed her quotations from Wilde with some epigrams of her own, all written in an unmistakably Wildean style: "To acknowledge the presence of fear is to give birth to failure." "Happy people are never brilliant. It implies friction" (p. 3). "Ambition is a curse if you are not proof against everything else—unless you are willing to sacrifice yourself to your ambition" (p. 10).

In an appreciative essay on the stylistic manifestations of Mansfield's debt to Oscar Wilde, the New Zealand poet and critic Vincent O'Sullivan demonstrates how Mansfield's interest in Wilde radiated outward to include as shaping forces the French symbolists, Walter Pater, and the decadents. O'Sullivan suggests that "the strongest indications of Mansfield's apprenticeship to Wilde were the supposition that one can give to life the shape one decides upon, and the demand that experience be intense."[1]

The standard critical opinion about Mansfield's influences until the 1970s had been that she was an imitator of Chekhov, from whom she learned how to construct a new kind of short story.[2] With Chekhov as her literary "father," Mansfield could be linked to a serious, "respectable" literary tradition. Katherine Mansfield herself encouraged this view. After she had developed her mature style and achieved critical recognition, she liked to think of herself as having a spiritual connection with the Russian writers, especially with their understanding of human suffering and intense emotion. Chekhov's struggle against the same disease (tuberculosis) that would cause her own death heightened such identification. Focusing on the Chekhovian model, however, tends to undercut her importance as an innovator of the modernist short story by ignoring the earlier, more profound sources of her creativity.[3] Her early writing was so clearly modeled after Wilde that it might easily betray the hidden reasons for her obsession with him. Katherine Mansfield became wary of Wilde's "influence" for good reason: the fear that literary influence might appear to merge with sexual influence. She would later prefer to bury those secret sources along with the figure of Oscar Wilde.[4]

[1]Vincent O'Sullivan, "The Magnetic Chain: Notes and Approaches to K.M.," *Landfall* 114 (June 1975), 100.

[2]The subject of Mansfield's debt to Chekhov is treated more fully in Chapter 11.

[3]A distinction between Mansfield's use of Chekhov and her earlier absorption of Wilde (and Pater) is made by Hanson and Gurr, *Katherine Mansfield,* p. 32.

[4]A number of critics note Wilde's influence; for example, Hanson and Gurr remark upon Wilde's effect on her notion of the artistic personality: "The Symbolist belief in the artist's ability to create himself, to *become* his mask, sustained her throughout her career" (p. 11). See also C. A. Hankin, *Katherine Mansfield and Her Confessional Stories,* pp. 41–42. Hankin explores a story fragment by Mansfield, written about 1907, called "The Man, the Monkey and the Mask," which was "obviously derived from *The Picture of Dorian Gray.*" Hankin draws attention to the bisexual aspects of the story, in which a man fights the "feminine aspect of his nature" embodied in a mask.

In contrast to O'Sullivan's appreciative account of the Mansfield-Wilde connection, some critics have approached it with edginess and condescension. V. S. Pritchett, for example, mentions that Mansfield "was soon raving . . . about the perversities and paradoxes of Oscar Wilde" ("Katherine Mansfield," *The New Yorker,*

# The Problem of Oscar Wilde

Yet Mansfield's adolescent obsession with the life and writings of Oscar Wilde needs to be discussed further if we are to explore the question of literary influence when it crosses traditional pathways of father-son, mother-daughter conventions. It is not difficult, for example, to see Mansfield's later interest in Chekhov in terms of those conventions, but her idolization of Wilde fits neither Harold Bloom's notion of the "anxiety of influence" nor Virginia Woolf's model of "thinking back through our mothers." What was the attraction of the famous homosexual writer for the adolescent Mansfield? Reverse muse? Her own father's "shadow" (although that approach verges into Jungianism)? Although such questions lead me to consider Mansfield's general responses to fathers and mothers— literary and biological—I am dubious of any explanation of her relation to Wilde based solely on the oedipal construct. It is necessary to consider such responses more as evidence of socially ascribed powers than as essential and unchanging constructs of the unconscious.

It should be noted that Wilde was Mansfield's principal stylistic influence in 1906–8, the years of her most active lesbian experiences.[5] Although her biographers differ in their interpretations of the significance and the number of these experiences, Mansfield only refers to two in her notebooks: one with her school friend Martha Grace Mahupuku (whom she called "Maata"), which may have occurred before her stay at Queen's College, and the other with Edith (Edie) Bendall, after her return to Wellington in 1907. There may have been other relationships with friends at Queen's College, and perhaps still others during her first years in London

---

October 26, 1981, p. 196); and Jeffrey Meyers explains that "Wilde . . . provided aesthetic justification for the rebellious and rarefied spirit whose clothes 'toned' with her 'cello and whose life was 'wrecked' by soiled linen" (*Katherine Mansfield: A Biography,* p. 25). The notable uneasiness of many writers on the subject of Wilde's "perversities and paradoxes" should make it clear that Wilde still has the power to make readers uncomfortable.

[5]In her notebooks of that time, Mansfield also referred to Whitman and Edward Carpenter as important influences, although, not surprisingly, she mentioned them not in a sexual context, but in terms of their liberating ideas, and in the case of Whitman, his technical innovation. It is not hard to see how she might use these writers as exponents for the artist's pursuit of experience. She needed outside justification for her own experimentation.

before she met J. Middleton Murry.[6] Her intimate friendship with Ida Constance Baker (who took the initials "L.M." [for Lesley Moore, a pen name derived, like Mansfield's, from her maternal heritage] at the same time Kathleen Beauchamp became "K.M.," when they were students at Queen's College) lasted for the rest of her life, and K.M. depended on her friend for emotional and domestic support throughout the latter stages of her illness, referring to L.M. as her "wife."[7] Although Mansfield's mother had suspected a lesbian relationship between K.M. and L.M., Tomalin doubts that it was ever particularly sexual, in spite of its "incipient eroticism."[8]

Richard Ellmann once remarked that "more than any other writer of his time in England, Wilde recognized that homosexuality was the great undercover subject. He relished belonging to an illegal confederation."[9] Mansfield might not have relished belonging to an illegal confederation, but her early notebooks give full evidence of a secret pride in her defiant identification with "Oscar." For example, consider the following entry in which she writes explicitly about her love for Edie Bendall:

> Never was the feeling of possession so strong, I thought. Here there can be but one person with her. Here by a thousand delicate suggestions I can absorb her—for the time. . . . O Oscar! am I peculiarly susceptible to sexual impulse? I must be, I suppose—but I rejoice. Now, each time I see her to put her arms round me and hold me against her. I think she wanted to, too; but she is afraid and custom hedges her in, I feel. (*Journal*, p. 14)

Wilde's power over Mansfield manifests itself in her attempts to find self-fulfillment through sensuality; his example allowed her to justify expressing her sexual desires for women, initially freeing her energies and developing her courage. Obviously, Wilde did not *influence* her desires, but his ideas allowed her a space in which such

[6]See Claire Tomalin, *Katherine Mansfield: A Secret Life*, pp. 24–26, 35–39, 225–26. Alpers mentions "two short love-affairs with girls," and notes that these "occurred now under the direct influence of her reading Oscar Wilde" (*The Life of Katherine Mansfield*, p. 46).

[7][Ida Baker], *Katherine Mansfield: The Memories of L.M.* (New York: Taplinger, 1972), p. 203.

[8]See Tomalin, p. 225.

[9]Richard Ellmann, "A Late Victorian Love Affair," *Oscar Wilde: Two Approaches* (Los Angeles: William Andrews Clark Memorial Library, 1977), p. 6.

desires might be recognized and named. She undoubtedly was impressed by such expansive descriptions of sexual release as the following from *Dorian Gray*:

> "I believe that if one man were to live out his life fully and completely, were to give form to every feeling, expression to every thought, reality to every dream—I believe that the world would gain such a fresh impulse of joy that we would forget all the maladies of medi- ævalism, and return to the Hellenic ideal. . . . But the bravest man amongst us is afraid of himself. The mutilation of the savage has its tragic survival in the self-denial that mars our lives. . . . Every impulse that we strive to strangle broods in the mind and poisons us. The body sins once, and has done with its sin, for action is a mode of purification. Nothing remains then but the recollection of a pleasure, or the luxury of a regret. *The only way to get rid of a temptation is to yield to it.* Resist it, and your soul grows sick with longing for the things it has forbidden to itself, with desire for what its monstrous laws have made monstrous and unlawful."[10]

Mansfield copied only the italicized sentence into her notebook.

As a young woman still in her teens, Katherine Mansfield boldly rejected any notion of art as replacement for sexual passion; outdated Victorian conceptions of sexual purity needed to be overcome if she were to fulfill her creative potential. She appreciated Wilde's recognition of the inseparability of body and language, as is apparent in the following quotation, which she attributed to "O. W." and copied into her notebook in 1907:

> 'The translation of an emotion into an act is its death—its logical end.... But... this way is not the act of unlawful things. It is the curiosity of our own temperament, the deliberate expression of our own tendencies, the welding into an art of act or incident some raw emotion of the blood. For we castrate our minds to the extent by which we deny our bodies.' (*Journal*, p. 11)[11]

Throughout this period of Mansfield's greatest admiration for Wilde, she delighted in outrageous and flamboyant assertions of

[10]Oscar Wilde, *The Picture of Dorian Gray*, ed. Isobel Murray (London: Oxford University Press, 1974), pp. 17–18; hereafter cited as DG. My emphasis identifies the sentence quoted in the *Journal*, p. 4.

[11]It is curious to hear the Wildean phrase echoed by the French postmodernist

sexual and artistic independence, sometimes expressed in Wildean epigrammatic phrasing. Wilde's "I like persons better than principles, and I like persons with no principles better than anything else in the world" (DG, p. 9; the last phrase is quoted in the *Journal*, p. 11) is echoed faintly in a letter Mansfield sent to her first publisher, saying that she was "poor—obscure—just eighteen years of age—with a rapacious appetite for everything and principles as light as my purse."[12]

Her enthusiastic association with Wilde also is reflected in the pseudonym she used in one of her earliest publications, a sketch, clearly in the tradition of the prose poem, entitled "In the Botanical Gardens," by "Julian Mark."[13] "Julian" neatly merges Dorian with Juliet, the name she gave her persona in an unfinished autobiographical novel that she was working on around the same time as the Wilde notebook entries. "In the Botanical Gardens" is filled with Wildean touches; for example: "Strange that these anemones—scarlet, and amethyst, and purple—vibrant with colour, always appear to me a trifle dangerous, sinister, seductive, but poisonous."

If we now return to the two quotations from Wilde at the beginning of this chapter, but put them back into their original context in *The Picture of Dorian Gray*, we can unveil Mansfield's unexpressed statement of connection:

> "*All influence is immoral—immoral from the scientific point of view*. . . . Because to influence a person is to give him one's own soul. He does not think his natural thoughts, or burn with his natural passions. His virtues are not real to him. His sins, if there are such things as sins, are borrowed. He becomes an echo of someone else's music, an actor of a

---

Hélène Cixous: "Censor the body and you censor breath and speech at the same time" ("The Laugh of the Medusa," trans. Keith Cohen and Paula Cohen, *Signs* 1 [Summer 1976], 880). Here and in other quotes from Mansfield's notebooks, letters, and manuscripts, I have used tightly spaced periods (as opposed to standard ellipses) to represent dots written by Mansfield herself.

[12]*Letters* I, p. 26. The first reference to the Wildean style of this letter was in the first biography of Mansfield (Mantz and Murry, *Life of Katherine Mansfield*, p. 274), and it contained a telling and fruitful misreading of Mansfield's handwriting. The last few words were rendered as "and principles as light as my prose."

[13]Julian Mark [pseud.], "In the Botanical Gardens," *The Native Companion* 2 (December 1907), 285–86. Reprinted in *Poems of Katherine Mansfield*, ed. Vincent O'Sullivan (Auckland: Oxford University Press, 1988), pp. 9–10.

part that has not been written for him. The aim of life is self-development. *To realise one's nature perfectly—that is what each of us is here for.*" (P. 17)

Mansfield feared influence as much as she was attracted, especially when she identified with Wilde's portrayal of the artist overwhelmed by his obsession with Dorian Gray, eventually destroyed by his love for the beautiful young man:

> "I knew that I had come face to face with someone whose mere personality was so fascinating that, if I allowed it to do so, it would absorb my whole nature, my whole soul, my very art itself. I did not want any external influence in my life." (P. 6)

In her wariness Mansfield remains close to Wilde. If his influences were "burning unicorn and uninflamed satyr," as Ellmann suggests,[14] it is clear that for Wilde too the anxiety of influence was different from the Bloomian notion of heterosexual father-son combat. For Wilde, and for Mansfield, literary influence was also connected with erotics, linking style with sexual desires. As such desires were socially forbidden, they had to express themselves through covert means.

Mansfield sensed the threat of sexual obsession lurking behind the merging of artist and art object in Wilde's novel. Ellmann remarks in his study of Wilde: "Dorian, like Mademoiselle de Maupin, does not limit himself to one sex. He ruins young men offstage and a young woman onstage."[15] This comment compares nicely with an entry in Mansfield's notebook of November 1906: "So, smiling at myself, I sit down to analyse this new influence: this complex emotion. I am never anywhere for long without a like experience. It is not one man or woman that is music and violins—it is the whole octave of the sex."[16] Mansfield's recognition of the fluidity of sexual attraction, the alternation of her objects of sexual desire between men and women, reflected as well her sense of herself as multiple,

[14]Richard Ellmann, *Golden Codgers: Biographical Speculations* (New York: Oxford University Press, 1973), p. 53.

[15]Ellmann, "A Late Victorian Love Affair," p. 6.

[16]*Journal*, p. 5, as emended from Mansfield Notebook 1, Alexander Turnbull Library, by Vincent O'Sullivan. Cited in O'Sullivan, "The Magnetic Chain," p. 118.

androgynous. In a diary entry a few pages after her quotations from Wilde she describes herself as "child, woman, and more than half man."[17]

Mansfield's absorption in Wilde could be said to go further than appreciative imitation. Near the end of her life—and in a quite different context—she acknowledged that "we all, as writers, to a certain extent, absorb each other when we love. . . . Anatole France would say we eat each other, but perhaps nourish is the better word."[18] Katherine Mansfield's identification with Wilde seemed to involve almost a kind of transmutation. Antony Alpers describes how her first husband, George Bowden, commented that she looked very different to him on his second meeting with her. The first time she had been "inconspicuous and somewhat demure," but now she was

> dressed "more or less Maori fashion," with some sort of scarf or kerchief over her shoulders, and there was "something almost eerie about it, as though of a psychic transformation rather than a mere impersonation." So much Mr. Bowden said in 1949, declining to elaborate. He has done so since: "She looked like Oscar Wilde."[19]

In spite of such intense identification with the figure of Wilde, there is clear evidence of Mansfield's growing rejection of his influence. Alpers refers to a letter she wrote in 1909, in which she asks: "Did you ever read the life of Oscar Wilde—not only read it but think of Wilde—picture his exact decadence? And wherein lay his extraordinary weakness and failure?" The letter, written so shortly after her intense enthusiasm for Wilde, gives clear and painful evidence of the ways that society's ingrained homophobia finally overcame her:

> In New Zealand Wilde acted so strongly and terribly upon me that I was constantly subject to exactly the same fits of madness as those which caused his ruin and his mental decay. When I am miserable now—these recur. Sometimes I forget all about it—then with awful recurrence it bursts upon me again and I am quite powerless to pre-

[17]*Journal*, p. 13, emended from Mansfield Notebook 39, Alexander Turnbull Library.

[18]*The Letters of Katherine Mansfield*, edited by J. Middleton Murry (New York: Knopf, 1929), p. 481.

[19]Alpers, *The Life of Katherine Mansfield*, p. 87.

vent it—This is my secret from the world and from you—Another shares it with me, . . . for she, too is afflicted with the same terror—We used to talk of it knowing that it wd eventually kill us, render us insane or paralytic—all to no purpose—

It's funny that you and I have never shared this—and I know you will understand why. Nobody can help—it has been going on now since I was 18 and it was the reason for Rudolf's death.

I read it in his face today.

I think my mind is morally unhinged and that is the reason—I know it is a degradation so unspeakable that—one perceives the dignity in pistols.[20]

In spite of Mansfield's expressed fear of her likeness to Oscar Wilde, she continued to absorb him whenever it suited her purpose. For example, compare the apparently unconscious connection in the language of two notebook entries, the first from 1907, the second from 1911:

Do other people of my age feel as I do I wonder so absolutely powerful licentious so almost physically ill—[21]

Do other artists feel as I do—the driving necessity—the crying need—the hounding desire that [will] never be satisfied—that knows no peace? I believe there was a time when I might have stopped myself, and days even weeks would have drifted by—but now there is not an hour. I breathe it in the air. I am saturated with it. Then Catherine what is your ultimate desire—to what do you so passionately aspire? To write books and stories and sketches and poems.[22]

What kind of transfer has taken place? Has Mansfield turned her immense sexual energy now to writing? Has she given up, through

[20]This is a fascinating letter. Its origin is unclear, and also its recipient. O'Sullivan and Scott (*Letters* I, p. 90) suggest it was written to Ida Baker. They mention that it was found among other papers at George Bowden's flat, and "on either side of the paper wrapped round it she wrote, 'Never to be read, on your honour as my friend, while I am still alive. K. Mansfield.'" Cited by Alpers, *Life*, p. 91. Tomalin is dubious, however, about the sincerity of Mansfield's *angst* in this letter, believing the letter might have played a role in her efforts to rid herself of her first husband, George Bowden. See p. 67.

[21]Quoted in Meyers, p. 10.

[22]*Journal*, pp. 47–48. This entry was incorporated by Murry from William Orton's autobiographical novel. Murry was convinced that it was written by Mansfield. See Orton, *The Last Romantic* (New York: Farrar & Rinehart, 1937), p. 283.

a more deeply final repression, her passionate longing for sexual interaction with women? In the 1909 letter quoted above, Mansfield reveals how she is hounded by feelings that "burst" upon her, that she is "powerless" to stop. In the 1911 journal entry Mansfield was ready to use similar phrasing—"the hounding desire that [will] never be satisfied—that knows no peace"—for an artistic purpose. It has become self-conscious. I am not referring simply to the Freudian notion of sublimation of sex to art. For Mansfield, art was not supposed to take the place of sexuality (although it appears that later in her life, because of illness, art may have had to suffice). What I am suggesting is the similarity of the two activities as expressed through the nearly identical *rhythms* of these sentences: the unconscious displacement of the sexual, which is forbidden, onto the artistic, which is allowed.

Yet an issue that troubles me as a feminist is how Mansfield's absorption in Wilde affected her sense of herself as a woman. Although Wilde provided her with the impetus to seek experience, to express sexuality and not deny the body, following such advice proved dangerous, as her later pregnancies, abortion, and related illnesses give sad evidence. Moreover, the call to burn oneself out for experience, to destroy the body in service to art, and all those other exaggerated aesthetic poses were intended rather to suggest a certain kind of *masculine* initiation into art. The physical beauty of Dorian was a lure for male sexual desire, his insatiable lust for experience a male prerogative. Wilde's focus is on men with the freedom of men; women are only the objects of their intermittent attention—and of their scorn. Lord Henry Wotton, for example, remarks: "No woman is a genius. Women are a decorative sex. They never have anything to say, but they say it charmingly. Women represent the triumph of matter over mind, just as men represent the triumph of mind over morals" (DG, p. 47). Some of Lord Henry's comments are not only trivializing, but ominous: "I am afraid that women appreciate cruelty, downright cruelty, more than anything else. They have wonderfully primitive instincts. We have emancipated them, but they remain slaves looking for their masters, all the same. They love being dominated" (DG, p. 102).

It is hard to believe that Mansfield would have enjoyed seeing herself in Lord Henry's characterizations of women. She also would have had trouble with Wilde's portrayal of Sibyl Vane, the only significant female character in the novel. Sibyl is both artist and woman, and the genius of her acting is the magnetic force attracting Dorian to her. (Sibyl is playing Juliet when Dorian first sees her, another point of Mansfield's identification with her.) Sibyl, like Mansfield herself, is a role-player, an impersonator. She even has the appropriate touch of androgyny, which would make her more attractive to Dorian; as Rosalind, in *As You Like It*, Sibyl is allowed to wear boys' clothes. Yet the woman artist in this novel is sacrificed because she lets "woman" take precedence over "artist." Dorian Gray rejects Sibyl when she appears to lose her talent in a test of his love for her "self" and not the illusion of her role. Of course it was the illusion brought about through art that was her alluring influence. "Woman" as a natural, physical creature quickly becomes a victim.

Katherine Mansfield would have had to read Wilde's novel always with a double consciousness. She would have had to split herself off from her female identity in order to continue to delight in Lord Henry's world-weary, cynical, antibourgeois witticisms. His caustic epigrammatic pronouncements were another alluring *influence*, but a potentially dangerous one. Although he is the one major character who is alive at the end of the novel, his life is ruined. (As life's "spectator," he cannot be said to have really "lived," but has set the dreary course of evil into action by giving Dorian "the fatal book."[23])

Of course one should not assume that Mansfield took Lord Henry's pronouncements at face value.[24] Her reading of the book had to

[23]For an excellent discussion of the entire question of "the fatal book" among the decadents, see Linda Dowling, *Language and Decadence in the Victorian Fin de Siècle* (Princeton, N.J.: Princeton University Press, 1986), pp. 104–74. Dowling remarks: "The fatal book *is* fatal, that is to say, not because of its power to kill outright, but because of its power decisively to change an individual life" (p. 164). On Wilde's particular use of the notion of "the fatal book," see esp. pp. 170–74.

[24]Wilde's own attitudes toward women are considerably more complex, as well as more sympathetic. Regenia Gagnier discusses the prominent role women played for Wilde as consumers of his writing. See her *Idylls of the Marketplace: Oscar Wilde and the Victorian Public* (Stanford: Stanford University Press, 1986), p. 66. Gagnier notes that in his role as editor of the *Woman's World*, Wilde reviewed positively many novels written by women, in particular, novels about artists and psychological novels "all concerned with the effects of 'sin' on personality." Gagnier states: "Just as Wilde had dedicated his stories and tales to women of Society who would thereby ensure his reputation, he constructed the narrative of *Dorian Gray* from the standard elements of a certain genre of upper-class women's literature: art, psychology, sin,

be selective and multilayered. The plot of *Dorian Gray* would have been distorted in line with her own self-division among the characters. She was already questioning the unified notion of "self" implicit in Sibyl Vane's destruction of her own creative brilliance. While Mansfield may have taken Lord Henry's cynicism as Wilde's own comments about art and life and imitated his style in her own attempts at Wildean epigrams, she must have seen another aspect of herself in the artist Basil Hallward, whose secret passion for Dorian inspired the destructive painting. The young Katherine Mansfield thus perceived how art may spring from sexual desire. But she also must have recognized that it was not the sexual passion itself that eventually destroyed Hallward: it was his fear of its public revelation. Basil admitted to Dorian that he did not want others to see the picture because "I grew afraid that others would know of my idolatry. I felt, Dorian, that I had told too much, that I had put too much of myself into it" (p. 115). The homosexual basis for this idolatry is much more apparent in the *Lippincott* version of the novel, which Mansfield first read in 1906. There, Basil says:

> "It is quite true that I have worshipped you with far more romance of feeling than a man usually gives to a friend. Somehow, I had never loved a woman. I suppose I never had time. . . . Well, from the moment I met you, your personality had the most extraordinary influence over me. I quite admit that I adored you madly, extravagantly, absurdly. I was jealous."[25]

The artist here is ruined as an artist even before he is destroyed as a living man. Mansfield could easily absorb the lesson that to reveal

---

and luxury. These elements often combined to form a particularly modern problem: the relation of influence and history to present action. This was certainly the Modern Woman's problem, and in this as well as in its thematic components, the novel was indeed 'effeminate.' The outcry against Wildean decadence on the part of gentlemen journalists was in part an outcry against the male author who won the support of Society—an institution managed by women—by writing a book that would appeal to women" (p. 66).

[25]DG, "Textual Notes," p. 236. Isobel Murray, editor of the Oxford University Press edition of *Dorian Gray*, provides a good summary here of the differences between the *Lippincott* version and later texts, pp. 230–37. The novel first appeared in *Lippincott's Monthly Magazine* in July 1890. Alpers (*Life*, p. 35) notes that Mansfield was lent the magazine by Vere Bartrick-Baker in 1906.

too much about forbidden sexuality is self-destructive. She must learn to hide her own impulses in her work and not admit their source.

The figure of Dorian Gray provided an aura of beauty and glamor to the novel, but to identify with Dorian, the art object itself (for Dorian was as much a "creation" of Lord Henry's as his painting was one of Basil Hallward's), would have been self-destructive for Mansfield. The art object does not shape experience into art. It embodies whatever conceptualization brought it forth, in this case what Mansfield would have seen as Wilde's own call for excess. Dorian's bisexuality linked with her own, and his "punishment" for his sinful life is reflected in her own fantasies of death and defeat. While the artist is destroyed by the inspiration for his own creation, the creation self-destructs.

Another lesson for Mansfield in her possible identification with Dorian Gray concerned the commodification of sexual object as art object. Dorian has to remain young and beautiful if he is to continue to serve as the object of others' passions. In a moment of self-recognition, he blurts out to Basil: "I am less to you than your ivory Hermes or your silver Faun. You will like them always. How long will you like me? Till I have my first wrinkle, I suppose. I know, now, that when one loses one's good looks, whatever they may be, one loses everything" (p. 26). This is more typically a woman's plight, and the story of women's pursuit of youth and beauty is all too familiar in contemporary culture. In some ways, Mansfield could view Dorian's plight as representative of her own situation as a woman—that is, when she longed to be loved by a man, since her personal situation was complicated by her alternating desires for men and women. As her identifications in Wilde's novel shifted between artist, art object, lover, observer, beloved, she wanted to be everyone: to be witty, cynical, removed from passion like Lord Henry Wotton; to be passionate, inspired, brilliantly creative like Basil Hallward; to be publicly acclaimed, absorbed in performance, and tragically in love like Sibyl Vane; and—most dangerous—to be desired, indulged, and feared like Dorian Gray. She wanted, especially, to have Dorian's freedom to experience everything. And she particularly enjoyed his penchant for being adored by both men and women. Her frequently expressed passion for living is not markedly dissimilar to Dorian's awareness that Lord Henry's influence has opened him to an unceasing search for more and more experience:

> "You filled me with a wild desire to know everything about life. For days after I met you, something seemed to throb in my veins. As I lounged in the Park, or strolled down Piccadilly, I used to look at every one who passed me, and wonder, with a mad curiosity, what sort of lives they led. Some of them fascinated me. Others filled me with terror. There was an exquisite poison in the air. I had a passion for sensations." (DG, pp. 47–48)

Oscar Wilde proved a difficult influence for Katherine Mansfield, and one she needed to control if she were to develop her own style as a woman and as a writer. If "Dorian Gray had been poisoned by a book" (DG, p. 146), there must have been times when Mansfield felt she had been poisoned also. Wilde spoke for her own awareness of the power of literary influence when he had Dorian remark: "Yet one had ancestors in literature, as well as in one's own race, nearer perhaps in type and temperament, many of them, and certainly with an influence of which one was more absolutely conscious" (DG, p. 144).

Accordingly, the complex interaction between Mansfield and Wilde continued throughout her career. It can be seen, for example, in her well-known story "Bliss" (1918), which uses symbolism, epigrammatic phrasing, and exaggeration to highlight its undercurrent of half-suppressed lesbian sexuality. For example: "Why have a baby if it has to be kept—not in a case like a rare, rare fiddle—but in another woman's arms?"[26] Or, take the following passage, also from "Bliss," describing Bertha's husband Harry (who later is revealed to be having an affair with Pearl Fulton, the same woman Bertha "had fallen in love with" [p. 340], and whose very touch "could fan—fan—start blazing—blazing—the fire of bliss that Bertha did not know what to do with" [p. 344]:

> Harry was enjoying his dinner. It was part of his—well, not his nature, exactly, and certainly not his pose—his—something or other— to talk about food and to glory in his "shameless passion for the white

---

[26] *The Short Stories of Katherine Mansfield* (New York: Knopf, 1937), p. 339. All future references to stories in this edition will be indicated parenthetically in the text.

flesh of the lobster" and "the green of pistachio ices—green and cold
like the eyelids of Egyptian dancers." (P. 345)

As Vincent O'Sullivan has observed, "Wilde's *presence* she left behind, but his traces will be in her work for the rest of her life. Her
way of describing flowers, for instance; her precision in parodying
the language of aesthetes; the brittleness of much of the conversation
in her fiction; those inversions which are a mark of her style
always."[27]
Many years after her initial enthusiasm for Wilde had passed, she
described his intrusion into one of her dreams, in which she met him
in a cafe and invited him home: "When I arrived home it seemed
madness to have asked him. Father & Mother were in bed. What if
Father came down & found that chap Wilde in one of the chintz
armchairs?"[28] The dream, with its obvious oedipal associations,
harks back to 1906–7, the time of her return to Wellington from
Queen's College in London—the same time when she quoted *Dorian Gray* in her journal—when she struggled with her parents for
permission to return to London and begin her career as an artist. She
had been especially angry then with her father's interference in her
activities, with his overbearing masculine presence, and with his
suspicions over her involvement with Edie Bendall. But her mother
too she had described as "constantly suspicious, constantly over-
bearingly tyrannous" (*Journal*, p. 7). Writing down the dream in a
letter to her husband, J. Middleton Murry, on November 1, 1920,
Mansfield was fully aware of its Freudian implications.[29] In fact, the
dream is probably as much a creative production as any story she
would designate as fiction. The letter describing the dream was
written from France, where she was battling her fatal illness, angry
with Murry for not being with her, suspicious of the possibility that
he might be involved with another woman.
In her telling of the dream, Mansfield vacillates between revulsion
and attraction to Oscar Wilde: he was "shabby," and he had "long
greasy hair." She remarks: "I couldn't help it. He *was* attractive—as a

[27]O'Sullivan, "The Magnetic Chain," pp. 98–99.

[28]Vincent O'Sullivan, ed., *Katherine Mansfield: Selected Letters* (Oxford: Clarendon, 1989), p. 185.

[29]I am indebted to my colleague Sara van den Berg for her perceptive psychoanalytic reading of this dream.

curiosity. He was fatuous & brilliant!" He was "very affected." She describes how he arrived with Lady Ottoline Morrell. Mansfield says, "I saw he was disgustingly pleased to have brought her," and cruelly describes "Ottoline in a red hat on her rust hair *'hounyhming'* along." The last part of the dream bears quoting in full; Wilde, now seated comfortably on the chintz armchair, speaks:

> 'You know Katherine, when I was *in that dreadful place* I was haunted by the memory of a *cake*. It used to float in the air before me—a little delicate thing *stuffed* with cream and with the cream there was something *scarlet*. It was made of pastry and I used to call it my little Arabian Nights cake. But I couldn't remember the name. Oh, Katherine, it was *torture*. It used to *hang* in the air and *smile* at me, and every time I resolved that next time *they let someone* come and see me I would ask them to tell me what it was but every time, Katherine, I was *ashamed*. Even now...'
>
> I said, 'Mille feuilles à la creme?' At that he turned round in the armchair and began to sob, and Ottoline who carried a parasol opened it and put it over him...

The dream combines Mansfield's own sense of herself as Wilde and as not-Wilde (a privilege of the dreaming subject), thus encapsulating her fear of *being* him and her separation from him through irony and humor. Her own imprisonment in illness has prevented her from enjoying a sexual relationship, and she ridicules Lady Ottoline's "hounyhming along" with its allusions to Swiftian coarseness, horsey sexuality, and erotic rivalry,[30] which is in contrast to her own delicate sensuality—what she has Wilde note as "'Katherine's hand—the same gentle hand!' as he took mine." Wilde's craving, while imprisoned, for the "cake" conflates both male and female sexual symbolism: it "used to hang in the air" but also to "smile," and it is "*stuffed* with cream and with the cream there was something *scarlet*." But to crave it, in fact, even to remember it, makes him "ashamed," again reinstating the motif of guilt over the patriarchally forbidden—especially oral—sexual desire. The *name* of that desire elicits the guilt—so much so that it cannot be said. Such linking of "name" and "ashamed" circles back to "Father and Moth-

[30]Sara van den Berg detects a pun in "hounyhming" (win-him-ing) that clearly links Ottoline Morrell and Murry.

er . . . in bed," and the oedipal/preoedipal desires and silences crystallized in the conflicts of this dream.

The Katherine figure in the dream gives the Wilde figure the *name* of the cream-filled pastry, "mille feuilles à la creme," which literally translated means "thousand leaves," suggesting book pages (and thus language itself) as well as the "Thousand and One Nights" of the "Arabian Nights," with its imprisoned storytelling heroine, who like Mansfield had to tell stories to stay alive.

For Katherine Mansfield, Oscar Wilde was not a mere adolescent obsession, as some of her critics—and her husband—have too readily assumed, but rather a continuing model and terror, her impetus toward the idolization of art as a means of *controlling* the forbidden while allowing it, nonetheless, oblique expression. Wilde himself gave her the clue to how she might continue to express the forbidden by accepting the transformative power of art: "It is a mistake to think that the passion one feels in creation is ever really shown in the work one creates. Art is always more abstract than we fancy. Form and colour tell us of form and colour—that is all. It often seems to me that art conceals the artist far more completely than it ever reveals him" (DG, p. 115).

In terms of the evolution of Katherine Mansfield's aesthetics, style emerged as the term for her earlier fusion of experience, imitation, and identification. It gradually was subsumed under the rubric of technique. Mansfield later referred to her "passion for technique,"[31] and in that phrase we can see both sexual passion and the controlling, impersonal mastery of art.

[31]Mansfield used this expression in a letter to her brother-in-law, Richard Murry, in February 1921. See O'Sullivan, ed., *Selected Letters*, p. 197.

# ∂ 3

# Sexuality Encoded

T his discussion of Mansfield's sexuality is grounded on some assumptions that need clarification. Most of Mansfield's critics and biographers tend to take a Freudian position in relation to her sexual proclivities; that is, her bisexuality is seen as either symbolic of a disturbance in her maturation process, a fixation at a particular stage of the oedipal crisis, or an unresolved conflict in gender role. Recent feminist psychoanalytic theory responds to the question of bisexuality in ways different from the classic Freudian interpretation. By emphasizing the pre-oedipal, the blurring of boundaries between mother and daughter, and the difficulties of separation, theorists such as Nancy Chodorow position themselves differently on the question of bisexuality. It becomes less a symptom of thwarted development toward a maturity defined in terms of its acceptance of patriarchal domination, and more the lifetime persistence of the original inseparability of mother and child. According to Chodorow's descriptions of the production of femininity, Katherine Mansfield's course of sexual development can be described in terms other than "perverse," "infantile," "regressive," etc. Chodorow states that "the asymmetrical structure of parenting generates a female oedipus complex . . . characterized by the continuation of preoedipal attachments and preoccupations, sexual oscillation in an oedipal triangle, and the lack of either absolute change of love object or absolute oedipal resolution."[1]

[1]Nancy Chodorow, *The Reproduction of Mothering: Psychoanalysis and the Sociology of Gender* (Berkeley: University of California Press, 1978), pp. 133–34.

Sexuality Encoded

Although both classic Freudian and revisionary feminist views may shed light on elements of Mansfield's development and frequently prove useful in interpreting images and motifs in her fiction, the limitation of all such approaches is their underlying essentialism. Mansfield's individual development is always explained by reference to an assumed standard of normality; the particular expressions of her sexuality are therefore deviations from the "norm." As C. A. Hankin remarks about Mansfield's early stories in which lesbian elements emerge, "In dealing with bisexuality, Katherine Mansfield was entering difficult territory. She was not only exposing in fiction the motivations of women whose psychology resembled her own; she was writing about a subject which in the aftermath of the Wilde trial was considered morally wrong, if not 'forbidden.'"[2]

Hankin stresses the conflict Mansfield faced in confronting her sexual attractions, but she tends to view that conflict as a stage in a development toward "normality," i.e., heterosexuality. Although much of this view conforms to Mansfield's own anxieties over lesbianism, it is important not to validate retrograde assumptions about some kind of "essential" sexual nature by accepting her own fears as indicative of underlying "truth" about her real self. As I have previously suggested, Mansfield was already suspicious of the idea of the *essential* self. Her emphasis on roles and role playing reflects her sense of self as a multiplicity, ever changing, dependent on the shifting focus of relationships.

Now there is no question that Mansfield defined herself at times as "deviant" (as the letter about Wilde quoted in the last chapter reveals), and her letters, diaries, and fiction offer many critiques of contemporary sexual standards in which she appears to take a defensive stand supporting conventional morals and behavior. The key word here is "defensive," and I explore that issue in Chapter 8 in more detail.

I emphasize that my discussion of Mansfield's sexuality depends on the axiom, articulated by Jeffrey Weeks, "that 'sexuality' is not an unproblematic natural given, which the 'social' works upon to control, but is, on the contrary, an *historical* unity which has been shaped and determined by a multiplicity of forces, and which has

[2]C. A. Hankin, *Katherine Mansfield and Her Confessional Stories*, p. 66.

undergone complex historical transformations."[3] Such an emphasis on the interplay between social, cultural, economic, political, and other factors in the establishment of sexual definitions is more useful, I believe, in discerning the significance of sexuality in Mansfield's artistic production than psychoanalytic assumptions alone. This emphasis is particularly helpful if we want to understand how Mansfield contributed to the development of literary modernism, and how her contribution reflects a new conjunction of forces in which the rise of feminism is a strong component. The arguments from psychoanalysis (either from the classic Freudian positions or the revisionary Lacanian versions of them) tend to isolate Mansfield from her milieu, preventing an analysis of the complicated negotiations she had to make between older, traditional definitions of female sexuality and the more experimental, constantly shifting definitions based on new forms of social practice brought about by rapid modernization.

It is important to remember that the Wilde influence gave Katherine Mansfield *male* models of sexuality: homosexuality and its punishment in Wilde's case were part of a history of men and men's power struggles. The very notion of homosexuality as an identity would have been a discovery she made through the public exposure of Oscar Wilde, confirming Jeffrey Weeks's observation that there was a shift in the latter part of the nineteenth century from defining homosexual acts to defining a homosexual person:

> The "homosexual" . . . belonged to a species, and it is this new concern with the homosexual person, both in legal practice and in psychological and medical categorisation, that marks the crucial change, both because it provided a new subject of social observation and speculation, and because it opened up the possibility of new modes of self-articulation.[4]

[3]Jeffrey Weeks, *Sex, Politics, and Society: The Regulation of Sexuality since 1800* (London: Longman, 1981), p. xi.

[4]Ibid., p. 102. Weeks illuminates the social significance of the Wilde trials and their aftermath: "The downfall of Oscar Wilde was a most significant event for it created a public image for the 'homosexual', a term by now coming into use, and a terrifying moral tale of the dangers that trailed closely behind deviant behaviour. The Wilde trials were in effect labelling processes of a most explicit kind drawing a clear border between acceptable and abhorrent behaviour. But they also of course had paradoxical effects. As Havelock Ellis said of the Oscar Wilde trials, they

Such "self-articulation," however, was still clearly based on the experiences and life-styles of male homosexuals. It is no suprise, therefore, to realize that Katherine Mansfield's absorption in Oscar Wilde involved models of sexuality based only on male desire. To *become* Wilde, on some level, would mean to become not only male, but homosexually male. She would turn to male objects of desire, but would love them in the *style* of a man loving other men.

Such imaginative displacement of her sexual identity onto a male subject was characteristic of Mansfield's early awareness of the possibility of manipulating gender roles. With the Wilde model, she was learning the art of *seeing through* gender as a given. When, at seventeen, she referred to "the whole octave of the sex" (quoted in the previous chapter), her awareness of the multiplicity of sexual desires was beginning to develop. In the same passage, written in November 1906 on her way home to New Zealand, we can observe an early attempt to write about her sexuality, and how that attempt was shaped by her Wildean influence. She describes her attraction to a Dorian-like young man. "His face is clean cut, like the face of a statue, his mouth absolutely Grecian" ( *Journal*, p. 5). She studies his "complete rhythmic movement, the absolute self-confidence, the beauty of his body." She notes his elegance and his volatility:

> He wore a loose silk shirt under his dress coat. He was curiously excitable, almost a little violent at times. There was a suppressed agitation in every look, every movement. He spoke French for the greater part of the time with exquisite fluency and a certain extreme affectation. He has spent years in Paris. The more hearts you have the better, he said, leaning over my hand. I felt his coat sleeve against my bare arm. If one heart is a very primitive affair, I answered, in these days one must possess many. We exchanged a long look and his glance inflamed me like the scent of a gardenia. ( *Journal*, p. 6)

Elements of this passage seem almost a parody of decadent style: the witty epigrammatic retort, the "exquisite" details, the gardenia.

---

appeared 'to have generally contributed to give definiteness and self-consciousness to the manifestations of homosexuality, and to have aroused inverts to take up a definite stand'. It seems likely that the new forms of legal regulation, whatever their vagaries in application, had the effect of forcing home to many the fact of their difference and thus creating a new community of knowledge, if not of life and feeling, amongst many men with homosexual leanings" (p. 103).

When she watches him play cricket on deck, she admires his "most marvellous force," and feels that "each ball seemed to be aimed at my heart. I panted for breath." Fittingly, she follows immediately with a reversal of the Wildean epigram quoted on page 23: "We deny our minds to the extent we castrate our bodies." But the parodic dissipates as she asks herself, "I am wondering if that is true and thinking that it most certainly is. Oh, I want to push it as far as it will go" (*Journal*, p. 6). No clearer statement can I find of Mansfield's recognition of role playing as a function of the creation of gender. She notes that "he has seen so much, it would be such a conquest." The Dorian-like use of others for the sake of experience is matched by her self-reflection; she admits that her motives are mixed—and not completely understood. She remarks: "I shall fight for what I want, yet I don't definitely [know] what that is."

A disturbing and, from a feminist perspective, ominous element of this journal entry is the way Mansfield alternates between the sense of adventure, conquest, and her right to sexual experience, and a countermovement of familiar, yet inappropriate, "feminine" masochism: "When I am with him a preposterous desire seizes me, I want to be badly hurt by him. I should like to be strangled by his firm hands" (pp. 5–6). Images of female masochism occur elsewhere in the *Journal* and in Mansfield's fiction ("The Swing of the Pendulum" is a good example); it is too large a subject to take up here, except to note that frequently Mansfield's sexual aggressiveness appears to turn back on itself with images of pleasure in pain.[5]

Vincent O'Sullivan calls attention to Mansfield's difficulties in shifting her feelings from women to men, and to the ways in which her lesbianism remains, although submerged, throughout her involvements with men. He quotes from the *Journal* her expressions

---

[5]The florid description in the journal entry may also be a manifestation of the influence of Gabriele D'Annunzio, whose novel *Il Fuoco* (Mansfield probably read the English translation, *The Flame of Life* [New York: Boni & Liveright, 1900]) would have set the tone for a female sexuality imbued with masochistic and violent impulses: "Mortal dismay was in the woman's voice. Her bare neck and her bare arms shuddered in the darkness; and she longed to deny herself and she longed to be possessed, and she longed to die and longed to be shaken by his man's hands. She trembled; her teeth trembled in her mouth. A stream that seemed to flow from a glacier submerged her, rolled over her, chilled her from the roots of her hair to the tips of her fingers" (p. 131).

of uncertainty over her feelings for Arnold Trowell, the first heterosexual focus of her desires:

> He must always be everything to me—the one man whom I can call
> Master and Lover too—and though I know I shall have many fascinat-
> ing connections in my Life none will be like this—so lasting—so
> deep—so everything—because he poured into my virgin soul the Life
> essence of Music. . . Never an hour passes free from his influence. I
> love him—*but I wonder with all my soul. And here is the kernel of the
> matter—the Oscar-like thread.*[6]

The Wilde dream quoted in the last chapter illustrates the results
of Mansfield's early linking of Wilde, male homosexuality, and her
ambivalence over her own similarity to Wilde: her penchant for
forbidden sexuality. It also contains as its central image the cake
whose name cannot even be brought to speech by the Wilde figure
in the dream. In Mansfield's writing, sexuality is often encoded in
objects to be eaten. For her, Kate Fullbrook remarks, "sexually, one
devours or is devoured."[7] C. A. Hankin notes the predominance of
eating symbols in Mansfield's work, especially in the *German Pension* stories (1911).[8]

The cake in the Wilde dream relates to many images of like sweets
in the stories, images that often have sexual overtones. In "Je ne
parle pas français," a story published in February 1920 (she began
writing it in January 1918), Mansfield uses a sweet cake in connection with sexuality, and more to the point, links it with a bisexual
*male* character, who combines several Wildean features. Raoul Duquette, the narrator of the story, recounts the origins of his diverse
sexuality in his childhood seduction by an African laundress. Raoul
remembers himself as having "a lovely little half-open mouth" (p.
355), and that the woman paid him for "kisses" in the outhouse with
"a little round fried cake covered with sugar" (p. 356). Raoul's
sexuality is conveyed as polymorphous here: the laundress first
rocked him in the laundry basket "while I held tight to the handles

---

[6]Quoted by O'Sullivan, "The Magnetic Chain," pp. 118–19, from the *Journal*, p.
16, supplemented by Mansfield Notebook 39, Alexander Turnbull Library. The
emphasis is O'Sullivan's.
[7]Kate Fullbrook, *Katherine Mansfield,* p. 88.
[8]Hankin, pp. 66–70.

and screamed for joy and fright." Raoul justifies his present mode of life on the basis of that childhood experience:

> As this performance was repeated once a week it is no wonder that I remember it so vividly. Besides, from that very first afternoon, my childhood was, to put it prettily, "kissed away." I became very languid, very caressing, and greedy beyond measure. And so quickened, so sharpened, I seemed to understand everybody and be able to do what I liked with everybody. (P. 356)

Now, whenever he is short of funds for his necessities, "quantities of good clothes, silk underwear . . . gloves and powder boxes and a manicure set, perfumes, very good soap. . . . there's always an African laundress and an outhouse, and I am very frank and *bon enfant* about plenty of sugar on the little fried cake afterwards" (p. 357).

Raoul Duquette is portrayed then as both writer and prostitute, Mansfield here clearly satirizing the parasitical features of the world of the artistic avant-garde. Raoul speaks with the cleverness and pointed wittiness of a Wildean character who has emerged into a surrealistic twentieth-century Paris where he draws images from the cinema rather than '90s decadence. Although he says, "I am going in for serious literature. I am starting a career," his thoughts continue to circle back to his obsessions with sexuality and his own narcissistic fixations. He describes his physical attractions—"olive skin, black eyes with long lashes, black silky hair cut short, tiny square teeth that show when I smile" (p. 357)—and is delighted when a woman in a bakery comments that "you have the hands for making fine little pastries." His androgyny is emphasized when he remarks, "I confess, without my clothes I am rather charming. Plump, almost like a girl, with smooth shoulders, and I wear a thin gold bracelet above my left elbow" (p. 358). The term "confess," as we shall see in Chapter 10, takes on significant implications for Mansfield. Here, it provides the entry into the encoded world of homosexuality.

Raoul as writer intends "to write about things that have never been touched before." He will "make a name for" himself "as a writer about the submerged world," and insists that he will write of that "submerged world" in ways that no one else has dared: "Very naively, with a sort of tender humour and from the inside, as though it were all quite simple, quite natural. . . . Nobody has ever done it as I shall do it because none of the others have lived my experiences" (p. 357). Although Raoul supposedly is based on the writer Francis Carco, with whom Mansfield had an affair in 1915, he reflects, as well, Mansfield's self-criticism of her earlier role as aesthete.[9] Her portrait of a Wildean figure is now laden with several layers of significance. She has rejected the glamorous if tragic appeal of the decadent Dorian Gray; rejected the claim of superiority of the artist who must experience everything; rejected her own likeness to a male homosexual role.

Complicating her attitude toward the male homosexual is a later element, which brings Mansfield back to her hastily rejected female role model in *Dorian Gray*: the victimized Sibyl Vane. That new element is competition, on the part of the victimized woman, with the homosexual man's desire for her own male lover. For Sibyl Vane, Dorian's rejection appeared to be due to her own refusal to continue to play a role. But a decoding of the subtext suggests that Dorian's "submerged" impulses would have forced a rejection somehow or other. Wilde did not simply position a rival male character for Dorian to choose instead of Sybil. But by 1918, Mansfield had experienced the situation of the woman caught between two men's desires for each other. Although Murry finally rejected D. H. Lawrence's attempts to establish a "blood brotherhood," Mansfield lived through many months of competition with Lawrence for Murry's attention. Mansfield does not tell the Lawrence/Murry story in "Je ne parle pas français," but it remains in the background. So does the fact that Francis Carco had been first Murry's friend, and then Mansfield's lover.[10] Mansfield also conflates Murry's late-

---

[9]Kate Fullbrook suggests that "in Duquette, Katherine Mansfield attacks a familiar view of the artist as an impresario of the emotions, and condemns it in her delineation of his moral bankruptcy" (p. 91).

[10]Hankin draws attention to the parallels between Murry and Katherine and Dick and Mouse, suggested by Francis Carco's description of the reception of Murry and Katherine when they arrived in Paris in 1913 when Katherine told him, "Je ne parle pas français." See Hankin, p. 162. Hankin's excellent discussion of the origin of this story as a response to Mansfield's disappointment with Murry and her substitution of L.M. as a rival to Murry takes a different direction from my argument here, but is compatible with it. My emphasis is rather on Mansfield's reactions to *male* homosexuality than on the reminder of her bisexuality that intimate contact with L.M. was again bringing into focus. Both elements are present and significant,

adolescent abandonment of his French lover, Marguerite, in this tale of duplicity and abandonment.[11]

Raoul Duquette reveals himself to be infatuated with Dick Harmon, the Murry-like, ineffectual Englishman who brings the naive, innocent young woman, "Mouse," to Paris and then abandons her. Dick's irresponsible behavior is the result of his fear of telling his mother that he has committed himself to another woman. (Mansfield here appears to draw on what was becoming the popular Freudian interpretation of latent male homosexuality: mother fixation.)

In "Je ne parle pas français" women's sexuality is portrayed completely from the point of view of the male narrator, who sees women as prostitutes, mother figures, or asexual innocents. The character of Mouse remains as elusive and one-dimensional as Wilde's depiction of Sibyl Vane. Unlike most of Mansfield's complex, many-sided female characters, Mouse is simply woman as victim. Kate Fullbrook suggests that "Mouse is self-endangered by her acquiescence to a tradition of feminine honour and feminine passivity expressed in her mouse disguise."[12]

Of course we know Mouse only through Raoul's descriptions of her. She is beautiful, exquisite, fragile; Raoul explains that "she came upon you with the same kind of shock that you feel when you have been drinking tea out of a thin innocent cup and suddenly, at the bottom, you see a tiny creature, half butterfly, half woman, bowing to you with her hands in her sleeves" (p. 368).[13] And like other images in Mansfield's fiction of tiny, living creatures (the fly in the story of the same name is the most brutal example), such intricate beings hover or "bow" in futile hope against the certainty of the attack that will annihilate them. The vulnerability of women

---

however. Hankin also clearly states that the story "is an extended and psychologically penetrating study of male homosexuality—from a woman's point of view" (p. 155).

[11]See F. A. Lea, *The Life of John Middleton Murry* (London: Methuen, 1959), pp. 25–26, and Sharron Greer Cassavant, *John Middleton Murry: The Critic as Moralist* (University: University of Alabama Press, 1982), p. 10.

[12]Fullbrook, p. 94.

[13]Hankin notes that Raoul and Mouse may also be seen as "doubles." She points out Raoul's description of himself as Madame Butterfly (p. 161) and several other elements of similarity and psychological opposition.

when they must depend on men for economic and emotional support is a continuing theme in Mansfield's writing.

As we have seen, *female* sexuality is a missing subject in *Dorian Gray*. Mansfield would not have found examples of lesbian behavior in Wilde's novel. In fact, she would not have had much knowledge of lesbianism, as a subject, when she read Wilde at Queen's College in 1906. The public discussion of homosexuality was based almost totally on relations between men. Weeks points out that "although the theorising of homosexuality applied indifferently to males and females, it is striking that it was male homosexuality that was chiefly subject to new regulation. Lesbianism continued to be ignored by the criminal codes."[14] Weeks explains that by the time of the Wilde trial,

> a recognizably "modern" male homosexual identity was beginning to emerge. . . . [But] it would be another generation before female homosexuality reached a corresponding level of articulacy. The lesbian identity was much less clearly defined, and the lesbian subculture was minimal in comparison with the male, and even more overwhelmingly upper class or literary.[15]

Katherine Mansfield's sexual awakening took place in the period between these two generations. By the time she wrote "Je ne parle pas français," a lesbian identity was beginning to take shape among some women in London, but in 1906 homosexual identity was formulated for her only in its male version. Lesbian sexual *behavior*, however, was a real possibility.

Mansfield had lived in an atmosphere of strong emotional connections between women during her years at Queen's College (1903–6). Much of the passionate life of the students revolved around the kinds of "romantic friendships" common in women's lives in the nineteenth century.[16] It is not clear from the biographies

---

[14]Weeks, p. 105. For a concise, well-documented review of attitudes about homosexuality in the nineteenth century, see his chap. 6, "The Construction of Homosexuality," pp. 96–121.

[15]Ibid., p. 115.

[16]A growing number of works on women's relationships have appeared during the last decade, following from Carroll Smith-Rosenberg's ground-breaking article in the inaugural issue of *Signs*, "The Female World of Love and Ritual: Relations between Women in Nineteenth Century America," *Signs: Journal of Women in Cul-*

whether Mansfield actually participated in sexual activity during her time at Queen's.[17] Nonetheless, she apparently wrote the highly erotic unpublished sketch "Summer Idylle. 1906" during the last months of her stay there (ca. May–October 1906), when she was only seventeen.[18]

Mansfield reverses the names of her characters in "Summer Idylle. 1906": Hinemoa, the Maori name, belongs to the character more like herself—that is, more European, and implicitly more inhibited sexually. Marina, the Maori character, is the initiator, the daring one. Marina appears to be based on her Maori friend from childhood, Maata Mahupuku. It is Maata who evokes the passionate longings and the terror and revulsion and guilt in the unpublished journal entries: "I alone in this silent clockfilled room have become powerfully—I want Maata—I want her as I have had her—terribly. This is unclean I know but true. What an extraordinary thing—I feel savagely crude—and almost powerfully enamoured of the child. I had thought that a thing of the Past—Heigh Ho!!!!!!!!!!"[19]

There are racist implications to Mansfield's assumptions about Marina's sexuality, which are drawn from colonialist stereotypes of the sexuality of the "other." A version of the expression "savagely crude" turns up again six months later in another diary entry, this

---

ture and Society 1 (Autumn 1975), 1–30. See in particular, Blanche Wiesen Cook, "'Women Alone Stir My Imagination': Lesbianism and the Cultural Tradition," *Signs* 4 (Summer 1979), 718–39; Lillian Faderman, *Surpassing the Love of Men: Romantic Friendship and Love between Women from the Renaissance to the Present* (New York: Morrow, 1981). Faderman's discussion of "romantic friendship" and its destruction through the increasing medicalization of the discussion of women's relationships after the turn of the century is especially illuminating.

[17]Alpers and Meyers date her lesbian experiences differently. Alpers, *The Life of Katherine Mansfield*, pp. 46–47, dates her relationship with Maata Mahupuku during the period of her return to New Zealand, in early 1907. Meyers, *Katherine Mansfield: A Biography*, p. 32, suggests that the two were lovers as early as 1903, when pupils at Miss Swainson's school in Wellington. Mansfield would have been fourteen at the time. Tomalin, *Katherine Mansfield: A Secret Life*, p. 16, is more tentative: "If a later entry in Katherine's journal is to be believed, she had some experience with Maata during their schooldays that was sexually disturbing; it seems to have been more than a matter of a schoolgirl crush, and it became the germ of her awareness of her own bisexuality."

[18]"Summer Idylle. 1906," in "The Unpublished Manuscripts of Katherine Mansfield," ed. Margaret Scott, *The Turnbull Library Record* 3 (n.s.) (November 1970), 133–36.

[19]Quoted in Alpers, p. 49, from Mansfield's Notebook 39, p. 17, Alexander Turnbull Library.

time in a description of a "young Maori girl" Mansfield encountered on her camping trip in the Ureweras: "All the lines of her face are passionate violent—crudely savage—but in her lifted eyes slumbers a tragic illimitable peace."[20] The reversal of the words "crude" and "savage" is reminiscent of the reversal of names in the "Summer Idylle" sketch. Both suggest at the same time self-identification and disassociation, the latter implied in the diary reference to the "unclean."

Margaret Scott, who painstakingly transcribed this sketch, noted: "It may be significant that 'Summer Idylle' is the most difficult to decipher of all the manuscripts. To the uninitiated it looks like the seismological chart of an unstable region."[21] If the handwriting in the manuscript is the physical symptom of the writer's emotional turmoil, the content of the sketch is equally explosive, regardless of its surface appearance of Edenic innocence and natural beauty. The sketch is a remarkable example of how Mansfield reworked '90s artificialities of style into an early modernist piece full of elusiveness, indirection, and sexual innuendo. Many of the features of her later style are already in embryo, demonstrating that her emergence into "modernism" was not derivative of other twentieth-century writers, but a function of her own synthesis and imaginative reworking of late nineteenth-century techniques and themes. The symbolists had given her a glimpse of a view of art in which abstract analysis was replaced by suggestive concrete images and symbols.[22] Organic unity was another requirement, and so she learned at the beginning of her career that each image, word, and sentence must contribute to the meaning of the whole.

One advantage of this de-emphasis of the analytical is that it allows for the expression of what had always been silenced by that older, dominant, authoritarian prose. Mansfield was attracted to the evocativeness of the symbolist prose style for reasons she would not have had the terminology to articulate. Jonathan Monroe sees the development of the prose poem itself as symptomatic of "the struggle . . . for the power of speech" by those who "have been con-

[20]Katherine Mansfield, *The Urewera Notebook*, ed. Ian A. Gordon (New York: Oxford University Press, 1978), p. 85.
[21]Scott, p. 128.
[22]For a discussion of symbolism and Mansfield's use of it in her early writings, see Hanson and Gurr, *Katherine Mansfield*, pp. 21–23, 27–31.

sidered by generations of writers and critics unworthy of literary attention."[23] Monroe illustrates how from "its very beginnings the prose poem anticipated the kinds of reversals of hierarchically dominant oppositional terms which the work of Jacques Derrida and his followers exemplifies" (p. 24). What Mansfield might have discovered in the prose poem was the possibility of deconstructing the phallocentric structures of conventional narrative and producing instead a kind of writing from the body, such as that advocated by contemporary postmodernists like Hélène Cixous. (Accordingly, many of the examples used by the French feminists come from the same symbolist writers about whom Mansfield was learning through reading Arthur Symons.) Cixous's questions—"What is feminine *sexual pleasure*, where does it take place, how is it inscribed at the level of her body, of her unconscious? And then how is it put into writing?"[24]—are correlatives of Mansfield's efforts in "Summer Idylle."

The first sentence of the sketch seems a holdover from the aestheticism of the prose poems: "A slow tranquil surrender of the Night Spirits, a knowledge that her body was refreshed and cool and light, a great breath from the sea that skimmed through the window and kissed her laughingly—and her awakening was complete." Mansfield used personification, especially of elements of nature, or of the city, over and over in her early sketches, as in her "London" vignette, written around the same time as "Summer Idylle," where "London stretches out eager hands towards me."[25] In one of her first published sketches, "Silhouettes" (the connection with Arthur Symons's collection of the same name should not be overlooked), she writes: "I want the night to come, and kiss me with her hot mouth, and lead me through an amethyst twilight to the place of the white gardenia."[26]

"Summer Idylle. 1906" begins with "awakening." The story is a highly encoded sexual awakening, and significantly, it involves the relationship between two young women. On the surface the "plot"

[23]Jonathan Monroe, *A Poverty of Objects: The Prose Poem and the Politics of Genre* (Ithaca: Cornell University Press, 1987), p. 10.

[24]Hélène Cixous, "Sorties," in *New French Feminisms: An Anthology*, ed. Elaine Marks and Isabelle de Courtivron (New York: Schocken Books, 1981), p. 95.

[25]Scott, p. 132.

[26]K. Mansfield, "Silhouettes," *The Native Companion*, November 1, 1907, p. 229. Reprinted in *Poems of Katherine Mansfield*, p. 8.

is simple and inconsequential: Hinemoa and Marina are alone in a beach cottage; they start their day with a swim to an island; Marina encourages Hinemoa to dive in spite of her fear of drowning; they swim back to the shore and return to the house where Hinemoa kisses her own reflection in the mirror to comfort herself after her terror out in the sea; she dresses and joins Marina who has prepared breakfast; she eats a peach but rejects the koumara (a New Zealand sweet potato that has a blue color to it) that Marina offers; Marina eats it herself and the story is over.

But the short piece is as dense and compact as poetry. As in the symbolist poetry Mansfield had been studying, each object radiates a multiplicity of meanings, and these meanings are intensified by clusters of archetypal as well as conventional connotations, many of which are related to the female body, such as water, flowers, and fruits of the earth. The only masculine image is the rata tree "with his tongues of flame," which "rose like a pillar of flame." The traditional association of fire with the masculine, water with the feminine is maintained throughout this story, but it is complicated by Mansfield's attempt to superimpose the relationship between the two young women on a Maori legend about Hinemoa, who swam to an island to meet her lover. Marina appears to be the leader, the one who initiates Hinemoa's awakening. At dawn Hinemoa looks out the window at the sea, which "flung itself onto the warm whiteness with so complete an abandon that she clapped her hands like a child." But then "she grew serious, frowned, and then smiled ironically. 'I'd forgotten she existed' she laughed, opening the door." The word "ironically" understates the overwhelming importance of the "she" in the next room. Thus the tightly worked opening lines already suggest an undercurrent of sexual excitement. Within the first two sentences Mansfield uses the words "surrender," "body," "kissed," "awakening," "danced," "flung itself," "abandon." In the next paragraph, Hinemoa enters Marina's room in which "the scent of the manuka was heavy and soothing." The imagery shifts to flowers:

> The floor was strewn with blossoms. . . . Marina lay straight and still in her bed, her hands clasped over her head, her lips slightly parted. A faint thin colour like the petal of a dull rose leaf shone in the dusk of her skin. Hinemoa bent over her with a curious feeling of pleasure,

intermingled with a sensation which she did not analyse. It came upon her if she had used too much perfume, if she had drunk wine that was too heavy and sweet, laid her hand on velvet that was too soft and smooth. Marina was wrapped in the darkness of her hair. Hinemoa took it up in her hands and drew it away from her brow and face and shoulders. (P. 134)

The "sensation which she did not analyse" becomes too intense to bear without release. Marina wakes up and kisses Hinemoa "just between her eyebrows." Hinemoa cries, "O come quick, come quick. . . . Your room is hot with this manuka and I want to bathe." Marina tosses blossoms into Hinemoa's hair and calls her "Snow Maiden." Hinemoa is linked through this image with the "beautiful green hair" of the fern trees, when Marina later refers to the Maori legend: "should a warrior venture through the bush in the night, they seize him and wrap him round in their hair and in the morning he is dead" (p. 135). But Marina underscores the sexual parallel between the male devastated by his entrapment by female desire and her own urgings to entice Hinemoa when she says, " 'They are cruel even as I might wish to be to thee, little Hinemoa.' She looked at Hinemoa with half-shut eyes, her upper lip drawn back, showing her teeth." (p. 135). (Mansfield would later use the half-shut eyes and drawn-back lip to suggest the animalistic nature of sexuality in a number of stories.) After the verbal enticement Hinemoa draws back.

The next paragraph deserves quoting in full:

'Now we dive' said Marina, rising and walking to the edge of the rock. The water was here in shadow, deep green, slumbering. 'Remember' she said, turning to Hinemoa, 'it is with the eyes open that you must fall—otherwise it is useless. Fall into the water and look right down, down. Those who have never dived do not know the sea. It is not ripples and foam you see. Try and sink as deeply as [you] can... with the eyes open, and then you will learn.' Marina stood for a moment, poised like a beautiful statue, then she sprang down into the water. To Hinemoa it seemed a long time of waiting, but at last Marina came up, and shook her head many times and cried out exultantly 'Come. Come.' A flood of excitement bounded to Hinemoa's brain. She quivered suddenly, laughed again, and then descended.

When she came up she caught Marina's hands. 'I am mad, mad' she
said. 'Race me back, quickly, I shall drown myself.'

Mansfield wrote this many years before she met D. H. Lawrence,
and it is apparent that her understanding of the symbolism of diving
and the terror of immersion in the body of the female long preceded
his version of sexual awakening through baptism by water in "The
Horse-Dealer's Daughter."[27] But as in Lawrence's story, the return
to the ordinary after the plunge contains elements of retrogression.
The dive is so overpowering, so destructive of the known and the
assured, that although everything is changed forever it seems necessary to seek, at least momentarily, comfort from the familiar. And
comfort as well from the protection of the shell of the ego. So
Hinemoa runs back to her room and kisses her reflection; so she
dresses "slowly and gravely in a straight white gown, just like a
child wears" (p. 135).

But she is drawn out of herself again by the sight of Marina
combing her hair in the sunlight:

> 'See how beautiful I am' she cried as Hinemoa came up to her.
> 'Come and eat, little one.' 'O I am hungry' said Hinemoa going up to
> table. 'Eggs and bread and honey and peaches, and what is in this dish,
> Marina?' 'Baked koumaras'... Hinemoa sat down and peeled a peach
> and ate it with the juice running through her fingers. 'Is it good?' said
> Marina. 'Very.' 'And you are not afraid any more?' 'No.' 'What was it
> like?' 'It was like... like...' 'Yes?' Hinemoa bent her head. 'I have seen
> the look on your face' Marina laughed. 'Hinemoa, eat a koumara.'
> 'No, I don't like them. They're blue, they're too unnatural. Give me
> some bread.' Marina handed her a piece, and then helped herself to a
> koumara, which she ate delicately, looking at Hinemoa with a strange

---

[27]In spite of Mansfield's often quoted remark about D. H. Lawrence's obsession
with Freudian symbolism ("And I shall *never* see sex in trees, sex in the running
brooks, sex in stones & sex in everything. The number of things that are really
phallic from fountain pen fillers onwards!" [*Letters* I, p. 261]), her own writing is
equally laden with sexual suggestion. Yet she differs from Lawrence in her attitude
toward it, either not taking it seriously at all and satirizing others' use of it, or using
it herself to encode the elements of sexuality most troubling to her. This deeper,
more subtle and diffused use of sexual symbolism is related both to her stylistic
inheritance from the symbolists and to an unarticulated, yet profound, understanding of female sexuality.

half-smile expanding over her face. 'I eat it for that reason' she said. 'I eat it because it is blue.' 'Yes' said Hinemoa, breaking the bread in her white fingers.

The child in white still resists the temptation of the "unnatural." The unspeakable spills out like the juice of the peaches, and though Marina playfully tries to make Hinemoa articulate it, she gets in return only "It was like... like... ." (Years later in "The Garden-Party," Mansfield would show us Laura's inability to speak her insight into the meaning of death in language very much like this.) But Marina responds not to Hinemoa's words but to her body, to the "look on [her] face," and takes it as a sign: "eat a koumara." As Marina asserts her own superiority to the conventions that bind Hinemoa—"I eat it because it is blue"—Hinemoa takes these same words as a question. Her response, "Yes," has all the resonance of Joyce's later use of that word at the end of Molly Bloom's soliloquy in *Ulysses*.

## 4

# "The Strange Longing
# for the Artificial"

**B**oth Katherine Mansfield and Oscar Wilde could be said to prepare for their own respective future tragedies. Ellmann points out that the notion of prison had certainly crossed Wilde's mind,[1] and Mansfield wrote an eerily prescient passage in a journal entry of December 21, 1908:

> I should like to write a life much in the style of Walter Pater's *Child in the House*. About a girl in Wellington; the singular charm and barrenness of that place—with climatic effects—wind, rain, spring, night—the sea, the cloud pageantry. And then to leave the place and go to Europe. To live there a dual existence—to go back and be utterly disillusioned, to find out the truth of all—to return to London—to live there an existence so full and strange that life itself seemed to greet her—and ill to the point of death return to W. and die there. A story—no, it would be a sketch, hardly that, more a psychological study—of the most erudite character—I should fill it with climatic disturbance—and also of the strange longing for the artificial. I should call it *Strife*—and the child I should call—ah, I have it—I'd make her a half-caste Maori and call her Maata. (*Journal*, pp. 37–38)

When Mansfield referred to the "style" of Pater's "Child in the House," she was reaching back through Wilde to one of *his* primary influences. Through Pater, she could still absorb Wilde,[2] especially

[1]Richard Ellmann, *Golden Codgers: Biographical Speculations* (New York: Oxford University Press, 1973), p. 75.
[2]Vincent O'Sullivan remarks: "Mansfield's conception of life was, I believe, close

since by December 1908 Pater must have seemed a safer model than Wilde. Her affair with another young woman, Edie Bendall, had taken place in June 1907; by August 1908 she had returned to England, so the belief that she was fated to die young, to be disillusioned, was already being nurtured by the city's effect on her in those first few months—the growing realization that her search for experience might culminate in disaster.

More significant, the interiority of Pater's "The Child in the House," as well as the prose poems of the symbolists, was more useful than *Dorian Gray* in her own search for alternative structures. She delighted in the Paterian emphasis on intensity in the midst of flux, although she was still responding to it as an adolescent who could not possibly understand the depths of melancholy implicit in Pater's concentration on the ephemeral or the rage it might have concealed against the certainty of change. She could use the methods and the moods of the period to express her own desires for growth, excitement, and passion, disregarding their more somber implications. She would understand those much later when she tried to assert the intensity of the moment in stories reflecting her certain knowledge of her own impending death.

Although Pater may have appeared "safer" than Wilde in that he was not associated with homosexuality in the public sense of Wilde's scandalous reputation, Mansfield's interest in him is still linked to the homosexual encoding represented by his elevation of the Greek ideal of male friendships. In his chapter on Johann Winckelmann in *The Renaissance,* for example, he refers to Winckelmann's "romantic, fervent friendships with young men," which "perfected his reconciliation to the spirit of Greek Sculpture."[3] Moreover, Mansfield's reference to Pater appears in the same notebook (no. 39) in which she writes about her sexual attraction to Maata and quotes the many epigrams from Wilde. (Wilde permeates Notebook 39, a fact not immediately apparent in the published

---

to Pater's own, before that scholar's views were touched by the temperament and performance of Wilde to become something rather more sensational than he should have cared to father. . . . Mansfield was in an intellectual stream whose current was wide at the end of the last century and strongest where it took its force from Pater" ("The Magnetic Chain," p. 101).

[3]Walter Pater, *The Renaissance: Studies in Art and Poetry* (London: Macmillan, 1910), p. 191.

# "The Strange Longing for the Artificial"

*Journal of Katherine Mansfield*, because Murry interspersed material from other notebooks in order to make it appear one chronological record.) There, in the entry referring to Pater, the Wildean touches emerge in the references to "dual existence"[4] and "the strange longing for the artificial." She had written in the same notebook earlier, on March 30, 1907, the following quotation from *Dorian Gray*: "Being natural is simply a pose—and the most irritating pose I know" (*Journal*, p. 11). Yet the "Child in the House" passage also contains an implicit contrast—and a potential conflict—between the natural ("climatic disturbance") and "the artificial" as the locus for the writer's attention. The natural for Mansfield would necessarily include a recognition of the interactions of external and internal reality: a romantic poetics of immanence. On the other hand, the ideal of artifice, while appearing to escape organicism, is equally romantic in its heroic despair over finality.

The opposition of natural and artificial has relevance to a feminist quandary as well, since nature is equated with the feminine in the ideological framework of western thought.[5] The romantic tradition posits nature as the foundation of wisdom, creative generativity, and inspiration, but it is still defined as source (or womb) rather than as agent. An implicit hierarchy of gender pervades much of the discussion of this dichotomy in the nineteenth century, as in Pater's apparent approval of Winckelmann's elevation of the masculine and his assertion of the superiority of artifice in the creative process. Thus in *The Renaissance* Pater quotes the following from Winckelmann:

> As it is confessedly the beauty of man which is to be conceived under one general idea, so I have noticed that those who are observant of beauty only in women, and are moved little or not at all by the beauty of men, seldom have an impartial, vital, inborn instinct for beauty in art. To such persons the beauty of Greek art will ever seem

[4]Dorian Gray felt the "terrible pleasure of a double life" (Wilde, *Dorian Gray*, p. 175).

[5]There is a growing body of feminist work on the nature/woman question. See, for example, Teresa de Lauretis, *Alice Doesn't: Feminism, Semiotics, Cinema* (Bloomington: Indiana University Press, 1984); Luce Irigaray, *This Sex Which Is Not One* (Ithaca: Cornell University Press, 1985). See also the essays (especially those by Julia Kristeva, Nancy K. Miller, and Christine Brooke-Rose) in *The Female Body in Western Culture*, ed. Susan Rubin Suleiman (Cambridge: Harvard University Press, 1986).

wanting, because its supreme beauty is rather male than female. But the beauty of art demands a higher sensibility than the beauty of nature, because the beauty of art, like tears shed at a play, gives no pain, is without life, and must be awakened and repaired by culture. (P. 131)

The implication that heterosexual men must be deficient in the "instinct for beauty in art" because of their desire for women—that is, their absorption in the possession and use of "nature"—results in an ultimate presumption of the superiority of the artificial. This superiority is to be achieved through a homosocial cultural arrangement, in which the female/nature is to be surpassed altogether. Again, in a manner similar to the elevation of the Greek ideal in *Dorian Gray*, Mansfield would find herself excluded as a woman from both the role of artist and—ironically—the role of art object as well.

Pater pulls back from a whole-hearted endorsement of Winckelmann's position, however, when he wryly notes the personal contradiction:

Certainly, of that beauty of living form which regulated Winckelmann's friendships, it could not be said that it gave no pain. One notable friendship . . . begins with an antique, chivalrous letter in French, and ends noisily in a burst of angry fire. Far from reaching the quietism, the bland indifference of art, such attachments are nevertheless more susceptible than any others of equal strength of a purely intellectual culture. Of passion, of physical excitement, they contain just so much as stimulates the eye to the finest delicacies of color and form. (P. 131)

In one of her first published sketches, "In the Botanical Gardens," which appeared in December 1907, Mansfield called an arrangement of flowers "such a subtle combination of the artificial and the natural—that is, partly, the secret of their charm."[6] In this prose poem, she contrasts the mannered garden—where all the visitors congregate—with the surrounding untamed bush, where she (paradoxically using a male—and Wildean—pseudonym, "Julian Mark") feels "old with the age of centuries, strong with the strength of savagery," and loses herself in a desire to merge with the ancient

[6]*Poems of Katherine Mansfield,* p. 9.

powers of the wilderness: "Remembrance has gone—this is the Lotus Land." She imagines "a great company moving towards me, their faces averted, wreathed with green garlands . . . following the little stream in silence until it is sucked into the wide sea." The imaginary crowd of ancient ritualists, with all its associations with orgiastic, Dionysian release, is counterbalanced by the narrator's return to the "civilised" crowd of visitors, proper in their conventional appreciation of the cultivated garden. The entire counterforce of the passage is the strength of its female imagery: the stream "sucked into the wide sea," the bush "strong with the strength of savagery." Such identification with the untamed world—what Mansfield once referred to as her "undiscovered country" (*Journal*, p. 94)—appears only fitfully in the course of her writing career. One wonders how much more of it there would have been had she never left New Zealand. It bursts forth for a moment here, but it is already mannered, stylistically akin to the arranged gardens, containing within it the impurities of nostalgia.

Several months after the publication of "In the Botanical Gardens," Mansfield's letters and notebooks indicate that her interest in aestheticism had not abated. In a letter to her sister Vera, probably in April or May of 1908, she wrote:

> I am ashamed of young New Zealand, but what is to be done. All the firm fat framework of their brains must be demolished before they can begin to learn. They want a purifying influence—a mad wave of pre-Raphaelitism, of super-aestheticism, should intoxicate the country. They must go to excess in the direction of culture, become almost decadent in their tendencies for a year or two and then find balance and proportion. (*Letters* I, p. 44)

It must have been around this time that she read Arthur Symons's *Studies in Prose and Verse*,[7] where she would have had her artistic

[7]Mansfield quoted from Arthur Symons's *Studies in Prose and Verse* (London: J. M. Dent, 1904) in Notebook 2 (Alexander Turnbull Library, Mansfield MSS). This notebook dates from November 14, 1907, to April 1909. It's likely that Mansfield wrote the notes from Symons while she was still in New Zealand, sometime before June 1908. My reading of these notes at the Turnbull Library was impeded by Mansfield's notoriously difficult handwriting. I am therefore indebted to Clare Hanson's excellent transcription of these notes and other unpublished passages from the early notebooks in *The Critical Writings of Katherine Mansfield* (New York: St. Martin's, 1987), pp. 140–44.

preferences confirmed. When she wrote the journal entry about the "girl in Wellington," she might have remembered Symons's description there of Walter Pater, with the characteristics of Pater's "service of art" so carefully delineated:

> It was not natural to him to be natural. There are many kinds of beauty in the world, and of these what is called natural beauty is but one. Pater's temperament was at once shy and complex, languid and ascetic, sensuous and spiritual. He did not permit life to come to him without a certain ceremony; he was on his guard against the abrupt indiscretion of events; and if his whole life was a service of art, he arranged his life so that, as far as possible, it might be served by that very dedication. With this conscious ordering of things, it became a last sophistication to aim at an effect in style which should bring the touch of unpremeditation, which we seem to find in nature, into a faultlessly combined arrangement of art.[8]

She might well have understood her own attempts to achieve "the touch of unpremeditation, which we *seem* to find in nature" (emphasis added) in such sketches as "In the Botanical Gardens" and "Summer Idylle"; and she certainly kept, throughout her career, a notion of the seriousness of the artistic life, which she could have described as "a service of art." But how much of Pater's work she actually had read is not clear from her letters and journals, where, aside from her remark on "The Child in the House" and a passing reference or two, Pater's name seems to disappear from the record. She probably read *The Renaissance* between 1903 and 1906 at Queen's College, where her professor Walter Rippmann had great enthusiasm for the creative work of the aesthetes and decadents; but there is no definite evidence for it. Undoubtedly, she would have been introduced to many of Pater's basic ideas about style through Rippmann, from whom she also learned about Symons's work on the French symbolists. What is most certain is that she read *about* Pater in Symons's *Studies in Prose and Verse* in 1908. This particular work may have had a greater impact on her than his better-known book, *The Symbolist Movement in Literature* (1899), because the former concentrates more fully on prose writers, especially English writers of the late nineteenth century such as Pater, Robert Louis Stevenson, and Oscar

[8]Symons, *Studies in Prose and Verse*, p. 76.

Wilde, whose styles would have provided her with models to emulate, admire, and eventually reject. (Significantly, she copied notes
from Symons on Balzac, De Quincey, Hawthorne, D'Annunzio,
Zola, and de Maupassant, as well.[9])

When Mansfield refers to "the singular charm and barrenness of
that place" in the "girl in Wellington" passage, we can recognize
echoes of Symons's phrasing in his description of Pater as "a personality singularly unconventional, and singularly full of charm."[10] Her
reference to Pater's "style" indicates her sympathy with certain
kinds of attitudes, with certain moods, as in this passage from
"Child in the House":

> A touch of regret or desire mingled all night with the remembered
> presence of the red flowers, and their perfume in the darkness about
> him; and the longing for some undivined, entire possession of them
> was the beginning of a revelation to him, growing ever clearer, with
> the coming of the gracious summer guise of fields and trees and per-
> sons in each succeeding year, of a certain, at times seemingly exclusive
> predominance in his interests, of beautiful physical things, a kind of
> tyranny of the senses over him.[11]

Mansfield must have been attracted to the notion of the "tyranny of
the senses," to the references to flowers and perfume, and to the

[9]It should be noted that in her letter to Vera Beauchamp, cited above in reference
to New Zealand and aestheticism, Mansfield suggests reading the following authors
as an antidote to provincialism: William Morris, Catulle Mendes, George Meredith,
Maurice Maeterlinck, Ruskin, Rodenbach, Le Gallienne, Symons, D'Annunzio,
Shaw, Granville Barker, "Sebastian Melmoth" (code for Wilde), Whitman,
Tolstoi, Carpenter, Lamb, Hazlitt, Hawthorne, and the Brontës. Of this list, Symons writes about the following in *Studies*: Morris, Meredith, Symons, D'Annunzio,
Wilde, Tolstoi, and Hawthorne. The other authors Symons includes are Balzac,
Merimée, Gautier, De Quincey, Pater, R. L. Stevenson, J. A. Symonds, de Maupas-
sant, Daudet, H. Crackanthorpe, Robert Buchanan, Gorki, Campoamor, Robert
Bridges, Austin Dobson, Yeats, Stephen Phillips, and Dowson. The book concludes with Symons's prefaces to the 2d ed. of his own "Silhouettes" and to the 2d
ed. of his "London Nights."

[10]Symons, *Studies*, p. 63. In her notes on the *Studies*, Mansfield quotes the following: "*Walter Pater* an exquisite fineness" (*Critical Writings*, p. 141). These words are
from the following discussion by Symons about Pater: "As a critic, he selected for
analysis only those types of artistic character in which delicacy, an exquisite fineness,
is the principal attraction" (p. 64).

[11]Walter Pater, "The Child in the House" (1878), in *Miscellaneous Studies: A Series
of Essays* (London: Macmillan, 1910), p. 186.

complex of meaning created out of a mingling of objects, memories, sense impressions, longings—that complex of meaning only expressible through the interaction of human emotion and physical object. But the syntax, the phrasing—these were far removed from her own style. Without articulating the difference, in 1907 she was already writing a prose different from the ornate style of Pater.

I do not believe, however, that Mansfield "rejected" Pater's prose style, or that she developed her own voice in reaction to his, as Perry Meisel implies was the case with Virginia Woolf and the Bloomsbury group. Meisel suggests that "the intricate diction of Pater's most characteristic sentences was one of Bloomsbury's principal and symbolic musts to avoid, and that the largely comma-free cadences of Woolf, Strachey, and Forster all may be accounted for by the reaction against such Victorian stylistic mannerisms for which all three writers are famous."[12] A study of Mansfield's earliest prose writings reveals that Pater's "intricate diction" was not a habit she needed to break. Her sentence structure from the *beginning* was easy and fluent, without "Victorian stylistic mannerisms," with the exception of occasionally archaic diction and personification. Some good examples of Mansfield's easy fluency, if one disregards their queasy sentimentality and mawkishness, are found in the stories about children she published in *The Queen's College Magazine* in 1903–4. Here her sentences resemble more the clarity and directness of Hans Christian Andersen than the style of Pater—or Wilde, for that matter. Even in adolescent work, Mansfield's voice is recognizable. One such story begins:

> He was a tall, stately pine-tree. So tall, so very tall, that when you stood underneath and looked right up through the branches you could not see the top. How very fond you were of that pine-tree! We used to go and see it every day. He sang the most beautiful songs and told the most lovely stories; but he always seemed a little sad, somehow.[13]

Rather than emulate Pater's prose style, Mansfield later incorporated his emphasis on interiority, his attitudes about the renuncia-

[12]Perry Meisel, *The Absent Father: Virginia Woolf and Walter Pater* (New Haven: Yale University Press, 1980), p. xiv.
[13]Kathleen Beauchamp, "The Pine-tree, the Sparrows, and You and I," *The Queen's College Magazine* 22 (December 1903), 74.

tion of the artist, and his appreciation for artifice into a style *already modern*.[14] It is likely that she absorbed these things from Symons's description of Pater.[15] For instance, in writing on Pater's style Symons locates exactly the elements that would have appealed to her: "An almost oppressive quiet, a quiet which seems to exhale an atmosphere heavy with the odour of tropical flowers, broods over these pages; a subdued light shadows them."[16]

Meisel remarks that Pater's portraits are usually criticized "for being 'static' compared to their modernist counterparts in Woolf or Joyce. . . . As a form . . . portraiture already means a bias against action and an emphasis instead on the contemplation of character."[17] In this instance, Meisel's observation is no less true of Mansfield than of Woolf and Joyce. Mansfield's talents of impersonation had already taught her to dramatize rather than describe the interactions of human beings with each other and with the natural environment. But she learned much from Pater's portraiture nonetheless. Surely she appreciated his emphasis on dreams and memories as components in evolving character—not in the sense of a scientific explanation for behavior, but rather as a means to artistic creation. For example, in "The Child in the House" Florian Deleal recalls in a dream the house he had lived in as a child: "And it happened that this accident of his dream was just the thing needed for the beginning of a certain design he then had in view, the noting, namely, of some things in the story of his spirit—in that process of brain-building by which we are, each one of us, what we are."[18]

That the components of the "design" are different for each individual and that each individual *perceives* uniquely details presented

[14]I wonder if in a time when academic prose itself has become overwhelmingly latinate and convoluted, a return to Paterian intricacies appeals to critics, while the seemingly transparent prose of some of the modernists—Hemingway, Sherwood Anderson, etc.—gradually is becoming devalued.

[15]Richard Ellmann's description of Symons's style suggests without stating it explicitly that Symons's methods derive from Pater: "His style is made up of delicacies and insinuations. Considering as he does that symbolist literature is 'a sacred ritual,' he treats each of his authors as a renunciant, who gives up contentment for the sake of his soul and art" ("Introduction" to Arthur Symons, *The Symbolist Movement in Literature* [1908; New York: Dutton, 1958], p. xiii).

[16]Symons, *Studies*, p. 65.

[17]Meisel, pp. 45–46. Meisel, pp. 34–36, also suggests that Bloomsbury seemed to avoid references to Pater and Wilde partly as a result of the Wilde scandal and its own members' homosexual proclivities.

[18]Pater, *Miscellaneous Studies*, p. 173.

by sense impressions are concepts also fully articulated in Pater: "Tracing back the threads of his complex spiritual habit, as he was used in after years to do, Florian found that he owed to the place many tones of sentiment afterwards customary with him, certain inward lights under which things most naturally presented themselves to him."[19] And Mansfield may have learned other things from Pater: that the artist must be "true from first to last to that vision within"[20] and that "the first step towards seeing one's object as it really is, is to know one's impression as it really is, to discriminate it, to realise it distinctly."[21]

Even if Mansfield had not actually read *The Renaissance*, she would have found a similar and more direct statement in Symons, and there she would have seen it framed within a discussion of the prose style of one of her most famous precursors in the genre of the short story, Guy de Maupassant: "The first aim of art, no doubt, is the representation of things as they are. But, then, things are as our eyes see them and as our minds make them, and it is thus of primary importance for the critic to distinguish the precise qualities of those eyes and minds which make the world into imaginative literature."[22] In her letter to Vera (ca. May or June of 1908), Mansfield mentions that she is reading de Maupassant and Balzac, and "I have had too, quite a mania for Walter Pater—and Nathaniel Hawthorne—and also Robert Browning—and Flaubert—Oh, many others" (*Letters* I, p. 46). This is a clue that the notes on Symons in her notebooks date from the same period as this letter, since Symons writes about most of these authors in *Studies in Prose and Verse*. Symons devotes whole chapters to Balzac, de Maupassant, Pater, and Hawthorne. In the letter to Vera, Mansfield comments about Balzac: "Yet—and this keeps him from being much read by young people—he deals with the senses *through* the intellect." The sentence is a slight revision of the phrase she quoted from Symons in her notebook: "He is concerned with the senses through the intellect."[23]

But what does Symons *actually* say about Balzac? The following is

---

[19]Ibid., p. 176.
[20]Walter Pater, *Appreciations* (London: Macmillan, 1897), p. 20.
[21]Pater, *The Renaissance*, p. xviii.
[22]Symons, *Studies*, p. 97.
[23]Quoted in *Critical Writings*, p. 140.

the complete passage from which Mansfield was quoting; what she did *not* quote is illuminating in itself, for her silence on Symons's phallocentric assumptions may reflect a culturally conditioned female self-suppression, or that same silence may be a symptom of Mansfield's underlying resistance to his confident sexism:

> "The physiognomy of women does not begin before the age of thirty," he has said; and perhaps before that age no one can really understand Balzac. Few young people care for him, for there is nothing in him that appeals to the senses except through the intellect. Not many women care for him supremely, for it is part of his method to express sentiments through facts, and not facts through sentiments. But it is natural that he should be the favourite reading of men of the world, of those men of the world who have the distinction of their kind; for he supplies the key of the enigma which they are studying.[24]

Note how Mansfield's remarks to Vera avoid placing herself within the hierarchy of readers of Balzac which Symons describes. She separates herself from "young people"—even though she is only nineteen—by implying that she and Vera are more mature than their compatriots. By omission, she separates herself from the category "women"—they are said to dislike Balzac, and she so obviously likes him. Therefore, the category for herself can only be the one Symons puts at the highest level: "men of the world." Consequently, according to this illogical syllogism, Mansfield is a man of the world! In such ways are the destructive self-deceptions of women under patriarchy brought to life.[25]

Inadvertently, Mansfield's reading about Balzac through Symons

---

[24]Symons, *Studies,* p. 22.

[25]There are several other places in *Studies in Prose and Verse* where Symons makes similar statements supporting the dominance of the masculine perspective, and Mansfield quotes from none of them, even though she quotes adjacent passages. Again, it almost seems a purposeful silence. For example, from Symons's chapter on Hawthorne Mansfield quotes: "His feeling for flowers was very exquisite—& seems not so much a taste as an emotion" (a quality very like her own), but she omits Symons's comment a few lines earlier: "Yet is there not some astringent quality lacking in Hawthorne, the masculine counterpart of what was sensitively feminine in him?" (p. 58). Similarly, Symons remarks a few lines later that "there is much in his sentiment and in his reflection which is the more feminine part of sensitiveness, and which is no more than a diluted and prettily coloured commonplace."

may have alerted her to a quality that would relate to her own later style. She would have read in this same essay Symons's analysis of the difference between Balzac and Tolstoi:

> He would never have understood the method of Tolstoi, a very stealthy method of surprising life. To Tolstoi life is always the cunning enemy whom one must lull asleep, or noose by an unexpected lasso. He brings in little detail after little detail, seeming to insist on the insignificance of each, in order that it may pass almost unobserved, and be realised only after it has passed. It is his way of disarming the suspiciousness of life.[26]

Pater and Symons provided techniques that Mansfield would use later to uncover, at its deepest level, the culturally determined condition of women. By importing symbolist devices into realistic fiction, Mansfield exemplifies how the male-bonded nineteenth-century aesthetes became absorbed into the twentieth-century feminist consciousness. Some of her brilliance lies in her realization that the symbolism of the aesthetes could be joined, as well, to a twentieth-century epistemology—partially Freudian, partially feminist. Her use of the '90s influences veers away from the occult, abstract direction it took with Yeats, for example, and it never goes to the extremes of Joyce with his preoccupation with symbolic language, myth, and metafiction.

Throughout her career, Mansfield would find conflict between the symbolist ideal of art as, in Symons's words, "a kind of religion, with all the duties and responsibilities of the sacred ritual"[27] and her desire to represent truthfully the social world in order to criticize its behavior and values. She may have found a clue to how that could be achieved through a welding of symbolism and realism in Symons's reference to Comte Goblet d'Alviella's definition of a symbol "as a representation which does not aim at being a reproduction."[28] But her project would never be the same as that of experimentalists like Gertrude Stein, whose concerns were far more centered on language itself and the ways its dominant structures could be changed. Mansfield's concentration on the symbol, the uses of sen-

[26]Ibid., p. 16.
[27]Symons, *Symbolist Movement*, p. 5.
[28]Quoted from d'Alviella's *The Migration of Symbols* by Symons in *Symbolist Movement*, p. 1.

sory images, and the problems of subjectivity always remained grounded in a belief in representation as a possibility for artists, but representation enlarged to include interiority, which itself becomes a prime subject for fictional treatment. Symons had defined symbolism as "a form of expression, at the best but approximate, essentially but arbitrary, until it has obtained the force of a convention, for an unseen reality apprehended by the consciousness."[29] Katherine Mansfield translated this conception from its metaphysical frame of reference to a psychological one. The "unseen reality" loses its occult and spiritual dimensions for the most part with Mansfield, but it takes on, instead, those of psychic alienation and problems in communication between human beings, as well as the dimension of the *social* construction of reality.

The emphasis on artificiality as a counter to the natural posed a particular dilemma for Mansfield as a woman writer. The preference for the artificial—linked as it was with a male-centered ideology—de-emphasized the authority of women. It devalued women's traditional powers as mothers and lovers, as objects of desire and inspirations for art. But those were the very "powers" that Mansfield already knew were the sign of women's entrapment in the patriarchy. An insistence on the primacy of the natural would be the means of keeping her safely within the generative cycle, dominated by bodily processes and the unconscious, locked into the inevitable repetition of the lives of her mother and grandmother. She would insist on artifice because to accept too much of the "natural" was to condemn herself to submission to patriarchal control. To elevate artifice over nature allows for the substitution of artistic control for passive acceptance of biological process. She would have read Symons's sacralization of the powers of the artist with a special awareness of its relevance to her own escape from the material:

> Here, then, in this revolt against exteriority, against rhetoric, against a materialistic tradition; in this endeavour to disengage the ultimate essence, the soul, of whatever exists and can be realised by the consciousness; in this dutiful waiting upon every symbol by which the soul of things can be made visible; literature, bowed down by so many burdens, may at last attain liberty, and its authentic speech. In attaining this liberty, it accepts a heavier burden; for in speaking to us

[29]Symons, *Symbolist Movement*, p. 1.

so intimately, so solemnly, as only religion had hitherto spoken to us, it becomes itself a kind of religion, with all the duties and responsibilities of the sacred ritual.[30]

Note how this elevation of literature to "a kind of religion" elevates the author as well to a higher function in society—as a priest, an initiator; all this is in reaction to "a materialistic tradition." It would appeal to a young woman who was searching for a way to achieve power in a society that limited the assertions of women.

The conflict between the natural and the artificial has a particular relevance to feminist inquiry. If "nature" is always *someone's* representation of it—that is, is always mediated through some kind of cultural ideology—it cannot be said that any one person, culture, race, is more "natural" than any other. The assumption of the intuitive apprehension of nature (often ascribed to women) is as culturally bound as the concept of woman *as* nature. What this suggests in terms of aesthetics is that all approaches to nature are "artificial," and the one stemming from "realism" is no less so than the one stemming from "symbolism." In fact, the approach from symbolism may go further in exposing the fallacies behind "representation," since it forces a self-consciousness about the method itself.

[30]Ibid., p. 5.

# ﾂ 5

## "A Gigantic Mother":
## Mansfield and the City

T he ultimate counter to the natural, obviously, is culture, or civilization: the organization of wildness into function and
beauty. For a young woman writer seeking the "modern," the location for culture would more logically be the city than the bush.
Accordingly, Mansfield's other prose poems from the same period
as "In the Botanical Gardens" suggest the additional influence of the
French symbolists, who turned to the city as the landscape best
representative of the modern consciousness.[1] In this respect, her
evolution of style from nineteenth-century aestheticism to modernism is comparable to that of other major modernists like Eliot and
Joyce, who turned to the city as subject for modernist stylistic experimentation. Yet the city's meaning for her, as a woman writer,
was compounded of different elements, different emphases, reflecting the realities of another experience of urban life.

The symbolist prose poem is clearly a precursor of the following
"vignette," one of Mansfield's earliest published writings (October
1907). Note its overobvious personification, romantic sense of cor-
respondences, and stilted nineteenth-century diction:

It is at this hour and in this loneliness that London stretches out eager
hands towards me, and in her eyes is the light of knowledge. "In my

[1]For a discussion of Mansfield's relationship to French symbolist poetry, see
Hanson and Gurr, *Katherine Mansfield,* pp. 21–23. On Mansfield's own experiments
in writing poetry, see Vincent O'Sullivan's introduction to *Poems of Katherine Mansfield,* pp. ix–xiii.

streets," she whispers, "there is the passing of many feet, there are lines of flaring lights, there are cafes full of men and women, there is the intoxicating madness of night music, a great glamour of darkness, a tremendous anticipation, and, o'er all, the sound of laughter, half sad, half joyous, yet fearful, dying away in a strange shudder of satisfaction, and then swelling out into more laughter. The men and women in the cafes hear it. They look at each other suddenly, swiftly, searchingly, and the lights seem stronger, the night music throbs yet more madly.

Out of the theatres a great crowd of people stream into the streets. There is the penetrating rhythm of the hansom cabs.

Convention has long since sought her bed. With blinds down, with curtains drawn, she is sleeping and dreaming.

Do you not *hear* the quick beat of my heart? Do you not *feel* the fierce rushing of blood through my veins?

In my streets there is the answer to all your achings and cryings. Prove yourself, permeate your senses with the heavy sweetness of the night. Let nothing remain hidden. Who knows that in the exploration of your mysteries you may find the answer to your questionings.[2]

Mansfield's persona and the personified city of London merge voices here. Her London is archetypically feminine—"she stretches out eager hands," "she whispers," and she is passionate: "the quick beat of my heart," "the fierce rushing of blood through my veins."

The London vignette, the first of three Mansfield published in the same issue, interweaves its description of the city with impressions of her room in Wellington, and it conveys the sense of distance and longing for London that several months at home after leaving Queen's College had produced. In the third vignette, the persona remembers her friend in London: "she and I, hand in hand, cheek to cheek, speaking but little," cuddled together because of the cold. "We talked of fame, how we both longed for it, how hard the struggle was, what we both meant to do." With a satiric thrust that counters the histrionic quality of the prose in the first vignette, the persona now wonders about their resolution to be famous in a year: "Today, at the other end of the world, I have suffered, and she, doubtless, has bought herself a new hat at the February sales. *Sic transit gloria mundi.*"[3]

[2]Katherine Mansfield, "Vignettes," *The Native Companion* 2 (October 1, 1907), 129–30. Reprinted in *Poems of Katherine Mansfield*, p. 4.
[3]*Poems of Katherine Mansfield*, p. 7.

The London vignette, with its sexualized language ("intoxicating madness," "strange shudder of satisfaction," "swelling out into more laughter," "penetrating rhythm of the hansom cabs"), comes to its climax with "in my streets there is the answer to all your achings and cryings." In an earlier version of this vignette in her notebooks, written around the same time as the "Summer Idylle" piece, and thereby associated with Maata and lesbian sexuality, Mansfield included a sentence omitted from the published version. After the phrase "blood through my veins," she had written: "Your hand can pluck away the thin veil, your eyes can feast upon my shameless beauties."[4] The earlier version is thus more blatantly sexual, as well as more nineteenth-century in its use of capitalized abstractions: "Night Music," "Darkness," "Anticipation," and so on.

Mansfield must have been aware of the sexual implications of her language in the vignette, since in "Juliet," an unfinished manuscript of a novel written around the same time as the first version of the London vignette, she states them explicitly. "Juliet" illuminates Mansfield's awareness of a special dimension of the city—that is, its potential as a catalyst for sexual release. When Juliet's roommate informs her that her restless mood has a physical cause—"You feel sexual"—Juliet responds with "Horribly—and in need of a physical shock or violence. Perhaps a good smacking would be beneficial." Juliet also explains: "I am in need of exercise. I shall go out, I think, for a walk, despite the fact that I shall become physically, mentally, and psychically damped. . . . I feel a need of a big grey sky, and a long line of lights. Also a confused noise of traffic, and the sense of many people—you know?"[5]

All of this helps us to interpret a characteristic feature of Mansfield's later fiction: she often portrays a female character rushing outside or desiring to be caught up in the rapid movement of life in the London streets. In "Revelations" (1920), Monica Tyrell, who "suffered from her nerves," feels "she could not stand this silent

[4]"The Unpublished Manuscripts of Katherine Mansfield," ed. Margaret Scott, *The Turnbull Library Record* 3 (n.s.) (November 1970), 133. Scott has dated this version from about the same time as "Juliet" and a few other pieces, including "Symmer Idylle. 1906," which apparently were written during the end of her stay in London. The three Beauchamp sisters left England with their parents in October 1906. Mansfield would have been just eighteen during their ocean voyage.

[5]"Juliet," in "The Unpublished Manuscripts of Katherine Mansfield," ed. Margaret Scott, *The Turnbull Record* 3 (n.s.) (March 1970), 16.

flat . . . this ghostly, quiet, feminine interior. She must be out; she must be driving quickly—anywhere, anywhere" (p. 428). And in "Bliss" (1918), Bertha Young asks: "What can you do if you are thirty and, turning the corner of your own street, you are over-come, suddenly, by a feeling of bliss...?" (p. 337). An unrecognized or at least undefined sexual restlessness affects a good number of Mansfield's city women, and that restlessness often is both a symp-tom of rebellion against confinement in stereotypically female spaces and a clue to the diction and rhythm of her prose in evoking women's responses to the city. It also displaces sexuality from the "natural" to the "artificial." Contrary to the conventional linkage of woman's sexuality with "natural" rhythms, passivity, and recep-tivity, Mansfield frequently portrays women's desire as stimulated by urban restlessness, technology (lights, traffic), and the longing for mastery.

"Juliet," the unfinished novel, is especially useful for analysis in this context because it is so much a projection of Mansfield's fan-tasies about what her own life in the city might be, should she ever gain the independence to live it. Juliet, her persona, emerges as a completely self-supporting "new woman," who lives in a dreary room "up five flights of stairs," where she reflects on

> the horror of the long white day. She could not endure another. Here in this twilight, shaking off her great chains of Commerce, London shone, mystical, dream-like. . . . This struggle for bread, this starva-tion of Art. How could she expect to keep art with her in the ugliness of her rooms, in the sordidness of her surroundings.[6]

Juliet has moments of triumph over "her fatigue, her doubts, her regrets," and expresses her author's own youthful wish for indepen-dence: "How weak I am. How I ought to be full of strength, and

---

[6]"Juliet," p. 13; another influence on this text is the fiction of the naturalists, who offered many examples of women struggling amidst the sordidness and hopelessness of the city. Malcolm Bradbury comments on the merging of influences in turn-of-the-century literature: "The London of strange, unreal contrasts and encounters had been in fiction since Dickens; it certainly has much to do with those strange ex-changes between Naturalism and Impressionism, Realism and Surrealism, Deter-minism and Aestheticism that make up the turn-of-century mood." "The Cities of Modernism," *Modernism: 1890–1930*, ed. Malcolm Bradbury and James McFarlane (New York: Penguin, 1976), p. 181.

rejoicing all the day. Relations at the other end of the world who have, thank Heaven, cast me off and my wish fulfilled. I'm alone in the heart of London, working and living" (p. 13). (Kathleen Beauchamp was actually living either at college or in her parents' huge house in Wellington when she described Juliet's "struggle for bread," her "starvation of Art.")

Juliet compares her present life with the boredom of the bourgeois colonial existence she left behind:

> On one hand lay the mode bohème, alluring, knowledge-bringing, full of work and sensation, full of impulse, pulsating with the cry of Youth Youth Youth. . . . On the other hand lay the Suitable Appropriate Existence, the days full of perpetual Society functions, the hours full of clothes discussions, the waste of life. (P. 25)

Compared with Mansfield's later, sharp-edged, unembellished depictions of London in stories like "Pictures," "Bliss," and "Life of Ma Parker," both "Juliet" and the London vignette may seem exaggerated and full of overly suggestive diction, but it is important to emphasize the youth of their author. Her first immersion into the life of the city had been as a student, during her three years at Queen's College (1903–6). From the protected environment of the college, London had suggested tentative adventures, moments of intrigue whose dangers were cushioned by the rules and regulations of the school. Although Kathleen Beauchamp and her friends might venture forth from the college on their way to music lessons wearing large artist hats and ties, they invariably had to return to their rooms on time. The darker sides of life in London appeared to them romantic and exciting, images of bohemia caught in glimpses. Even their introduction to the art and literature of the '90s—Beardsley, Symons, and Wilde—came from their professor of German, Walter Rippman, whose "chosen" pupils they were, invited to tea and to enjoy their taste of "decadence" in the comfortable surroundings of his artistically decorated flat.

Nonetheless, in contrast with her classmates' attitudes, Mansfield's devotion to the '90s went deeper than fashionability and had a permanent effect on her literary career. After her return to New Zealand, where she longed for London from her room in her parents' expensive Wellington house, that devotion provided her with an ideal of the city which became linked with her own intensifying sense of sexual ambivalence and urge toward sexual experimentation. She had perceived that the world of the decadents was one of sexual ambiguity, a place where sexual boundaries broke down for the pure artist, where experience led to artistic creation. Her sexual ambivalence is apparent in a notebook entry written not long after the London vignette was published: "Here in my room, I feel as though I was in London. In London! To write the word makes me feel that I could burst into tears. Isn't it terrible to love anything so much? I do not care at all for men, but *London*—it is life" (*Journal*, p. 21).

That unconscious remark, "I do not care at all for men," reveals how her sense of self-division was affecting her attitudes about the city itself, her simultaneous longing for and rejection of London. It also relates to a characteristic feature of her style. Antony Alpers observes that in a considerable number of early Mansfield sketches and stories we can see the author or her persona at a window, either longing for greater life or observing others experiencing it. (The London vignette is a good example.) Alpers remarks: "A trick of her mind is evident: she is constantly inhabiting one space while observing another, and has her characters doing the same."[7]

Juliet's choice of London is in accord with Malcolm Bradbury's remarks on the vital link between artistic emancipation and the drift toward the city in the fiction of this period:

> If one theme of Modernist literature is disconnection and loss, then another is that of artistic emancipation—so that not only Dedalus in *A Portrait of the Artist as a Young Man* but Paul Morel in *Sons and Lovers*, George Willard in *Winesburg, Ohio*, and many another literary hero all stand at the end of their novels on the edge of some urban redefinition of themselves—as if the quest for self and art alike can only be carried out in the glare and existential exposure of the city, where, as Julius Hart puts it in a compelling phrase in his poem *Journey to Berlin*, one is "born violently into the wild life."[8]

But Bradbury neglects a most crucial point. Obviously, as the works he lists so boldly announce, the literary "hero" is only de-

[7]Alpers, *The Life of Katherine Mansfield*, p. 53.
[8]Bradbury, "Cities of Modernism," pp. 100–101.

fined as masculine. Stephen, Paul, and George face very different futures from that of Juliet.

Although it is abundantly clear if we look at Mansfield's diaries, letters, and early writing that she was seeking "artistic emancipation" for *herself* in moving to London, it would be hard to find examples in her fiction of female heroes who stand "on the edge of some urban redefinition of themselves" and actually achieve it. Mansfield does not allow Juliet the fulfillment she seeks in the city; the novel ends tragically, self-destructively, with Juliet's death after an abortion. In fact, one by one Mansfield's city women retreat into fantasy and personal isolation. The "wild life" degenerates into disappointment, as well as an alarmingly female sense of terror.[9]

Consequently, the example of Mansfield's own later experiences in London—both imaginative and literal—may lead a feminist to question the effects of aesthetic doctrine on the art and—even more significant—the life of the female artist. The aesthetes' emphasis on the pursuit of sensual gratification, their belief that the artist's duty is to experience *more* than the ordinary person—experience cultivated for its own sake—may have pernicious consequences for women who seek such experience. What Katherine Mansfield feared, as is clearly evidenced in Juliet's defeat, became all too true in her own life. She underwent numerous disillusioning experiences during the tumultuous first years in London, including those of misplaced trust, loss of love, pregnancy, abortion, and illness. A few lines from an unfinished story of 1909 allow us a glimpse of her growing disenchantment: "Surely after my terrible sorrow, London seems to lose all her reality. I had thought of her as a gigantic mother in whose womb were bred all the great ones of the earth—and then—suddenly—she was barren, sterile."[10]

Mansfield's vulnerability as a woman alone in London surfaces in several stories in which women are victimized by predatory males, such as "The Swing of the Pendulum" (1911) and "The Little Governess" (1915). There is also the unmarried pregnant woman in "This Flower" (1919), who is attended by a "leering" doctor with "a rather shady Bloomsbury address." But one of the best examples of her depiction of women's victimization in the urban setting is "Pic-

[9]See especially "The Tiredness of Rosabel" (1908) and "The Little Governess" (1915) for examples of disappointment and fear.
[10]Quoted in Mantz and Murry, *Life of Katherine Mansfield*, p. 321.

tures" (1919). In this story the city both determines and reflects the main character's dilemma. Miss Ada Moss is an unemployed singer, middle-aged and overweight, out of place as an operatic contralto in the new world of popular entertainment dominated by the cinema. The story takes us through one day of her life: a "voyage" about the city as she searches for work in order to pay her landlady, who threatens to kick her out of her seedy Bloomsbury room, which "smelled of soot and face powder and the paper of fried potatoes she brought in for supper the night before" (p. 393). There are Prufrockian echoes in Miss Moss's impression of the street as she begins her futile rounds from one theatrical agent to another:

> There were grey crabs all the way down the street slopping water over grey stone steps. [Eliot's "pair of ragged claws" comes to mind here.] With his strange hawking cry and the jangle of the cans the milk boy went his rounds. Outside Brittweiler's Swiss House he made a splash, and an old brown cat without a tail appeared from nowhere, and began greedily and silently drinking up the spill. It gave Miss Moss a queer feeling to watch—a sinking—as you might say. (P. 396)

There are more reasons for that "sinking" feeling as the day goes on. When she stops first for a cup of tea (planning to use her last few cents), she finds that she is too early:

> When she came to the ABC she found the door propped open; a man went in and out carrying trays of rolls, and there was nobody inside except a waitress doing her hair and the cashier unlocking the cash-boxes. She stood in the middle of the floor but neither of them saw her.
> "My boy came home last night," sang the waitress.
> "Oh, I say—how topping for you!" gurgled the cashier. (P. 396)

Miss Moss is only an object of indifference to them—"neither of them saw her"—and the repetitive, mindless dialogue that continues between them establishes a rhythm that points ahead to Eliot's later use of the barroom conversation in *The Waste Land*. "Pictures" is a perfect, modernist city piece in miniature, with its use of the stream of consciousness, its rhythms of London waking up, its snatches of conversation overheard. Ada Moss is much like

Joyce's Leopold Bloom walking through *his* frustrating morning rounds. Also like Bloom, she is a city person who is totally without status or power. A taxi driver yells at her as she crosses the street: "Look out, Fattie; don't go to sleep!" Her movement through the city is marked by such indignities, and she suffers them with remarkably good humor and with considerable courage. Miss Ada Moss ends her day by allowing a "stout gentleman," who tells her "I like 'em firm and well covered," to pick her up and presumably to help her pay her rent that evening. Mansfield's last words in the story remind us, with disturbing irony, of Miss Moss's "voyage": "And she sailed after the little yacht out of the café" (p. 401).

It is troubling to find Miss Moss defeated by the end of the story, especially by a victimization that is ultimately sexual. Yet Mansfield's awareness of what produces Ada Moss's desperation is precisely the point where her vision differs from that of T. S. Eliot, her contemporary. Rather than use her alienated city characters as symbols of the breakdown of western civilization or as contrasts with the great figures of the past, Mansfield identifies with them. It would be hard to imagine her describing the young typist in *The Waste Land*, who "lights / Her stove, and lays out food in tins," with such cruel disdain. Neither would she phrase a line like Eliot's reference to the typist's "carbuncular" lover: "one of the low on whom assurance sits / As a silk hat on a Bradford millionaire." Mansfield's stories are much more likely to turn upon an instance of inhumanity or social injustice (see in particular "Miss Brill" and "Life of Ma Parker").

It was during the early stage of her friendship with T. S. Eliot that Katherine Mansfield wrote the first version of "Pictures," which appeared in *The New Age* on May 31, 1917, under the title "The Common Round." She had met the poet at a party at Lady Ottoline Morrell's on December 3, 1916.[11] The following June, she read aloud Eliot's "Love Song of J. Alfred Prufrock" at Garsington. Not long afterward, she recorded in a letter to Lady Ottoline the following description of the conclusion to another party: "I came away with Eliot and we walked past rows of little ugly houses hiding behind bitter smelling privet hedges; a great number of amorous

[11] Alpers, *Life*, p. 410.

black cats looped across the road and high up in the sky there was a battered old moon. I liked him very much and did not feel he was an enemy."[12]

They had, in fact, some important things in common: they were exactly the same age (Eliot was born September 26, 1888, Mansfield on October 14, 1888) and they were both outsiders in London—he an American, she a New Zealander. Yet most of the similarities between these two writers appear to be the result of parallel development rather than influence. Critics of modernism make much of the fact that Eliot read Symons's book on symbolism in December 1908 and that it catapulted him into his first efforts at modernist verse.[13] Mansfield's knowledge of Symons came even earlier than Eliot's and her awareness of symbolism independently shaped her first creative attempts.[14] Aside from the initial devotion to the symbolists, Mansfield's career corresponds with Eliot's in another way. As Malcolm Bradbury suggests in his discussion of the modernist writer and the city (although, characteristically, he does not include Mansfield in his comments), "frequently it is emigration or exile that makes for membership of the modern country of the arts." Surely Katherine Mansfield can be grouped with those other modernists as one who "perceives from the distance of an expatriate perspective of aesthetic internationalism."[15]

I wish we could know the conversation between Mansfield and Eliot during that walk because Mansfield's picture of "ugly houses," "amorous black cats," and "battered old moon" evokes a city not completely unlike the "certain half-deserted streets" and "yellow fog that rubs its back upon the window-panes" in "Prufrock."[16]

[12]Letters I, p. 312. O'Sullivan notes that "Lady Ottoline would have appreciated KM's parody of the imagery of 'Rhapsody on a Windy Night' and 'Conversation Galante', poems in T. S. Eliot's Prufrock and Other Observations (1917), published that month by the Hogarth Press" (Letters I, p. 313).

[13]Lyndall Gordon, Eliot's Early Years (Oxford: Oxford University Press, 1977), p. 29.

[14]Hanson and Gurr suggest that Mansfield's "early attempts to piece together an aesthetic rely almost entirely on the writings of Symons, and to a lesser extent Wilde." And what she learned from Symons was "the condensed version of Symbolist aesthetic theory" (p. 22).

[15]Bradbury, p. 101. For an excellent discussion of Mansfield as an expatriate writer, see Andrew Gurr, Writers in Exile: The Identity of Home in Modern Literature (Atlantic Highlands, N.J.: Humanities Press, 1981), pp. 33–64.

[16]Mansfield would have noted the similarities to London in Eliot's description, even though "Prufrock" is set in Boston.

These are not the only ironic references to "Prufrock" in her writing; in her journal of the same year she notes: "Is that all? Can that be all? That is not what I meant at all."[17] Katherine Mansfield's enthusiasm for Eliot subsided, however, as we can see in the following remarks she made to Virginia Woolf after the publication of Eliot's *Poems* by the Hogarth Press in 1919:

> Eliot—Virginia? The poems *look* delightful but I confess I think them unspeakably dreary. How one could write so absolutely without emotion—perhaps thats an achievement. . . . I don't think he is a poet—Prufrock is, after all a short story. I don't know—These dark young men—so proud of their plumes and their black and silver cloaks and ever so expensive pompes funebres—Ive no patience. (*Letters* II, p. 318)

But is it the "dreariness" of the male point of view that really marks her divergence from Eliot? If we pay attention to Mansfield's *tone* when she describes urban details similar to those of Eliot, we may approach their differences in response. The few lines from the letter to Lady Ottoline give us a clue: Mansfield nearly *delights* in the squalid features of nighttime London. She views them with affection and humor. Her description emphasizes the remote and the diminutive: "rows of ugly little houses hiding," the faraway "battered old moon"; all true danger and threat seem absent. For Mansfield, it is a relief to be out in the streets and away from the party; for the party, rather than the streets, is the locus for social hostility and competition, the real limitations of city life.

Earlier in the same letter to Lady Ottoline, Mansfield had complained that most parties are "too infernally boring" and was upset that one man there was "so stupidly callous about the war." But for her the streets—even this night with Eliot—were a source of creative energy. She would use the "amorous cats" some months later in "Bliss" ("A grey cat, dragging its belly, crept across the lawn, and a black one, its shadow, trailed after" [p. 341]) and in the same story satirize the London avant-garde and the absurd young poet Eddie

---

[17]*Journal*, p. 124. See also the letter to Murry, more than three years later, where she remarks in relation to Murry's review of Baudelaire: "I could not help comparing Eliot and you as I read. Your patient never dies under the operation. His are always dead before he makes an incision." *Katherine Mansfield's Letters to John Middleton Murry 1913–1922* (New York: Knopf, 1951), p. 572.

Katherine Mansfield

Warren, with his exaggerated city metaphors: "I saw myself *driving* through Eternity in a *timeless* taxi" (p. 343).

A letter to Murry on November 4, 1917, provides another illustration of Mansfield's ironic, energetic response to the city at this time, a city undergoing the trauma of World War I:

> By the way—isn't *Furnished Rooms* a good title for a story which plays in the Redcliffe Road—I cant resist it. . . . The meeting on the dark stairs—you know, someone is coming down & someone is coming up. . . . Then the whole Street—And for back cloth, the whole line of the street—and the dressmakers calling to the cat, the chinamen, the dark gentlemen, the babies playing, the coal cart, the line of the sky above the houses, the little stone figure in one of the gardens who carries a stone tray on his head . . . the lamenting piano, and all those faces behind the windows—& the *one* who is always on the watch. (*Letters* I, p. 339)

A journal entry nearly six months later expresses her continued interest in the same setting:

> If I had my way I should stay in the Redcliffe Road until after the war. It suits me. Whatever faults it has it is not at all bourgeois. There is 'something a bit queer' about all the people who live in it; they are all more or less 'touched.' They walk about without their hats on and fetch and carry their food and even their coal. There are nearly four bells to every door—the curtains are all 'odd' and shabby. The charwomen, blown old flies, buzz down each other's basements.[18]

There simply is not the same quality of hopeless impersonality in Mansfield's "there are nearly four bells to every door—the curtains are all 'odd' and shabby" as in Eliot's lines from "Preludes": "One thinks of all the hands / That are raising dingy shades / In a thousand furnished rooms."

While Mansfield recognized the elements of despair and danger for women in the city, she did not lose her equally powerful sense of the city as a catalyst for adventure, creativity, and women's poten-

[18]*Journal*, pp. 132–33. Mansfield was no stranger to the concept of the transiency of urban life; Alpers notes that she "had amassed a total of twenty-nine postal addresses since coming to London in 1908" (*Life*, p. 201).

tial independence. Her reaction to the city would continue to reflect the same ambivalence, the same self-division that characterized her sexuality. Gilbert and Gubar relate much of the "waste land" atmosphere of the work of male modernists to a crisis in "masculine confidence" which was connected not only with industrialism and loss of faith in traditional religion, but also with "the rise of women." For their female counterparts, however, new visions of achievement became possible, "not just because of their own new strength but also because of their antagonists' new weakness."[19] Mansfield's career illustrates her eagerness to participate in these new visions, but also her fluctuating disillusionment with the allures this entry into equality provided.

Some of the disappointments Mansfield experienced during her first years in London may have been temporarily submerged during the better stages of her relationship with John Middleton Murry,[20] when she was caught up in the enthusiasm over new friendships (Lawrence, Woolf, Eliot) and new discoveries in technique and conceptualization as her skills as a writer increased. Later, those disappointments would resurface, intensified by the suffering and despair resulting from her worsening tuberculosis. Her illness forced a change in her viewpoint from one of experience to one of observation. In this respect, Alpers's comment about her use of the window as both an opening into the world and a symbol of her own self-division is particularly relevant. As her illness progressed, the window became nearly her only way to connect with the city outside. With more distance in feeling now between herself and what she could observe, she gave expression rather to her delight in the city as *spectacle*, as in the following letter to Virginia Woolf in April 1919. Here Mansfield captures moments almost cinematic in their quick-flashing movement:

> But what I chiefly love, Virginia, is to watch the people. Will you laugh at me?—It wrings my heart to see the people coming into the open again, timid, airing themselves; they idle, their voices change & their

[19]Gilbert and Gubar, *No Man's Land,* vol. I, pp. 89–90.

[20]For J. Middleton Murry's own account of his impressions of London during this time, see *Coming to London,* ed. John Lehmann (London: Phoenix, 1957), pp. 94–107.

gestures. A most unexpected old man passes with a paper of flowers (for whom?), a soldier lies on the grass hiding his face; a young girl *flies* down a side street on the—positive—*wing* of a boy—[21]

I also notice a resemblance in tone and phrasing between this letter to Woolf and the passage, appearing a few years later in *Mrs. Dalloway*, where Clarissa expresses her delight in city people and the city panorama: "what she loved was this, here, now, in front of her; the fat lady in the cab."[22]

In moments of despair and depression Mansfield might turn against her pleasures in the real city and try to invent an ideal one—but not very often:

> Why isn't there some exquisite city where we all have our palaces and hear music—very often—and row upon the water, and walk in heavenly landscapes and look at pictures and where all the people are beauties—moving in the streets as it were to a dance. I am quite serious. I *pine* for lavishness. For the real fruits of the earth tumbling out of a brimming horn. (Perhaps it is four years of Khaki). (*Letters* II, p. 277)

Mansfield would ultimately reject London, but not by completely free choice. To escape London's cold and dampness she was uprooted over and over again as she moved from pension to hotel, hotel to pension, in France and Italy and Switzerland. It is no wonder that her nostalgia for New Zealand intensified. Her longing for "lavishness" blurred with memories of Wellington's crisply blue harbor, the dense bush surrounding its hills of wooden houses. Many of her greatest stories are set in New Zealand rather than London: "Prelude," "At the Bay," "The Garden-Party."[23] In the last year of her life she wrote to her father about her memories and the pain of separation:

> The more I see of life the more certain I feel that it's the people who live remote from cities who inherit the earth. London, for instance, is an awful place to live in. Not only is the climate abominable but it's a

---

[21]*Letters* II, p. 310. In the same letter, incidentally, Mansfield tells Woolf that she had read her "article on Modern Novels."

[22]Virginia Woolf, *Mrs. Dalloway* (New York: Harcourt, Brace, 1925), p. 12.

[23]For an extensive collection of Mansfield's writings about New Zealand, gath-

continual chase after distraction. There's no peace of mind—no harvest to be reaped out of it. And another thing is the longer I live the more I turn to New Zealand. I thank God I was born in New Zealand. A young country is a real heritage, though it takes one time to recognise it. But New Zealand is in my very bones. What wouldn't I give to have a look at it![24]

This wish is as close as she would get to the fate projected in her journal for the "girl in Wellington," who would finally return to Wellington to die.

Yet it would be a mistake, I believe, to consider London the destroyer of Katherine Mansfield. She was one of our first true contemporaries, one of the first notable women writers who attempted to live on equal terms with men in the city at a very young age. It was, after all, the only place she could have lived that way at all; such a life would have been impossible in Wellington, with its cultural isolation and with her socially minded parents always on watch. If she failed it was because her body failed, not because her ideal of independence was wrong. As much as she turned against London, she still knew the secret of its attraction for her and its power to inspire her. It was in London that her talent ripened and sharpened; it was there she developed the techniques that allowed her to express her unique vision. Her role as an outsider in the city strengthened her powers of observation. Mansfield knew how to look at people and see what was important in their lives, but she knew also that "one wants to feel a stranger, for these things to have their charm."[25] She questioned herself about her interest in charwomen, shabby streets, coal buckets: "But do you like this sort of talk? This kind of thing? What about the Poets and—flowers and trees?" Her answer comes from the "real" Katherine Mansfield: "As I can't have the perfect other thing, I *do* like this. I feel, somehow, free in it. It has no abiding place, and neither have I. And—and—Oh well, I *do* feel so cynical" (*Journal*, p. 133).

---

ered from her journals, letters, sketches, and stories, see Ian A. Gordon, ed., *Undiscovered Country: The New Zealand Stories of Katherine Mansfield* (London: Longmans, 1974).
[24]*Letters of Katherine Mansfield*, p. 456.
[25]Ibid., p. 408.

#  6

# The Question of Genre

$\mathbf{A}$s influential as *Dorian Gray* had been for Mansfield, it was so primarily at the level of subject matter and style: the encoding of the forbidden and its articulation in terms of the problems of art, the artist, sexuality, and gender roles. The narrative technique of *Dorian Gray*, however, with its omniscient point of view, its use of explicit statement, its theatrical dialogue, and its extravagant tone of allegory, followed nineteenth-century conventions she needed to leave behind.[1] The young Katherine Mansfield immersed herself in those genres that, in E. D. H. Johnson's words, were most appropriate to the spirit of this period:

> The best *fin-de-siècle* art impressionistically records the poignancy of fleeting moods. Symons spoke of 'this endeavor after a perfect truth to one's impression, to one's intuition.' The lyric, the Wildean epigram, the short story, the sketch, and the dialogue—these are the modes which most vividly embody the temper of an age obsessed with mutability.[2]

By the age of seventeen, Katherine Mansfield was writing narratives that did not rely on plot for their organization—narratives

---

[1]Wilde's shorter fictions, such as his fairy tales, might have provided more promising models for imitation. O'Sullivan ("The Magnetic Chain," p. 99) suggests that Mansfield's "A Fairy Story" (in *The Open Window* 1 [October–March 1910–11], 164–76) descends from Wilde's "The Selfish Giant." For an excellent discussion of Mansfield's juvenilia, in which fantasy elements predominate, see Hankin, *Katherine Mansfield and Her Confessional Stories*, pp. 3–24.

[2]E. D. H. Johnson, "The Eighteen Nineties: Perspectives," in *Wilde and the Nine-*

centered on mood, rhythm, and sensory impressions. Unlike many older writers who had learned their craft through imitation and refinement of traditional narrative conventions, Mansfield—at the very beginning of her career—began, through the dominant influence of the symbolists and decadents, to write fiction committed to the possibilities of narrative experimentation.

Her sketches and prose poems seem to be written as exercises, preliminaries to a major work. "Summer Idylle. 1906" prefigures Katherine Mansfield's later development of a new kind of short fiction, a remarkable flowering of the genre which has influenced writers up to our own times.[3] Yet there is rich irony in her success with the short story, since she never accepted it as the highest form of fiction. She was affected, of course, by the example of the literary greatness—critical acclaim and public success—of the major Victorian novelists. As an aspiring writer, she believed that becoming "great" meant, finally, that she must write a major novel. At first, the influence of the symbolists prevented her from becoming locked into an obsession with the tradition of Victorian fiction. Yet that tradition exerted a force too powerful to ignore for long, even if it proved difficult for her to reconcile the social vision of the Victorian novelists with her own tendency to escape from the social through the idealization of "Art."[4]

Mansfield planned more than once to write a novel, but she never completed one. Claire Tomalin suggests that "she soon realized that

---

ties: *An Essay and an Exhibition*, ed. Charles Ryskamp (Princeton: Princeton University Library, 1966), p. 28.

[3]Clare Hanson makes an important distinction between the "short story" and "short fiction," considering Mansfield's writing as the latter: "The modernist short story grew out of the psychological sketch of the 1890s. Like the psychological sketch it is more properly called a type of short fiction for one of its leading characteristics is a rejection of 'story' in the accepted sense. Modernist short fiction writers distrusted the well-wrought tale for a variety of reasons. Most importantly they argued that the pleasing shape and coherence of the traditional short story represented a falsification of the discrete and heterogeneous nature of experience" (*Short Stories and Short Fictions, 1880–1980* [London: Macmillan, 1985], p. 55).

[4]Of course, as Terry Eagleton has observed, "deprived of any proper place within the social movements which might actually have transformed industrial capitalism into a just society, the writer was increasingly driven back into the solitariness of his own creative mind. . . . The assumption that there was an unchanging object known as 'art,' or an isolatable experience called 'beauty' or the 'aesthetic,' was largely a product of the very alienation of art from social life" (*Literary Theory: An Introduction* [Minneapolis: University of Minnesota Press, 1983], pp. 20–21).

her gifts did not lie in the direction of a long book. As a writer, she always lacked stamina" (p. 120). Certainly, Mansfield's tumultuous life, filled with emotional upheaval, ceaseless travel, and illness—especially illness—would have made difficult the sustained, lengthy process of novel writing. She once wrote to Murry about Virginia Woolf: "How I envy Virginia; no wonder she can write. There is always in her writing a calm freedom of expression as though she were at peace—her roof over her, her possessions around her, and her man somewhere within call."[5] Although Mansfield's assumptions about Woolf's "calm freedom of expression" reveal her lack of knowledge of Woolf's own personal torments, her assertion about the contrast between their styles of living was true enough. Still, Mansfield's choice of genre was influenced by far more than her physical condition or financial circumstances. The novel presented her with narrative conventions she found troubling and limiting, especially in their encodings of concepts about women's roles.

Such awareness of the relationship of narrative convention to women's victimization made the choice of genre a problematic one for Mansfield. Although she was liberated in some ways by the flexibility of the newer, mixed genres, the levels of fantasy, dream, and artful arrangement of mood required by the prose poem or fairy tale were frequently countered by her even stronger impulses toward realism, especially in her struggle to understand her own situation as a woman and to achieve autonomy as a writer.[6]

From the beginning of her writing career, she was aware of the socially determined imperatives of narrative conventions, especially as embodied in the dominant narrative pattern of romantic love. In "The Tiredness of Rosabel" (1908), for example, the young working woman's romantic fantasies—of escape from her exhausting life through marrying a handsome, rich man—are based on the plots of the sentimental novels of the time. But these fantasies are shown in bold relief against the realities of Rosabel's impoverished life and the

[5]*Letters to John Middleton Murry*, pp. 419–20.

[6]As an example of Mansfield's interest in realism, Alpers refers to her penchant for "sordid detail" in her notebook sketches in 1908, and sees these leading to the story "The Tiredness of Rosabel." Alpers describes Mansfield at this time as "a girl in a hostel writing things, struggling quite alone to discover a form, with no idea where to turn for the critical guidance that every young writer needs" (*Life of Katherine Mansfield*, p. 80).

narrator's awareness of the impossibility of their resolution in the class-bound society Rosabel inhabits. In a double gesture that underscores her point that Rosabel's fantasies are products of the fiction she reads, Mansfield describes another young woman reading a typical romantic novel while Rosabel watches her as she rides the omnibus home from work. By introducing the other young woman, Mansfield enlarges her criticism of novel reading as escapism to show that it is not merely an individual response to personal disappointment, but a socially determined and sanctioned method of maintaining women's conformity to traditional roles.

Yet Mansfield's attack on the conventions of the novel in "Rosabel" is really against only one version of the genre, the popular sentimental novel. She had no *conscious* quarrel with the major Victorian novelists, whose works she held in awe. The solid grounding in observation of the "real" world called for by the novel would provide eventually a different direction for her fiction. It would also provide her with different influences from Wilde, Pater, and the decadents. As I have suggested, the latter are largely masculine influences, but Mansfield's "realistic" impulses necessarily involve her in a confrontation with powerful and significant "foremothers."[7]

Hanson and Gurr point out that Mansfield copied as many quotations from George Eliot's *Daniel Deronda* as she did from Oscar Wilde, and suggest that

> in her early struggle to become an artist, she felt the need to liberate herself from her weak position as a woman quite as strongly as she felt the impulse to flee from her bourgeois home. The dual nature of her struggle to become an artist is neatly exemplified in two sets of quotations copied into her early notebooks. In the 1954 *Journal* Murry printed all the aphorisms from Wilde urging the artist to self-development and rejection of convention. He omitted, however, almost all of an equally

[7]Although I consider the influence of the aesthetes and decadents to be largely masculine, it should be noted that their effect on modernist women authors often was to encourage an emphasis on the feminine. Cassandra Laity says they "provided . . . a 'female' tradition for modernist women poets . . . who, unlike twentieth-century women novelists, did not claim to 'think back through' their mothers, the strong women poets of the past." "H. D. and A. C. Swinburne: Decadence and Modernist Women's Writing," *Feminist Studies* 15 (Fall 1989), 462.

large number of quotations from *Daniel Deronda*. This was the book in which George Eliot explored more openly than in any of her other books the pressures on the woman-artist.[8]

Accordingly, George Eliot was an important influence of another sort than Wilde and the symbolists: she provided a deep moral seriousness, a concern with social life and injustices, and a realistic depiction of ordinary life which was in direct conflict with aestheticism. But stylistically, as her involvement with the possibilities of symbolism indicates, Mansfield chose not to confront this most powerful of women novelists. Sandra Gilbert and Susan Gubar have termed such a confrontation the female "affiliation complex," in which the modern woman writer, in discovering that she has female as well as male precursors, "fears the consequences of both renunciation and rivalry: to renounce her precursors' pain or to refuse to try to rival them may be to relinquish the originatory authority their achievements represent."[9]

Mansfield's development as a modernist writer is exceedingly complex and multifaceted; it demonstrates repeatedly her imaginative interaction with nineteenth-century precursors and her deconstruction of traditional conventions of fiction which restrict the roles of women. Although Mansfield would never attempt to write in the style of George Eliot, or to approach Eliot's breadth of intellectual interests or vision of the social structure, she could not avoid being influenced by Eliot's treatment of women's self-development when she first attempted to write a novel about her own life. It is not surprising, therefore, that Mansfield's excursions into the genre of the novel were limited to the subgenre of the *bildungsroman*. Her contemporaries Lawrence, Joyce, Richardson, and Woolf also struggled with the *bildungsroman*, but with the exception of Richardson, they moved on to new narrative possibilities, to different kinds of novels. Their encounters with the *bildungsroman* allowed them to isolate the elements of conflict: the battle between selfhood and the demands of society. Dorothy Richardson never moved beyond it, but found that by exploding the conventions of the genre she could use it to create a form completely new, flexible, and with the potential

[8]Hanson and Gurr, *Katherine Mansfield*, p. 13.
[9]Gilbert and Gubar, *No Man's Land*, vol. I, p. 199.

for illuminating the special features of a world as perceived by women.[10]

The developmental novel, focused on the self, assumes a particular kind of unfolding depending on education and experience. For women writers, however, until recently, the restrictions on education and experience inhibited the flowering of the genre.[11] Nineteenth-century novelistic conventions concerning women's development focused primarily on the marriage question.[12] Rita Felski observes that in the fiction of the nineteenth century, "the only choices available to a female protagonist are frequently revealed as negative ones: a stifling and repressive marriage or a form of withdrawal into inwardness which frequently concludes in self-destruction."[13] In George Eliot's *The Mill on the Floss*, for example, a woman is defeated by aspiring to more than the traditional givens of women's lives. Such scenarios occur even as late as Virginia Woolf's *bildungsroman*, *The Voyage Out* (1915), which defeated its central character and gave a vision of female development thwarted and finally destroyed by the marriage question. Clearly, the developmental novel would need to take a different shape when it was about a woman rather than a man, as Dorothy Richardson discovered in writing *Pilgrimage*.

If Mansfield had published a *bildungsroman* based on her own life, how easily it might have followed the classic plot line summarized by Jerome Buckley in *Season of Youth*:

A child of some sensibility grows up in the country or in a provincial town, where he finds constraints, social and intellectual, placed upon the free imagination. His family, especially his father, proves doggedly hostile to his creative instincts or flights of fancy, antagonistic to his ambitions, and quite impervious to the new ideas he has gained

---

[10]See my discussion of Dorothy Richardson and the female *bildungsroman* in *Feminine Consciousness in the Modern British Novel* (Urbana: University of Illinois Press, 1975), pp. 8–46. See also DuPlessis, *Writing beyond the Ending*, pp. 143–56.

[11]A useful collection of essays on the female *bildungsroman* is *The Voyage In: Fictions of Female Development*, ed. Elizabeth Abel, Marianne Hirsch, and Elizabeth Langland (Hanover, N.H.: University Press of New England, 1983).

[12]For a discussion of the hegemony of the marriage plot in nineteenth-century fiction, especially the two-suitor convention, see Jean E. Kennard, *Victims of Convention* (Hamden, Conn.: Archon, 1978).

[13]Rita Felski, *Beyond Feminist Aesthetics: Feminist Literature and Social Change* (Cambridge: Harvard University Press, 1989), p. 124.

from unprescribed reading. His first schooling, even if not totally inadequate, may be frustrating insofar as it may suggest options not available to him in his present setting. He therefore, sometimes at a quite early age, leaves the repressive atmosphere of home (and also the relative innocence), to make his way independently in the city (in the English novels, usually London). There his real "education" begins, not only his preparation for a career but also—and often more importantly—his direct experience of urban life. The latter involves at least two love affairs or sexual encounters, one debasing, one exalting, and demands that in this respect and others the hero reappraise his values. By the time he has decided, after painful soul-searching, the sort of accommodation to the modern world he can honestly make, he has left his adolescence behind and entered upon his maturity. His initiation complete, he may then visit his old home, to demonstrate by his presence the degree of his success or the wisdom of his choice.[14]

The young Kathleen Beauchamp was in Buckley's words "a child of some sensibility," who grew up in a colonial town where she was misunderstood by her bourgeois family. She received a gloss of sophistication at Queen's College in London, and then, after a struggle with her parents, left "the repressive atmosphere of home . . . to make her way independently in the city." So far, her *bildungsroman* fits Buckley's schema perfectly. The problem begins with the "preparation for a career," which in the case of a female protagonist runs counter to societal expectations. But when Buckley notes that his "hero" has "at least two love affairs or sexual encounters, one debasing, one exalting," at this juncture the plot pattern would have to break down in Mansfield's case. Her sexual experiences would not fit neatly into this dichotomy; in fact, because of their bisexual nature, the rules of literary decorum of her day would not even allow her to refer to them.[15] To include her own sexual experiences within the boundaries of a novel form known by its readers to be confessional would have been impossible for her during the early part of this century. Now I am not suggesting that women did not write about their sexual experiences, even

[14]Jerome Hamilton Buckley, *Season of Youth: The Bildungsroman from Dickens to Golding* (Cambridge: Harvard University Press, 1974), pp. 17–18.

[15]Virginia Woolf has written eloquently about the societal imperatives that prevent women from writing the truth about themselves as sexual beings. See in particular, Woolf's discussion of "the Angel in the House" in "Professions for Women," *Collected Essays*, vol. II (New York: Harcourt, Brace & World, 1967).

experiences society defined as "deviant"; rather, they could not *publish* truthful accounts of them.[16]

Accordingly, among Katherine Mansfield's papers can be found two early, aborted attempts at *bildungsromane*. The first is "Juliet," and Mansfield began working on it around the same time as "Summer Idylle. 1906," about May 1906, when she was only seventeen years old and still a student at Queen's College. She continued working on the novel briefly after her parents made her return home to New Zealand, but it appears that she had put it aside by January 1907. "Juliet" is of special interest as a version of Mansfield's self-development in that it is both a fairly transparent account of her early adolescence and an unnervingly prescient projection into a life she had not yet lived.

Her impulse to escape the provincialism of New Zealand and the bourgeois values of her parents was as significant a desire as her need for sexual expression. In "Juliet" Mansfield also asserts her rejection of women's traditional roles, her distrust of marriage, and her respect for work. At one point, she describes Juliet living happily with a woman friend who remarks that they have "all the comforts of matrimony with none of its encumbrances." Juliet agrees:

'As it is we are both individuals. We both ask from the other personal privacy, and we can be silent for hours when the desire seizes us. . . . I loathe the very principle of matrimony. It must end in failure, and it is death to a woman's personality. She must drop the theme and begin to start playing the accompaniment.'[17]

Whereas a contemporary feminist might very well end her novel at this point, the seventeen-year-old author must have felt too threatened by the implications of Juliet's independence, and perhaps unconsciously felt the need to punish herself for her own assertions. As the novel continues, Mansfield does not allow Juliet the fulfillment she seeks in independence. She closes off all possibilities for

---

[16]Gertrude Stein's novel about lesbian relationships, *Q.E.D.*, remained unpublished for decades; H. D.'s *Hermione* has only recently been published, long after the author's death. How many more confessional manuscripts by women modernists will turn up someday is anyone's guess. Correspondingly, E. M. Forster's *Maurice* also had to wait until after the author's death for publication.

[17]"Juliet," in "The Unpublished Manuscripts of Katherine Mansfield," ed. Margaret Scott, *The Turnbull Library Record* 3 (n.s.) (March 1970), 16–17.

her, taking her through a tragic course of events including seduction and betrayal, pregnancy, abortion, and death. Although Kathleen Beauchamp was making plans for her own escape into an independent life at the same time as she was writing "Juliet," it is clear from these fragments that she could not imagine what independence might really mean. She could only envision a typically *female* tragedy. This vision is not surprising; neither in life nor in literature did she find satisfactory models for the woman artist she longed to become.

Compared with the symbolist prose poems and other '90s-influenced sketches that Mansfield was writing at the same time, "Juliet" is strikingly realistic and psychologically astute. A sentence describing Juliet's father, for example, displays the same kind of careful observation, epigrammatic phrasing (certainly a Wildean carry-over), satirical tone, and pointed wit that characterizes her most sophisticated later writing: "Mr Wilberforce [was] wrapping up his throat in a great silk handkerchief, with all that care and precision so common to perfectly healthy men who imagine they wrestle with weak constitutions" (p. 9).

Mansfield's persona, Juliet, is a young New Zealander like her author. At the beginning of the story she is fourteen years old, restless, dreamy, longing to begin her life. Mansfield describes her as

the odd man out of the family—the ugly duckling. She had lived in a world of her own, created her own people, read anything and everything which came to hand, was possessed with a violent temper, and completely lacked placidity. She was dominated by her moods which swept through her and in number were legion. She had been as yet, utterly idle at school, drifted through her classes, picked up a quantity of heterogeneous knowledge—and all the pleading and protestations of her teachers could not induce her to learn that which did not appeal to her. She criticised everybody and everything with which she came into contact, and wrapped herself in a fierce white reserve. 'I have four passions' she once wrote in an old diary, 'Nature, people, Mystery, and—the fourth no man can number.' Of late she had quarrelled frequently with the entire family, through pure lack of anything definite to occupy her thoughts. She had no defined path ahead, no goal to reach, and she felt compelled to vent her energy upon somebody—and that somebody was her family. (P. 8)

The accuracy of Mansfield's self-reflections and the fluency with which she conveys them are remarkable for a writer of seventeen. That she could combine that ease of analytical statement with an extraordinary sensitivity to sensory stimuli and visual imagery is even more stunning. Here is a characteristic descriptive passage:

> When she pulled up the blind next morning the trees outside were being tossed to and fro, and the sea lashed into fury by a wild southerly gale. Juliet shuddered. The wind always hurt her, unsettled her. . . . She wandered about all the morning, and in the afternoon put on her reefer coat and tam-o'-shanter and went for a walk up the hill that spread like a great wall behind the little town. The wind blew fiercer than ever. She held on to bushes, and strong tufts of grass, and climbed rapidly, rejoicing in the strength that it required. Down in a hollow where the gorse spread like a thick green mantle she paused to recover breath. The utter loneliness of it filled her with pleasure. She stood perfectly still, letting the wind blow cold and strong in her face and loosen her hair. The sky was dull and grey, and vague thoughts swept through her—of the Future, of her leaving this little island and going so far away, of all that she knew and loved, all that she wished to be. 'O I wish I was a poet' she cried, spreading out her arms. 'I wish I could interpret this atmosphere, this influence.' She found a little bird fluttering near in a bush, its wing broken by the storm, and held it close to her, overcome with a feeling of tenderness. 'I am so strong' she said, 'and the strong are never hurt. It is always the weak who are pained.' She walked home more slowly. Now that the excitement of climbing had left her she felt tired and depressed. Clouds of dust whirled up the road, dry particles of sand stung her face. She longed for the evening to come, yet almost dreaded it. (Pp. 10–11)

This passage is a "realistic" treatment of a character's interaction with nature, compared with the stylized, "symbolic" treatment of that interaction in the prose poem "In the Botanical Gardens," written a few months later. I say "realistic" because the passage is embedded in a narrative sequence organized around details supposedly garnered from the writer's own experience, and based in a representational aesthetic mode. Yet Mansfield already was impatient with the conventions of representation. The climb and descent correspond with the alternation of moods from excitement to depression, and the "realistic" details are as artificially arranged to convey the nature/culture conflict as they are in the prose poem.

This passage corresponds with numerous "moments" of romantic transcendence in the prose narratives of women writers.[18] As in many of these other novels of the late nineteenth and early twentieth centuries, the young woman protagonist links her achievement of a sense of power to her experience of solitude in nature. She frees herself, even if only momentarily, from the shackles of societal expectations, and frees her imagination to envision other possibilities, using solitude as a force to overcome cultural resistance to women's autonomy. But as we can see here, Mansfield already knew that she would not allow Juliet to succeed in her pursuit of such autonomy. First of all, the "excitement of climbing" is not relieved through any total release of tension. Her climax was to be her achievement—her ability to "interpret this atmosphere, this influence," but that is put off to the "Future," and the intrusion of the "little bird" breaks the momentum of her climb. Her sudden, protective gesture also breaks the momentum of her hope for release through artistic generativity. With this maternal gesture, she simultaneously burdens herself with the maternal role and identifies herself with the broken "child" that the bird suggests. It is also a clever bit of foreshadowing, since Juliet will die of an abortion after pregnancy disrupts her plans for an artistic career.

"Juliet" gives evidence that even at seventeen Mansfield was moving toward the kind of "free indirect style" of narration she would handle later with such brilliance.[19] Her problem with the *bildungsroman* as a genre was, from the beginning, more one of narrative structure (and its encoded conventions) than of prose style. Her description of Juliet's first response to David when he plays the cello is a careful melding of sexual awakening and artistic aspiration securely centered in Juliet's own consciousness:

> Her whole soul woke and lived for the first time in her life. She became utterly absorbed in the music. The room faded, the people faded. She saw only his sensitive inspired face, felt only the rapture

[18]I consider this subject more fully in *Feminine Consciousness in the Modern British Novel* in relation to instances of such experience in novels by Dorothy Richardson, May Sinclair, Virginia Woolf, Rosamond Lehmann, and Doris Lessing. See also Annis Pratt, *Archetypal Patterns in Women's Fiction* (Bloomington: Indiana University Press, 1981), pp. 16–24, for a discussion of the prevalence of the "naturistic epiphany" in the novel of development by women writers.

[19]For an excellent theoretical discussion of this method, with examples from

that held her fast, that clung to her and hid her in its folds, as impene-
trable and pure as the mists from the sea.... Suddenly the music
ceased, the tears poured down her face, and she came back to reality... She put her handkerchief to her eyes and when she looked round
became aware of the amused glances of the company, and heard the
steady almost prophetic-sounding voice of David's Father: "That
child is a born musician." (P. 11)

The passage is noteworthy for its interiority, its concentration on
Juliet's sense impressions: sight, sound, internal feeling. Impressions
not relevant to the central emotion are ignored, so that only the
voice of David's father reaches her out of all the other sounds from
people peripheral to Juliet's concerns.

This growing ability to handle a multiplicity of sensory detail was
a necessary step in Mansfield's evolution as a modernist. In a later
section of the manuscript there is a description of Juliet out walking
in the street. Mansfield dispassionately renders Juliet's complex of
feelings as she walks and juxtaposes those feelings with the impersonal intrusions of other lives and adjacent physical objects into her
consciousness, so that her consciousness appears flooded with
impressions:

Once out in the streets Juliet walked very fast, her head bent. She was
thinking, thinking. How absurd everything was. How small she was.
She walked along Holborn, and into Oxford Street. The restaurants
were full of light, and the sound of laughter seemed to be in the air. A
curious helplessness took possession of her—an inability to speak or
to stop walking. Half way down Oxford Street she suddenly heard a
hoarse cry in the street. There had been an accident. In an instant there
had sprung up scores of people who were all hurrying forward. Juliet
ran with them. As she neared the place she heard "'E's done for, poor
feller. 'E caught 'im fair on the leg." "Hit 'is head too—'e was in the
hansom." (P. 17)

Margaret Scott, who transcribed the manuscript of "Juliet," notes
that the entire second half of the paragraph, from "a curious helplessness," has been scored out, presumably because Mansfield was

---

Mansfield's "Bliss," see Wallace Martin, *Recent Theories of Narrative* (Ithaca: Cornell
University Press, 1986), pp. 136–40.

dissatisfied with it. Yet it is on the edge of something new, some-
thing more modernist perhaps than anything she had yet written.
She was experimenting with a technique approaching Virginia
Woolf's years later in *Mrs. Dalloway*, when Woolf described
Clarissa Dalloway on her walk down Bond Street.

Juliet's death appears to serve as a way to position her back into
the role of woman as muse, woman as inspiration. Mansfield shows
us the would-be writer silenced. Bitterly, she reveals how after
Juliet's death her seducer produces "a very charming little mor-
ceau—'Souvenir de Juliet'. It created quite a quiver [uncertain read-
ing] at the London concerts—and it was reported on highest authority that the original MS was stained with tears" (p. 18). Moreover,
Juliet's first lover, David, and her best friend, Pearl, marry after her
death and name their first child Juliet. With biting irony, Mansfield
consigns them all to mediocrity in the very bourgeois mold she
made Juliet flee from: "They bought a nice little house . . . and
David achieved no small measure of success with his gardening" (p.
17). Pearl, the dilettante, publishes "a little volume which she called
'Mother Thought'... somehow the title does not seem intensely
original" (p. 17).

The death of Juliet is in accord with Marianne Hirsch's observations about the prevalence of early death in the female *bildungsroman*:

> How are we to read these deaths [of female heroes in nineteenth-
> century *bildungsromane*]? . . . Seen in the context of the *Bildungsroman*'s
> valorization of progress, heterosexuality, social involvement, healthy
> disillusionment, "normality," adulthood, these deaths are pointless,
> violent, self-destructive. Yet if we look at what adulthood and matu-
> rity mean for the female protagonists of these texts, at the confine-
> ment, discontinuity, and stifling isolation that define marriage and
> motherhood, they do not present positive options. . . . I submit that
> the heroines' allegiance to childhood, pre-Oedipal desire, spiritual
> withdrawal, and ultimately death is not neurotic but a realistic and
> paradoxically fulfilling reaction to an impossible contradiction. By
> showing death to be the only viable response to deep inner needs,
> these texts lead us to question the very values of *Bildung* itself, as it has
> traditionally been understood. . . . These novels do lead us, however,
> to examine a pattern of spiritual development in male heroes, the
> *Künstlerroman*. Similarly dissatisfied and led to withdraw into the inner
> life, its male heroes find a solution that saves them from the heroines'

death, the solution of art which is virtually unavailable to the young woman in the nineteenth-century novel. The story of female spiritual *Bildung* is the story of the potential artist who fails to make it.[20]

Juliet's seduction by Rudolf is played out in a scene where the power of music is destructive, not like its effect earlier in the novel when David's playing evokes in Juliet intense aspiration, a striving after her *own* creativity, which, like the sexuality implicit behind it, would flower in fullness and purpose. With Rudolf, it is a sexuality controlled, manipulated by the male intrusion of power. He, as seducer, tries to show her how convention holds her back, spouting the message of artistic freedom, abandonment: "Did Chopin fear to satisfy the cravings of his nature, his natural desires?" (p. 20). Juliet is overcome, but Mansfield must have already known the implicit dangers in the artist's willful appropriation of the concept of sexual liberation.

In terms of technique, Mansfield uses the aftermath of the seduction as an avenue toward stream-of-consciousness fiction. Yet it is still conveyed with clear control by an omniscient narrator:

I wonder why I am crying, she thought. Am I sad? Am I, am I? She crept over to the lounge and lay down, her head buried in the cushions. She was assailed with the most extraordinary thoughts. They seemed to be floating towards her, vast and terrible. I feel as though I was on a great river, she thought, and the rocks were all closing around me, coming towards me to sink me. . . And now and again Rudolf's face came before her—the broad low brow, the great sweep of hair, the fire of the eyes, the eager curve of his mouth—almost just a trifle mocking, but also concerned, just a trifle concerned. She saw the strong supple hands, hands such as Aubrey Beardsley would have given an Artist. It is Rudolf—and Rudolf, and Rudolf, she said to herself. Then suddenly a fierce thought sprang to birth in her brain. . . Did he ever think—that there might be consequences to his act? Did he ever for one moment dream that Nature might cry to the world what was so hidden, so buried? Terror took possession of her. 'O no—not that' she said, 'never, never that. That would be diabolical, and the world isn't diabolical—at least it can't be.

---

[20]Marianne Hirsch, "Spiritual *Bildung*: The Beautiful Soul as Paradigm," in Abel, Hirsch, and Langland, eds., *The Voyage In*, pp. 27–28.

Nothing would exist if it was.' But if—if—then if she were certain she
(Pp. 22–23)[21]

Aside from the nineteenth-century stylistic remnants ("Nature
might cry to the world," "Terror took possession of her"), the
intermingling of Juliet's thoughts and the narrator's interpretative
intrusions is surprisingly sophisticated. Mansfield goes even further
in the direction of stream-of-consciousness fiction in the surrealistic
effects produced in Juliet's mind as she listens to David respond to
the dilemma of her current life:

> 'You have made a mistake, for the sake of your old view. Juliet try and
> go back. We shall both help you... Pearl and I...' Juliet looked up into
> [his] face. How very very heavy she had grown. She could hardly
> hold up her head now... It is quite extraordinary—like a dead body,
> she thought. All the six undertakers couldn't lift her now. How
> curious—two Davids. How strange—two huge gigantic Davids,
> both of them thundering 'Pearl and I'... What colossal Davids. She
> must run away and tell Grannie. She started to her feet... and
> fell... (P. 23)[22]

Less than a year after she gave up writing "Juliet," Mansfield
sailed to England to take up the life she had projected in her fragments of the novel. That she felt confused by her decision to leave
New Zealand and take up life as an "independent" woman in London is reflected in the journal entry on "a girl in Wellington." Written in December 1908, a few months after she had arrived in England, the entry shows how much she was torn between her
attraction to London and her fears of failure there. It also gives

---

[21]In her editorial notes to "Juliet," Margaret Scott comments that the manuscript
is broken off at this point: "The passage which once followed, whether one page or
more, was torn out prior to the numbering of the remaining pages" ("The Unpublished Manuscripts of Katherine Mansfield," p. 28).

[22]Margaret Scott notes that "all through *Juliet* and many other of the unpublished
pieces of this period, is the recurring crisis of falling" (p. 5). Aside from the possible
psychoanalytic interpretations of this trope, there are cultural imperatives as well.
Nina Auerbach discusses the relation between prevalent Victorian treatments of the
fallen woman in literature and painting and the fate of Milton's Eve: "It seems that
an age of doubt has grafted the doom of Milton's Satan onto the aspirations of his
Eve, generating a creature whose nature it is to fall—the sexual trespass that produced that fall is almost elided in British treatments—and whose identity defines
itself only in that fall." *Woman and the Demon* (Cambridge: Harvard University
Press, 1982), p. 155.

evidence of her attempt to combine the stylistic features of aestheticism with a psychological projection of her own life (in retrospect, of course, it is painfully prophetic).

This is not the place to describe the tumultuous events of Katherine Mansfield's early years in London; the biographies supply the relevant details. It is enough to say that she underwent numerous disillusioning experiences in her pursuit of independence and sexual freedom. Her predictions in "Juliet" contain many truths, but luckily, one glaring deviation from the plot. Katherine Mansfield did not die in those early years in London, and she would turn back to these same events a few years later and attempt to come to terms with them again within the constraints of the traditional novel form.

Mansfield's second attempt at a *bildungsroman* was not until 1913, in the months between August and November. She had been living with J. Middleton Murry and they had recently become friends with D. H. and Frieda Lawrence. Mansfield and Murry read *Sons and Lovers*, Lawrence's *bildungsroman*, that very summer. Much had happened to her since 1907, and she was now a relatively well-known young author; her first collection of short stories, *In a German Pension*, had been published in 1911. Her world now included an involvement with the avant-garde through her joint editing, with Murry, of *Rhythm* and *The Blue Review*, and she was exploring an interest in current painting, sculpture, and literature. But in spite of the intensity of these new experiences, she discovered that life with Murry had sapped much of her creative energy. In her new role as a "wife" who was not legally a wife, she discovered that she was expected to conform to the role of housekeeper in spite of Murry's relatively advanced egalitarian attitudes. In late spring of 1913, she wrote to Murry: "Ive heard you and Gordon talking while I washed dishes. . . . Yes, I hate hate HATE doing these things that you accept just as all men accept of their women. I can only play the servant with very bad grace indeed. Its all very well for females who have nothing else to do. . . . I loathe myself, today, I detest this woman" (*Letters* I, pp. 125–26).

Later that summer, Mansfield began to work on her second *bildungsroman*, "Maata." [23] By August 2, 1913, she had drafted a plan for a novel of thirty-five chapters; by August 13, she had completed

---

[23] "Maata," in "The Unpublished Manuscripts of Katherine Mansfield," ed. Margaret Scott, *The Turnbull Library Record* 12 (May 1979), 11–28.

the first chapter. She wrote only one more chapter before abandoning "Maata," and that was finished on November 16.

Whereas "Juliet" is a projection into a life Mansfield had not yet lived in London, "Maata" is based on her actual experiences after arriving there at the end of 1908, at the age of nineteen. If reading Lawrence's *Sons and Lovers* was the impetus for beginning "Maata," as Claire Tomalin suggests (p. 119), imitating his approach to his material and his narrative method would not sustain Mansfield's attention. Lawrence's emphasis on the powerful effects of parental influence on the sexual life of his protagonist was not the subject Mansfield felt ready to explore. (Tomalin points out the absence of "Oedipal conflict" in "Maata.") Rather, she chose the "formative experiences through various friendships and love-affairs, some morbid and destructive" (Tomalin, p. 120) as the subject matter for her novel. In some ways this focus makes it far more a *künstlerroman,* an exploration of the development of an artist. It is closer to that tradition than *Sons and Lovers*—which may certainly be classified as a *künstlerroman,* but shows Lawrence far more concerned with the dynamics of Paul's sexual development and the deathly struggle for freedom from his mother's power than with the particulars of Paul's actual artistic career. In choosing to develop "Maata" around the artistic career itself, rather than around the psychosexual elements of its origin, Mansfield faced enormous problems in providing the kind of emotional intensity that the oedipal situation fueled for Lawrence. This lack of emotional intensity also has something to do with narrative technique.

Although Mansfield's short fiction already gave evidence of her preoccupation with new techniques for portraying states of consciousness, her projected new novel shows peculiarly little evidence of experimentation. "Maata" is as conventional as "Juliet" in its plot structure. In the earlier novel, Juliet loves David, a cellist, who deserts her for her best friend. Juliet is seduced by Rudolf, David's decadent, bohemian friend. In the later novel, Maata is in love with Philip, a violinist. (Both David and Philip are based on the Trowell brothers, the young musicians Mansfield loved—first Arnold and then Garnet.) Mansfield's most important female friend, Ida Baker (L.M.), appears in these fragments as Rhoda. This time, with more experience behind her, Mansfield allows Maata to enjoy a sexual relationship with Philip. There is no question of forced seduction.

But now there is pressure from Philip's family, as well as prospects of poverty for the young couple, and Maata turns from Philip to make a marriage of convenience with an older, more established man. This turnabout reminds us of Katherine Mansfield's own precipitous marriage of one day to George Bowden and her return to Garnet Trowell immediately afterward. Significantly, Mansfield does not victimize her protagonist; Maata does not die from an abortion. This time Mansfield does not destroy her persona; but she does destroy the man who loves her. Philip commits suicide after Maata's marriage.

The available fragments of this proposed novel are not especially promising. Tomalin remarks:

> This is no lost masterpiece, but it is a considerable curiosity. It is unlike anything else that has survived of Katherine's work. Throughout the synopsis Maata is shown as powerful and dominant in her relations with the other characters; even when she suffers, she does not behave like a victim, but more like a Nietzschean figure who makes her own fate, without regard for morality or kindness. She also justifies her behaviour by referring to the needs of her art, in line with the view of the divine rights of artists expressed in the editorials of *Rhythm* which she and Murry had concocted in 1912. (P. 120)

Maata's apparent disregard for others in her pursuit of artistic achievement corresponds with Rachel DuPlessis's observation about the female *künstlerroman* that "making a female character be a 'woman of genius' sets in motion not only conventional notions of womanhood but also conventional romantic notions of the genius, the person apart, who, because unique and gifted, could be released from social ties and expectations. Genius theory is a particular exaggeration of bourgeois individualism."[24]

In her first notes toward a *bildungsroman*, then, the inexperienced Mansfield punished herself for sexual assertion. Juliet is victimized, and "the divine rights of artists" reside only with the male seducer. The second time around, in "Maata," she punished the man. In terms of creative power, the assertions of artistic freedom in the later novel seem to lead to a confusing and ambivalent impasse, and to a corresponding diminishment of energy.

[24]DuPlessis, pp. 84–85.

Dissatisfaction with plot clearly was a factor in Mansfield's inability to finish "Maata." She had retained the two-suitor convention (which, ironically, corresponded with her own life and her decision to marry George Bowden as a temporary means of resolving her deterred relationship with Garnet Trowell). Yet she knew, in retrospect, that her own experiences—in their multiplicity and diversity—were so vastly different from the implications of that convention that to continue to follow the latter could only lead to boredom and artistic dishonesty. She knew that there was more to her own conflict as an artist than either the standard marriage-versus-career dilemma or the choices between male suitors. Mansfield must have sensed how inadequate a response to the conflict of the female artist "Maata" would have turned out to be. She would have been writing with a bitter awareness of the downward motion her own career was taking now that she was living with Murry, and of the dissipation of creative energy which was affecting her output of short fiction as well. The events of the novel so closely repeated her own experiences that if she were to be truthful to fact, she would have to admit that she had not realized the goals she had set forth when she arrived in London in 1908.

Although Lawrence ends *Sons and Lovers* with Paul Morel heading toward the city, drained of emotion and nearly defeated by the familial struggle, he implies that Paul is now freed to begin his life as an artist. Moreover, Lawrence wrote *Sons and Lovers* during a period of personal revolution and self-discovery. He had, as well, a sense of professional success following the critical acclaim of his first novels. Mansfield could not write her novel with the same confidence. While "Maata" begins at the place *Sons and Lovers* ends—the arrival in the city of the would-be artist—Maata's life as an artist in the city quickly begins to devolve primarily around the marriage question. At the end of the synopsis of the novel, Mansfield briefly sketches a Maata as depleted as Paul Morel by the destruction of relationships, but approaching the future with cynicism rather than guarded hope. Here are the last lines of the synopsis: "There is only one thing. Are you happy. Life is not gay. Life is never gay" (p. 20).[25]

---

[25]Although Mansfield discarded "Maata," she must have culled her notes for it later, for there is a reminiscent phrase in a sketch she published in *The New Age*,

An intriguing link between Mansfield's two attempts at the *bildungsroman* is revealed in the "girl in Wellington" journal entry of December 21, 1908, quoted previously. Aside from the fact— obvious to anyone familiar with the course of Mansfield's bio- graphy—that the diary entry nearly prefigures her life in actuality, it also contains the threads of the two incomplete "novels," the one she had just attempted to write a year or so earlier, and the one she would attempt five years later. It also hints at another major reason why Mansfield would never write a complete novel that described her coming of age.

In the diary entry she imagines a "dual existence" for the "girl in Wellington," but what did she mean by "dual existence?" What would have been the two lives she projected for her protagonist? In "Juliet" and later in "Maata" that duality is not clearly revealed. The novels end before the subject is even introduced. At the end of 1908, then, Mansfield projects a "sketch" about Maata's future life, but the story she outlines becomes, in reality, her own life. That she decided—both in the sketch and in the novel five years later—to name her persona "Maata" and to make her experience a future that might belong to herself is puzzling only until one realizes that Mans- field had been writing about the real Maata in the diary entries of the same notebook, and that she had transposed her name and Maata's even earlier in the "Summer Idylle" sketch.

Daniel Albright has remarked that "every literary act is at once self-disclosure and self-evasion."[26] With Katherine Mansfield, how- ever, it seems that the problem goes beyond the "literary act." It must include the act not completed, the act interrupted, the act prevented from being. Mansfield could not take her own conflicts through to their conclusion—even imaginatively. There was always material that resisted her attempts to shape it. The two unfinished novels obliquely hint at experiences and feelings that she dared not bring to light.[27] She was silenced by the strictures of the genre,

more than three years afterward: "One says: 'Life is not gay, Katherine. No life is not gay.'" Quoted in Alpers, *Life*, p. 243.

[26]Daniel Albright, *Personality and Impersonality: Lawrence, Woolf, and Mann* (Chicago: University of Chicago Press, 1978), p. 14.

[27]Mansfield apparently began a third novel in December 1913, "Young Country," of which she wrote only two chapters. See Gillian Boddy, *Katherine Mansfield: The Woman and the Writer* (New York: Penguin, 1988), pp. 158, 315.

which encoded conventions from which she needed to break free. Yet it may well be that Mansfield's failure to write the novel of her life, her *bildungsroman*, is the key to her artistic breakthrough. By rejecting the conventions of the genre, its plot-generated structure, she also rejected its implications about women's possibilities. Setting the novel aside in frustration, Mansfield began to experiment with techniques that might allow her to reveal and conceal at the same time: moments of revelation illuminating instances of growth, but not assuming a linear progression. Two years after "Maata" became impossible, Mansfield was to start writing a novel again. No less autobiographical than "Juliet" or "Maata," this novel would be based on her own family, the Beauchamps, and located in Wellington (in a way, this "return" is in accord with Buckley's paradigm). Like *Sons and Lovers*, it would be a return to origins and to the initiating moments of the awakening consciousness. But Mansfield's return would produce a text completely different from Lawrence's chronologically structured novel, as we shall see in the next chapter. In "Prelude"—and in the other great New Zealand stories that followed—the "child of some sensibility" awakens to consciousness at the same time as her author recognizes her own essential connection with the family and the country she once left behind.

# 7

## From *The Aloe* to "Prelude"

A certain strangeness, something of the blossoming of the aloe, is
indeed an element in all true works of art.

Walter Pater, *The Renaissance*

The evolution of "Prelude" from its initial conception as a
novel, *The Aloe*, in 1915[1] to its publication by the Woolfs in 1918
demonstrates Mansfield's intensified process of technical and concep-
tual experimentation, the true beginning of her *conscious* sense of a
new shape for prose fiction.[2] What began as a "novel" eventually
became something new: a mixed genre, a multileveled, spatially
ordered narrative. Katherine Mansfield remarked in a letter in response to a question about "Prelude": "What form is it? you ask. . . .
As far as I know, it's more or less my own invention" (*Letters* I, p.
331). Some years later she referred to "the *Prelude* method—it just
unfolds and opens."[3]

But what was the impetus for this new kind of narrative? The

---

[1] *The Aloe* has been printed along with "Prelude" in a beautiful edition arranged by
Vincent O'Sullivan with the two stories set side by side. See Katherine Mansfield,
*The Aloe: With Prelude*, ed. Vincent O'Sullivan (Wellington, N.Z.: Port Nicolson,
1982). Page references to *The Aloe* cited in the text are to this edition, which
supersedes the version edited by Murry and published by Knopf in 1930.

[2] Virginia Woolf refers to the first printing of "Prelude" in a letter on November
13, 1917, in *The Letters of Virginia Woolf*, vol. II, p. 196. See also Quentin Bell,
*Virginia Woolf: A Biography*, vol. II (New York: Harcourt Brace Jovanovich, 1972),
48.

[3] *Letters of Katherine Mansfield*, p. 359.

usual account of her new direction has the flavor of Murry's style of public relations about it: Leslie Beauchamp, Mansfield's brother, arrives from New Zealand on his way to the front and renews her connections with her childhood. He is killed almost immediately after leaving for the continent, and then, through her grief and final acceptance of his death, Mansfield experiences a sudden burst of creative energy. Yet even a brief study of the chronology of her writing process provides a more complicated story, and one that begins *before* the death of her brother.

The period between "Maata" and *The Aloe* was not very productive for Mansfield in terms of writing and publication.[4] By December 1913, she and Murry had moved to Paris, where she met the writer Francis Carco for the first time. Returning to England at the end of February 1914, she found her attention diverted by volatile relationships with friends, new and old. Her journal reveals a preoccupation with disturbing and sexual dreams,[5] memories of New Zealand, and vacillating feelings for her friend L.M. (Ida Baker), intensified by L.M.'s imminent departure for Rhodesia at the end of March. By April 2, Mansfield recorded her concern over her difficulties in writing: "If I could write with my old fluency for *one day*, the spell would be broken. It's the continual effort—the slow building-up of my idea and then, before my eyes and out of my power, its slow dissolving" (*Journal*, p. 58). On April 4, she wrote: "Nothing that isn't satirical is really true for me to write just now. If I try to find things lovely, I turn pretty-pretty. And at the same time I am so frightened of writing mockery for satire that my pen hovers and won't settle" (pp. 58–59).

But alternating with lethargy and depression were moments of recognition and expansion. Only three days later, her journal records:

> The heavens opened for the sunset to-night. When I had thought the day folded and sealed, came a burst of heavenly bright petals.... I

[4]Alpers (*Life*, p. 407) mentions that Mansfield wrote only one story in 1913: "Something Childish but Very Natural."

[5]For example, on March 6, 1914, she has a dream about walking with her sister along cliffs with "points of teeth"; other elements of the dream include a black fur muff, a charioteer with a quiet evil smile, horses galloping backwards, and "a dark serene rider in a wide hat, gliding past them like a ship through dark water" (*Journal*, pp. 52–53).

sat behind the window, pricked with rain, and looked until that hard
thing in my breast melted and broke into the smallest fountain, murmuring as aforetime, and I drank the sky and the whisper. Now who
is to decide between 'Let it be' and 'Force it'? J. believes in the whip: he
says his steed has plenty of strength, but it is idle and shies at such a
journey in prospect. I feel if mine does not gallop and dance at free
will, I am not riding at all, but just swinging from its tail. For example, to-day... To-night he's all sparks. (Pp. 59–60)

The implicit commentary on the differences between male and
female modes of creativity—and of sexuality—is undeniable. But
Mansfield would participate later that year in an incessant and elec-
trifying discourse on "the masculine" and "the feminine" as her
relationship with D. H. Lawrence deepened.

Lawrence and Frieda von Richthofen had returned from Italy on
June 24, and on July 13 their marriage took place. Only one month
later the First World War began. Throughout these same months,
Mansfield grew increasingly unhappy with her life with Murry.
Then, on October 26, after spending ten days as guests of the Lawrences, she and Murry moved to Rose Tree Cottage, only three
miles away. Devastated by his publisher's rejection of his first version of *The Rainbow*, Lawrence was in the thick of revising it.
Apparently, during this time Mansfield had many conversations
with the Lawrences about her problems with Murry and gained
their support for her side of the conflict.

Frieda Lawrence, in particular, was sympathetic to Mansfield's
longing for a lover more intense and sensual than Murry and abetted
her in her romance by mail with Francis Carco. On November 16,
Mansfield received a letter from Carco and implicitly contrasted
him with Murry by referring to "his warm sensational life" (*Journal*,
p. 62), using a typically Lawrencian phrase. It is interesting to note
how her interest in Carco countered some of Lawrence's prescrip-
tions on male authority. Carco seemed to Mansfield soft and feminine, "with his laughing face, his pretty hair, one hand with a bangle
over the sheets, he looked like a girl"(*Journal*, p. 78). She thought of
Carco while riding on top of a bus in London, on January 6, 1915,
and remarked in her notebook: "I longed for him so, and yet I dare
not push my thoughts as far as they will go" (*Journal*, p. 66). Note
how her phrasing here is the same as in the quote from Wilde in her
journal of 1906: "Push everything as far as it will go" (p. 3).

# Katherine Mansfield

Undoubtedly, these days with the Lawrences must have encouraged Mansfield's own analysis of sexuality, childhood, and parental influences. Not that these were new topics of concern for her. The earlier stories "New Dresses" (1910) and "The Little Girl" (1912) already show how astute she could be about the dynamics of family life and the power struggles inherent in a patriarchal society. But what the Lawrences may have provided was an awareness of the Freudian theory behind the observations she had already made. (Of course Lawrence's versions of psychoanalysis deviated greatly from their original sources.)

Mansfield must have been influenced as well by Lawrence's theories about "true marriage" and especially by his notions about the essences of the male and the female[6]—although, as I suggest later, much of this influence has its effect in reaction and rejection, rather than in enthusiastic acceptance.[7] At about this time Lawrence was working on the long, windy disputations on sexuality in his "Study of Thomas Hardy," and it is not improbable that Mansfield would have heard him speak of ideas like these from the "Study":

> But except in infinity, everything of life is male or female, distinct. But the consciousness, that is of both: and the flower, that is of both. Every impulse that stirs in life, every single impulse, is either male or female, distinct, except the being of the complete flower, of the complete consciousness, which is two in one, fused. These are infinite and eternal. The consciousness, what we call the truth, is eternal, beyond change or motion, beyond time or limit.[8]

[6]See Paul Delany, *D. H. Lawrence's Nightmare* (New York: Basic Books, 1978), p. 27, on Lawrence's completion of *The Rainbow* in winter 1914. Delany remarks that "Lawrence must have seen his celebration of Ursula's exuberant femininity as a phase of consciousness that already lay behind him. From now on he would view the relations between men and women as more deeply contradictory, and place a higher value on manly self-reliance."

[7]Interestingly, Murry was also uneasy with Lawrence's notions about the essential female. He writes in his autobiography: "Rightly or wrongly, it seemed to me that Lawrence did not serve Frieda as a person, or an individual, but as a sort of incarnation of the Female principle, a sort of Magna Mater in whom he deliberately engulfed and obliterated himself. And I felt a morbidly fastidious aversion to this. It produced in me a kind of nausea." *Between Two Worlds: The Autobiography of John Middleton Murry* (New York: Julian Messner, 1936), p. 312.

[8]D. H. Lawrence, "Study of Thomas Hardy," in *Phoenix: The Posthumous Papers of D. H. Lawrence*, ed. Edward D. McDonald (New York: Viking, 1972), pp. 443–44.

This work of Lawrence's reflects his interest in Otto Weininger's ideas about the essential bisexuality of human beings. Mansfield must have found such ideas intriguing if unsettling, and they might have encouraged her to reexamine her own sexual experiences. There may even be a connection (although the notion is purely conjectural) between Lawrence's analysis of the "flower," which like "the complete consciousness" is "two in one, fused," and Mansfield's later use of the aloe in "Prelude," where it seems to connote both the masculine and the feminine.

Tomalin remarks that Katherine Mansfield told Frieda much about herself during those months at the end of 1914. She might have told Frieda about her youthful sexual experiences, perhaps the affair with Edith Bendall.[9] Frieda probably told Lawrence about Mansfield's experiences or he was present himself at these story-telling sessions. Tomalin makes a convincing case that these stories influenced Lawrence. She believes that Lawrence drew on them for the chapter "Shame," about Ursula's lesbian relationship with Winifred Inger, which he added to *The Rainbow* that winter.[10]

The intensity of the atmosphere around the Lawrences confirmed Mansfield's belief that she needed independence and isolation in order to write.[11] By February 1915, she was anxious for escape. Her brother had arrived in England, and although it is true that she enjoyed their reminiscences about childhood, her greater impulse at this time was to run away to France and Francis Carco, and to escape the emotional complexities of her current life with Murry and the Lawrences. Her brother gave her the money to go to Paris on February 12. Her journey was to be a brief escape of only a few days, and by mid-February she was back in England with Murry, apparently reconciled with him.

By March 18, however, Mansfield had again returned to Paris to use Carco's flat in order to do some serious writing—writing that would become the first sections of *The Aloe* and would be dominated by a preoccupation with gender differences. This preoccupation is, I believe, a direct consequence of Mansfield's interaction with the Lawrences. But there were other influences connected with

[9]Tomalin, *Katherine Mansfield: A Secret Life,* p. 38.

[10]See Tomalin, pp. 37–39. Delany, p. 397, dates the composition of the chapter as December 1914.

[11]Claire Tomalin describes beautifully the details and stresses of this period; see pp. 115–44.

the origins of *The Aloe*. Partly, there was the atmosphere of Paris itself—wartime, air raids, a tumultuous visit with her old friend Beatrice Hastings, perhaps a lesbian flirtation (she wrote to Murry about a party at Hastings's where she met "a very lovely young woman—married & *curious*—blonde—passionate—we danced together" [*Letters* I, p. 164]), the suggestiveness of the sights, colors, and scents of early spring. Finally, in a letter to Murry on March 25, 1915, she mentions the originating moment for her new work:

> I had a great day yesterday. The Muses descended in a ring like the angels on the Botticelli Nativity roof—or so it seemed . . . and I fell into the open arms of my first novel.[12] I have finished a huge chunk but I shall have to copy it on thin paper for you. I expect you will think I am a dotty when you read it—but—tell me what you think—won't you? Its queer stuff. Its the spring makes me write like this. Yesterday I had a fair wallow in it and then I shut up shop & went for a long walk along the quai—very far. It was dusk when I started—but dark when I got home. The lights came out as I walked—& the boats danced by. Leaning over the bridge I suddenly discovered that one of those boats was exactly what I want my novel to be—Not big, almost 'grotesque' in shape I mean perhaps *heavy*——with people rather dark and seen strangely as they move in the sharp light and shadow and I want bright shivering lights in it and the sound of water. (This, my lad, by way of uplift) But I *think* the novel will be alright. Of course it is not what you could call serious—but then I cant be just at this time of year & Ive always felt a spring novel would be lovely to write (*Letters* I, pp. 167–68)

She returned to London on March 31 but was back in Paris on May 5. Several days later she told Murry:

> I have been writing my book all the afternoon. How good the fatigue is that follows after! Lovers are idling along the quai. They lean over the parapet and look at the dancing water and then they turn and kiss each other—and walk a few steps further arm in arm and then stop again and again kiss. It *is* rather the night for it, I must say. (P. 180)

12Open arms had long been associated for her with female sexuality. See *Journal*, p. 12, on one lesbian relationship: "Last night I spent in her arms"; "Nothing remains except the shelter of her arms" (p. 13); and "Now, each time I see her to put her arms round me and hold me against her" (p. 14).

It is clear from these first few remarks about the novel that Mansfield saw it originally as a lighter piece than it became, and one connected with spring, her own sexual frustration, and perhaps with a re-awakened lesbian desire. By May 12, she was writing to Murry: "My book *marche bien*—I feel I could write it anywhere—it goes so easily—and I know it so well. It will be a funny book—"(*Letters* I, p. 186). Only two days later, however, she told him: "My work is finished my freedom gained. . . . Besides which I have only to polish my work now; its all really accompli" (p. 188).

According to Vincent O'Sullivan, Mansfield at this point had only written "to the end of the dance scene in Chap. II."[13] If so, certain themes in the story were already in place, but other significant ones had not yet appeared. In place were Linda's distance from her children, the emphasis on defining gender differences, an awareness of the creative potential of the matriarchal order, and the women's responses to the masculine intrusion in their domain. Mansfield had yet to include Stanley's point of view, Linda's ambivalent feelings about Stanley, Linda's delusions about inanimate objects becoming alive, and the aloe itself. In fact, it is not clear yet that the aloe will be the story's central symbol.

After returning to England on May 19, 1915, Mansfield did not work on the story for nearly ten months. Lawrence's presence was again very much a factor. In August, he and Murry founded a new magazine, *The Signature*, for which Mansfield wrote some short stories, including "The Little Governess." Then, on September 30, while the sexual issues in *The Aloe* were still not fully articulated and the manuscript itself had almost been abandoned, Lawrence's *The Rainbow* was published. There is no written account of Mansfield's reaction to the lesbian episode within it. Murry's explanation of her response to the book only reflects what he believed she felt—and what she was willing to tell him. (His knowledge of her past sexual experiences was very limited.) Murry writes:

> We neither of us liked *The Rainbow* and Katherine quite definitely hated parts of it—in particular the scene where Anna, pregnant, dances naked before the mirror. That, Katherine said to me, was 'female'—her most damning adjective—and an apotheosis of the

---

[13]Vincent O'Sullivan, "Introduction" to *The Aloe* (London: Virago, 1985), p. ix.

'female': a sort of glorification of the secret, intimate talk between women, the sexual understanding of the female confraternity, which Katherine could not abide. But whereas Katherine in a sense understood the book and hated it positively, I could not understand it at all. I disliked it on instinct. There was a warm, close, heavy promiscuity of flesh about it which repelled me, and I could not understand the compulsion which was upon Lawrence to write in that fashion and of those themes.[14]

Mansfield's own treatment of pregnancy in her half-abandoned manuscript was completely at odds with Lawrence's. Linda's pregnancy is never stated explicitly; her mother looks for "smelling salts" to give her during the excitement of loading the buggy at the beginning of the story. Later, when Mansfield continued working on *The Aloe*, she developed the section of the story which emphasizes Linda's abhorrence of pregnancy and childbirth.

Katherine Mansfield spent quite a bit of time with her brother during that summer, and his visits helped to focus her imagination on their shared New Zealand past. During this period she wrote a story about a brother and sister, "The Wind Blows," which was published in *The Signature*. It is filled with the emotional intensity of adolescent anticipation, of the urge to start a new life, of escaping from family restrictions. It is also a story about awakening sexuality.[15] This energy of anticipation was broken by tragedy when Leslie Beauchamp was killed in France on October 7, 1915. Mansfield's reaction was intense and profound. A month later she wrote in her journal: "I am just as much dead as he is" (*Journal*, p. 89). "Then why don't I commit suicide? Because I feel I have a duty to perform to the lovely time when we were both alive. I want to write about it, and he wanted me to" (p. 90).

Consequently, by January 22, 1916, after Murry had joined her in Bandol, where she had gone to recuperate, she considered how her attitude toward her writing had been transformed by her brother's death:

Only the form that I would choose has changed utterly. I feel no longer concerned with the same appearance of things. The people who

[14]See Murry, *Between Two Worlds*, p. 351.
[15]"The Wind Blows" retains the suggestiveness of the symbolist work she did

*110*

lived or whom I wished to bring into my stories don't interest me any more. The *plots* [she underlined this word in her notebook, but Murry printed it without emphasis] of my stories leave me perfectly cold. (P. 93)

She writes here about her desire to "write recollections of my own country" (p. 93), "to make our undiscovered country leap into the eyes of the Old World" (p. 94). And then she refers to "a kind of *special prose*": "No novels, no problem stories, nothing that is not simple, open" (p. 94).

On February 16, 1916, she mentions in her journal that she had "*found The Aloe* this morning" (p. 97) and that

> *The Aloe* is right. *The Aloe* is lovely. . . . And now I know what the last chapter is. It is your birth—your coming in the autumn. You in Grandmother's arms under the tree, your solemnity, your wonderful beauty. Your hands, your head—your helplessness, lying on the earth, and above all, your tremendous solemnity. That chapter will end the book. The next book will be yours and mine. And you must mean the world to Linda; and before ever you are born Kezia must play with you—her little Bogey. (P. 98)

She also comments further in her "Notes for the Aloe": "They cut down the stem when Linda is ill. She has been counting on the flowering of the Aloe" (p. 99).

Although Mansfield wrote in her journal that the story was to be an elegy for her brother and that she intended it to end with his birth, her final version in "Prelude" did not include that birth. Her brother is the absent center, the son whose meaning to his parents is still incipient, in potential. Stanley looks at his family at the table and thinks, "That's where my boy ought to sit" (p. 244). But the *active* center is Kezia, the young girl; it is her en-gendering that the reader experiences, her realization of male dominance. The girl-child's later displacement by her brother, the brother who will receive the mother-love denied to her from birth, would not be treated in "Prelude." Mansfield would not introduce it until her later story about the Burnells, "At the Bay" (1921).

---

much earlier. Hanson and Gurr comment that it "is the most purely symbolist of her stories to this date" (*Katherine Mansfield*, p. 45).

Yet the terrible sense of loss and grief which followed her brother's death also might have included a suppressed element of relief—with its accompanying guilt.[16] For after all, the death of that masculine intruder, the longed-for male child, must have involved some of her most deeply suppressed childhood feelings. Her renewed friendship with him in adulthood must have reawakened those feelings, but she again submerged them by absorbing him into her own self-identity. Again and again she stresses their likeness, their being two halves of one whole, as in "The Wind Blows" with its duplication of brother and sister on shore and on board—the same two in two time zones, but composed spatially in the same picture—and in the unspoken "understanding" between the two of them, with its unfocused, diffused quality of sexual excitement.

Mansfield apprently stopped work again on *The Aloe* when she and Murry left Bandol to join the Lawrences in Cornwall in April 1916. O'Sullivan and Scott mention that "KM wrote nothing in Cornwall, nor for several months afterwards, apart from letters and occasional jottings in her notebooks" (*Letters* I, p. 259). There is a lapse of an entire year between the move to Cornwall and the moment when Virginia Woolf asked for a story for the Hogarth Press on April 26, 1917. While the story lay dormant, however, much was happening in Mansfield's life which would eventually influence its final shape. First of all, there was the disintegrating relationship with the Lawrences, including Lawrence's abortive attempt at a *blutbruderschaft* with Murry, the violent intensity of the fights between Lawrence and Frieda, and Mansfield's increasing disgust with Lawrence's incessant theorizing about sex. Next was Mansfield's first visit to Garsington in early July, which brought her into close contact with Bloomsbury, broadening her circle of friendships and associating her with the center of British modernist activity, introducing her subsequently to Lytton Strachey, Maynard Keynes, Aldous Huxley, Dorothy Brett, Dora Carrington, Mark Gertler, Bertrand Russell, and T. S. Eliot. And finally, as a consequence of her new involvement with Bloomsbury, came her significant friendship with Virginia Woolf.

After Woolf's request for a story, in April 1917, Mansfield spent

[16]See Hankin's discussion of Mansfield's guilt feelings after the death of her brother, which "must have seemed in some odd way the logical outcome of her years of battling with male adversaries" (*Katherine Mansfield and Her Confessional Stories,* pp. 105–15).

the summer revising *The Aloe*. It was not until July 10, 1918, that the first copies of "Prelude" were published. Mansfield's process of revision between *The Aloe* and "Prelude" reveals her continuing attempt to eliminate the personal intrusion—the cutting away of the author's voice. Many of Mansfield's alterations serve to bring the narration closer to a specific character's consciousness and away from interpretation by an omniscient narrator. These changes result in a more complex rendering of several female points of view. Other alterations eliminate a nostalgic, personal tone. In the earlier version she retained the second-person "you" as part of several descriptions: "From the window you saw beyond the yard a deep gully filled with tree ferns" (*The Aloe*, p. 35). The narrator seems to insinuate herself into the narrative at this point. She also inserts, in parentheses, information that Kezia would not have been able to explain: "(Kezia had been born in that room. She had come forth squealing out of a reluctant mother in the teeth of a 'Southerly Buster' . . .)" (*The Aloe*, p. 35). The expression "reluctant mother" bears some resemblance to Lawrence's diction.

Some of Mansfield's thematic concerns are strengthened, made more explicit through revision. In other places the revisions tone down a reference. For example, in *The Aloe*, the Samuel Joseph family is described as the "swarm" (p. 27); the overriding impression of too many children in messy familiarity and antagonism contrasts with Linda's desire not to have any more children. The contrast works thematically, but in revising, Mansfield de-emphasized the Josephs altogether, eliminating large sections of which they were a part. To make a simple point of contrast did not warrant allowing the story to take in so much extraneous narration. Neither did overobvious humor—even if it contributed to larger themes—remain in the final version. In a scene at the Josephs' excised in "Prelude," Mansfield originally wrote:

> "You've only got one w. at your place," said Miriam scornfully. "We've got two at ours. One for men and one for ladies. The one for men hasn't got a seat."
> "Hasn't got a seat!" cried Kezia. "I *don't* believe you." (P. 31)

This incident is actually the first of the several contrasts between male and female that Kezia encounters in the story; these contrasts contribute to a pattern of emphasis on the process of awakening to gender differences, a pattern that includes Kezia's later conversation with the storeman about the difference between sheep and rams. But in a section of description like "Sunlight, piercing the green chinks, shone once again upon the purple urns brimming over with yellow chrysanthemums that patterned the walls—" (*The Aloe*, p. 35), Mansfield makes changes in "Prelude" that help to situate these descriptive lines more firmly in a discourse on sexuality: "Long pencil rays of sunlight shone through and the wavy shadow of a bush outside danced on the gold lines" (*Stories*, p. 222). In this way the masculine, in the image of the sun with its "long pencil rays," intrudes into the child's perception of the abandoned house.

*The Aloe* becomes, through its evolution into "Prelude," an awakening into female sexuality. It is also a rejection of male modes, and this strategy is apparent in its all-over structure: its multiplicity, its fluidity, its lack of a central climax, and its many moments of encoded sexual pleasure. What makes "Prelude" so revolutionary as a narrative is its implicit statement that the construction of gender should be the motivating center of the text. The technical innovations are devices to reveal this process of reproduction. Reproduction in several forms dominates the text: in terms of procreation—Linda's pregnancy, the blossoming of the aloe; re-production of gender roles in the games of the children and in Kezia's questioning about sexual differences; and the re-production of bourgeois family life in the interactions of the family members as they respond to the pressures of their "roles." This reproduction assumes the continued dominance of the patriarchal society—the dominance of Stanley as businessman, rule-maker, center of authority—and it occurs in a world of upward mobility—"fleets of aloes," more children, more property. And it relies on the proficiency of the matriarchal center in Mrs. Fairfield: her managing, bringing order, situating the process of reproduction within an aesthetically satisfying and efficient home. But "Prelude" also reveals that a counter-process of resistance and rebellion is always at work within these dynamics. Linda's resistance counters Stanley's demands, but ineffectively. Hers is primarily a negative force: passive resistance. The imaginative powers necessary for active rebellion are not brought into force. She fantasizes escape but cannot envision what shape it should take. Yet the imaginative powers, the talents she will never develop, are also in her daughter Kezia, who shares so many of her mother's internal responses:

fears of rushing animals, a sense of things coming alive through a force that Kezia calls "It" and Linda, "THEY."

Three modes of female sexual response are suggested in this story: First, Linda's initial attraction to sexuality (the baby bird in her dream), revulsion when the bird swells, and fear when it turns into a human baby; second, Beryl's fantasies of romance, centered in self-love, narcissism, and envy, a body-consciousness purely visual—specular. The third response is that of Kezia, the child not yet completely gendered, who longs for her grandmother's arms, to be stroked and to stroke, to experience the tactile pleasures. She is still polymorphous, responsive to a whole range of stimuli. But she already fears any that might overpower her. Her sexuality requires mutuality, not assault.

A fourth possible mode is one that Mansfield deleted from "Prelude," and that is the implied sexuality of Mrs. Trout, Linda's other sister. No less a participant in fantasy than her two sisters, as neurasthenic as Linda appears to be, Mrs. Trout has sexual fantasies bound up in violence and injury; her imaginary "novels" always include the death and destruction of the male.

In "Prelude" we are presented with multiple viewpoints, nearly all those of female characters. Only the short sections from the point of view of the father, Stanley Burnell, allow for the intrusion of the masculine. His consciousness works as counterpoint in a minor key. It strikes me that the story is structured like a female organism (which invariably contains some subordinated masculine characteristics). In working on this story, nearly a decade before Woolf's *Mrs. Dalloway*, Mansfield was already attempting a spatial rendering of a few days in the inner lives of her characters (she was even closer to Woolf's technique in revealing several minds living through *one* day in the later story about the Burnells, "At the Bay").

Remarkable as it is as a piece of experimental fiction, "Prelude" is even more immediately accessible to us as an exploration of feminine consciousness. Within the story Mansfield grapples with her own relationships with the members of her family—mother, father, grandmother, aunt, sisters. It is her most directly autobiographical story, but she discovers a way of exploring these relationships without centering them in the mind of a fictional alter ego. Although the child, Kezia, is a re-creation of the author herself, Kezia's consciousness is but one focus of attention in the story. Mansfield establishes connections, psychic connections that link all of the female characters. The overriding theme of the story is female sexual identity. Linda Burnell, Kezia's mother, strains against her given role and does not want to be a mother. She avoids her children and dreads the sexuality that might lead to the birth of yet another one. She thinks of her husband with a mixture of affection and revulsion: "For all her love and respect and admiration she hated him. And how tender he always was after times like those, how submissive, how thoughtful. . . . There were all her feelings for him, sharp and defined, one as true as the other. And there was this other, this hatred, just as real as the rest" (p. 258).

Linda's ambivalence toward her role is one possible direction for female sexual identity which Mansfield explores in this story. Linda's unmarried sister Beryl represents another. Her outlet is fantasy; she imagines a lover while she gazes at herself in the mirror for self-gratification. And yet another direction is embodied in the grandmother, who represents the earlier, more traditional generation and totally accepts her role. She gives Kezia the affection she craves and is always generous, practical, hard-working, and sensitive to everyone's feelings. Kezia adores her grandmother, but Mansfield makes us see that Kezia shares more deeply the fearsome personal isolation and acute imagination of the mother she does not really know very well than the placid, assured rootedness of the grandmother she hugs, strokes, and calls her "Indian brave."

Early in the story Kezia asks the storeman the difference between a ram and a sheep, expressing the central question of her awakening consciousness. The storeman, embarrassed, typically avoids the truth by saying, "well, a ram has horns and runs for you." But Kezia intuitively knows what he means:

> "I don't want to see it frightfully," she said. "I hate rushing animals like dogs and parrots. I often dream that animals rush at me—even camels—and while they are rushing, their heads swell e-enormous."
> (P. 225)

Kezia's language here is nearly identical to her mother's later in the story when she alludes to her husband with:

> If only he wouldn't jump at her so, and bark so loudly, and watch her with such eager, loving eyes. He was too strong for her; she had always hated things that rush at her, from a child. (P. 258)

Such similar thought patterns establish a psychic connection between mother and daughter deeper than the external aloofness of their behavior with each other. "Prelude" is filled with points of connection like this one: images repeated in new contexts, phrases echoed or parodied by different characters, daydreams merging into waking reality.

Older Freudian readings of "Prelude" often consider how Kezia's response to the killing of the duck relates to castration anxiety. But in terms of feminist revisionary theory, the most noteworthy aspect is that it is the "head" that is cut off. To lose the head—mind, intellect, consciousness—is to participate in women's fate as constructed in masculine definitions of women's position in relation to civilization. Kezia responds with excitement and then with fear. She wants the head put back on. She would like genders to be as interchangeable as the earrings she suddenly notices on Pat's ears—to recognize that one can go back and forth in the costumes of gender, that the roles are as simple as impersonation, that "death" is not permanent and loss can be reversed.[17]

"Prelude" breaks the form of the *bildungsroman* but is a narrative of *bildung* nonetheless. The spatial organization suggests simultaneity, but the typical linear pattern of individual development is rather spread out among the female characters, who tend to represent the central consciousness at various stages of her life: early childhood, late adolescence, young motherhood, and old age. The child, aunt, mother, and grandmother embody the female life cycle. But the inevitability of the continuation of conventional female roles seems implicit in this structuring. The only opening is for Kezia, the child yet unformed, but already containing within herself the inner structure to be unfolded.

[17]Fullbrook remarks on Kezia's reaction to the beheading of the duck: "In this very ritualistic scene she assumes the position of suppliant before the man who has demonstrated his power of imposing death in an ordinary yet godlike display of authority. The scene is of a primal fall from innocence, and it is also a scene in which a male parent-figure initiates the children into slaughter. In 'Prelude' this is the core of masculine gender. The male is the devourer of life, the killer, and Pat's act is completed as male ritual later in the story when we see Stanley—associated with knives like the butcher in Kezia's nightmare in 'The Little Girl'—carving the same duck with professional manly pleasure. . . . Kezia is only recalled from her terror through the evidence of Pat's likeness to women" (*Katherine Mansfield*, pp. 74–75).

## ∂ 8

# The Feminist Imperative

**N**ot long before Katherine Mansfield began to write the first chapters of *The Aloe* (spring 1915), she completed a story similarly innovative in technique: "The Little Governess."[1] If *The Aloe* seems a response to memories of childhood, questions of engendering, and women's relations with one another, "The Little Governess" seems a response to women's victimization, isolation, and lack of support for one another. "The Little Governess" serves as a reminder of the difficulties Mansfield faced as a woman alone, traveling abroad, difficulties that competed for attention with her attempts to write her retrospective probings of a family-centered, less alienated environment.

"The Little Governess" belongs with the "realistic" rather than "aesthetic" strand of Mansfield's thematic concerns as a writer of fiction; it focuses on the vulnerability of women in a world dominated by male power. As I discussed in relation to Mansfield's difficulties with the *bildungsroman*, this subject is bound to the female line of influence, the tradition of women's writing which is enmeshed in a conflict of competing fictional conventions. "The Little Governess" follows a line of development in Mansfield's work originating with "Juliet" (1906–7) and "The Tiredness of Rosabel" (1908) and continuing in some of the stories in her first published collection, *In*

---

[1]Mansfield refers to S. S. Koteliansky's favorable response to "The Little Governess" in a letter to him on March 10, 1915. The story was not published, however, until late autumn 1915, in two issues of *The Signature* (October 18 and November 1), under the pseudonym "Matilda Berry." See *Letters* I, p. 153.

*a German Pension* (1911). But "The Little Governess" is more sophisticated in both technique and psychology than these (or than the
discarded novel "Maata" which immediately preceded it). Ian Gordon dates Mansfield's "new method" of writing fiction to "The
Little Governess," although he sees the earlier version of "Prelude"
as the place where "she finally broke through to a new structure and
a new technique."[2] The story is centered in the protagonist's perceptions and holds the reader tightly within her misconceptions of
reality. However, by situating this young female protagonist in an
alien environment, alone, without the traditionally supportive interactions of female community, Mansfield exposes women's vulnerability in the world of men. Aside from the kind stewardess in
the "Ladies Cabin" on the evening boat, who serves as a watchful,
maternal figure, with "a long piece of knitting on her lap" (p. 202),
no women protect the governess on her journey to Bavaria. Like
Kezia in "Prelude," fearful of things "rushing" at her, "the little
governess" fears "a stamping of feet and men's voices" (p. 203).
Men are again intruders in Mansfield's fictional world: they are
loud; they push their way in; they rush at you.

The old man on the train seems in counterpoint to the old woman
in *The Aloe*, the grandmother whose protective arms symbolized
maternal love for Kezia. Kindly, sentimental, on the surface the old
man appears capable of providing a masculine form of sympathy
complementary to that of Mrs. Fairfield. Sylvia Berkman, writing
in 1951, believed that Mansfield had shifted her attitude in this story
"from that of the early German stories with their fierce antagonism
against the male, for although the little governess is set upon by a
philandering old gentleman, we are given to see clearly that her own
ignorance and unworldliness largely bring about her discomfiture."[3]
Feminist theory helps us interpret Mansfield's response in a different
way. In fact, she is even more antagonistic against the male here
than she was in many of the earlier stories. For by now, she appears
to understand that the victimization of women by men is systemic
and that "blaming the victim"—as Berkman's reading tends to do
by suggesting that the little governess brings on her own
catastrophe—merely ignores the methods that patriarchal ideology

[2]Ian Gordon, ed., *Undiscovered Country: The New Zealand Stories of Katherine
Mansfield* (London: Longman, 1974), p. xix.
[3]Berkman, *Katherine Mansfield: A Critical Study*, p. 80.

sets in place to condition the dependency of women. The "ignorance and unworldliness" that Berkman describes are the end result
of that conditioning, which sets women up to fail. The little governess is not merely an emblem of woman as victim, but a representation of ideology's construction of woman as a *target* for victimization. En-gendering, therefore, is as much a theme of this story as it
is of "Prelude."

Treated to an education compiled of warnings, women are punished when they assert themselves beyond those strictures, when
they seek freedom and adventure. The story begins with exactly
such warnings. "Don't go out of the carriage. . . *be sure* to lock the
lavatory door," the young woman is cautioned at the Governess
Bureau; "it's better to mistrust people at first rather than trust them"
(p. 201). Her fear makes her tight, miserly, sure she is being taken
advantage of. She refuses to give the porter his rightful tip, angers
him, and "trembling with terror she screwed herself tight, tight,
and put out an icy hand and took the money—stowed it away in her
hand" (p. 203). She catches sight of herself in a mirror and sees that
her face is white, her eyes round: " 'But it's all over now' she said to
the mirror face, feeling in some way that it was more frightened
than she" (p. 203). The mirror face is "more frightened"; it is separate from the governess herself. (This kind of dissociation of mind
and body recurs with frequency in the thought patterns of Mansfield's women characters; it is notable in "Prelude" when Beryl
holds a discussion with her own mirror face.)

Her rudeness to the porter disregarded, the little governess settles
into a false security on the train: "She looked out from her safe
corner, frightened no longer but proud that she had not given that
franc. 'I can look after myself—of course I can' " (p. 203). But she
fears the young men in the compartment next door, whose "singing
gave her a queer little tremble in her stomach" (p. 205), and is
relieved when an old man arrives to share her compartment.

Mansfield gives us the mixed point of view of a narrator who sees
only part of the truth—almost with the naiveté of the young woman herself. But the imagery reveals more than the governess can
understand about herself:

> How kindly the old man in the corner watched her bare little hand
> turning over the . . . pages, watched her lips moving as she pro-

nounced the long words to herself, rested upon her hair that fairly blazed under the light. Alas! how tragic for a little governess to possess hair that made one think of tangerines and marigolds, of apricots and tortoise-shell cats and champagne! Perhaps that was what the old man was thinking as he gazed and gazed, and that not even the dark ugly clothes could disguise her soft beauty. Perhaps the flush that licked his cheeks and lips was a flush of rage that anyone so young and tender should have to travel alone and unprotected through the night. Who knows he was not murmuring in his sentimental German fashion: "*Ja, est is eine Tragodie!*" (P. 206)

In whose mind are these thoughts formulated? Would the little governess have described herself with such sensuous imagery? Would she have moved her gaze from hand to lips to hair? At this moment there is no mirror available to capture her self-admiration, her pleasure in narcissistic self-objectification. As a matter of fact, her pleasure is increased by the mirror's absence and the accompanying freedom to indulge her powers of imagination, which provoke her drastic misreading of the old man's gestures. This seeming pleasure, however, is the sign of how deeply she is entrapped in what Luce Irigaray calls the "dominant scopic economy."[4] She must become the object of desire for the other, the passive recipient of the other's lust. Ignorant of the nature of female sexuality, which Irigaray believes "takes pleasure more from touching than from looking," she distorts it and projects it into the innocent-seeming, grandfatherly gaze of the stranger. In a sense she transports herself into a creature looking *through* the old man's eyes, as the following description of the young woman's response to the old man's gift of fresh strawberries suggests: "They were so big and juicy she had to take two bites to them—the juice ran all down her fingers—and it was while she munched the berries that she first thought of the old man as a grandfather" (p. 209).

So the association made first by the narrator, who only surmises (for we never actually penetrate the mind of the old man), is made explicit as the governess eats and the old man tells her that it has been twenty years since he "was brave enough to eat strawberries." Mansfield employs the same symbolist technique here that she used

[4]Luce Irigaray, *This Sex Which Is Not One* (Ithaca: Cornell University Press, 1985), p. 26.

years earlier in "Summer Idylle," where eating and sexuality are interchangeable. The charged sexuality of this encounter may be unconsciously perceived by the young woman who misplaces its meaning. The old man asks: "Are they good? . . . As good as they look?" The governess really *wants* pleasure, life, excitement, and gives in to these desires as she relaxes her guard. For after all, she *loves* the strawberries. And after she agrees to the old man's invitation, "the little governess gave herself up to the excitement of being really abroad, to looking out and reading the foreign advertisement signs, to being told about the places they came to—having her attention and enjoyment looked after by the charming old grandfather" (p. 210). By giving "herself up" to the agency of the old man, she loses her own. The sentence poses her in dependency: "being told about," "having her attention . . . looked after." Consequently, her pleasured passivity is destroyed by the old man's attempted sexual assault. After running away from his apartment, she boards a tram and carries with her an image, a physical one, of "a world full of old men with twitching knees" (p. 214). In a flamboyant metonymic transposition, Mansfield describes a woman on the tram who notices the upset young woman and says to her companion, "She has been to the dentist." The substitution of body parts could not be more appropriately euphemized: the governess has been assaulted in either case. Once again, in Mansfield's fiction, sexuality is dangerous, and a woman becomes a coconspirator in her own destruction when she incorporates the ideology of her oppressor into her sense of identity.[5]

I have no doubt that the technical advance of "The Little Governess"—noticeable in its sophisticated and intricate interplay between a diffused narrative voice and a character's stream of consciousness, and also in its skillful yet unobtrusive handling of sexual symbolism—is a function of Mansfield's struggle to discover narrative techniques to convey the contradictions and ambiguities of women's encounters with the world at large. She needed to find a method flexible enough to incorporate both a character's self-division and her self-deception, both her impulses toward freedom and her conditioned responses of self-denial.

[5]In an earlier story, "Millie," Mansfield shows a woman joining in the blood-lust of men who try to capture a young fugitive to whom she had been sympathetically—and sexually—attracted.

Antony Alpers draws an important connection between Mansfield's education at Queen's College (which was founded in 1848 to improve the lot of governesses) and the title of this story.[6] Of course, making her woman alone a governess is the key to Mansfield's feminist statement. In this way she links the victimization of her protagonist to the history of women's limited opportunities, as well as to the literary history of women writers and the predominance of governesses as major characters in novels of the last century. This use of the governess figure, consequently, becomes a conscious assault on the conventions of fiction. Mansfield depends on the reader's familiarity with the governess figure in fiction in order to deconstruct the convention by treating it ironically. By choosing a governess for her central character as late as 1915, Mansfield sets up an atmosphere of disjunction. It is almost like setting Jane Eyre down in the midst of the First World War, too late for Jane's kind of innocence.[7] Alpers calls the type of character in this story (along with other single women in Mansfield's fiction, such as Miss Brill, the Lady's Maid, and the two sisters in "The Daughters of the Late Colonel")

Edwardian victims of an age in which Queen's College itself had represented an attempt to do something humane for England's surplus women; [note how Alpers's use of the word "surplus" connotes that women's true function—as wives and mothers—is oversubscribed. These are the leftovers!] that is what Queen's was founded for, and it was there that Kass Beauchamp was educated. Her *dame seule* stories have more of history in them than has been acknowledged.

[6]Alpers, *Life*, p. 23. In addition to its historical connection with the improvement of the lives of women through education, Queen's College must have provided Mansfield with an atmosphere conducive to discussion of feminist issues. One small notation from *The Queen's College Magazine* of December 1904 gives us a clue to that ongoing concern: thanks are given to a Professor Hudson for presenting the college library with a collection of books and periodicals in French on "La Femme, et le Féminisme" (p. 222).
[7]Did Mansfield read Beatrice Hastings's description of her departure from Paris in July 1914, published in *The New Age*, where Hastings describes how she seated herself across from a woman who looked like a governess, and was relieved to find that the woman was not offended by her smoking, and even accepted a cigarette from her, "though she will never be much of a hand at it"? Quoted by John Carswell, *Lives and Letters: A. R. Orage, Katherine Mansfield, Beatrice Hastings, John Middleton Murry, S. S. Koteliansky, 1906–1957* (New York: New Directions, 1978), p. 96.

They don't, of course, have an overt message for society with re-gard to the roles of women. Kass Beauchamp was never an incipient feminist—even if reading Elizabeth Robins briefly made her feel and talk like one in Wellington.

Yet in spite of his assurance that Mansfield "was never an incipient feminist," Alpers goes on to quote from a story fragment of hers about the anxieties of women traveling alone, and then to explain that in spite of her insistence on Art, in and of itself, "the founders of Queen's College, and the ghosts of the first sad occupants of its gracious rooms, had left their mark upon her practice of the Art."[8]

Alpers's remark about Elizabeth Robins refers to a passage in Mansfield's journal of May 1908, which in the context of feminism is especially revealing. It gives evidence of the struggling young woman just emerging from adolescence, who longed for freedom and independence, who experimented, suffered, and most crucially, *understood* the social and psychological basis for her own personal revolt:

> I have just finished reading a book by Elizabeth Robins, *Come and Find Me*.[9] Really, a clever, splendid book; it creates in me such a sense of power. I feel that I do now realise, dimly, what women in the future will be capable of. They truly as yet have never had their chance. Talk of our enlightened days and our emancipated country— pure nonsense! We are firmly held with the self-fashioned chains of slavery. Yes, now I see that they *are* self-fashioned, and must be removed. Eh bien—now where is my ideal and ideas of life? Does Oscar—and there is a gardenia yet alive beside my bed—does Oscar now keep so firm a strong-hold in my soul? No; because I am grow-ing capable of seeing a wider vision—a little Oscar, a little Symons, a little Dolf Wyllarde—Ibsen, Tolstoi, Elizabeth Robins, Shaw, D'An-nunzio,[10] Meredith. To weave the intricate tapestry of one's own life,

[8]Alpers, *Life*, pp. 327–29.

[9]In this novel Elizabeth Robins writes of Alaska, of the men who went to find gold there and the women who stayed behind. Throughout the novel are references to the different needs of men and women, and especially to the conflict between the "energetic pursuit of fortune" and the demands of maternity. Alaska becomes for the woman "her and her babies' rival in this man's thoughts." *Come and Find Me* (New York: Century, 1908), p. 46. I have not found evidence that Mansfield read Robins's more explicitly feminist novel, *The Convert* (1907), based on her play *Votes for Women*. Robins was president of the Women Writers Suffrage League in 1908.

[10]The reference to D'Annunzio is provocative and suggests a connection not yet adequately explored by critics. For example, a fruitful comparison might be made

it is well to take a thread from many harmonious skeins—and to realise that there must be harmony. Not necessary to grow the sheep, comb the wool, colour and braid it—but joyfully take all that is ready, and with that saved time, *go* a great way further. Independence, resolve, firm purpose, and the gift of discrimination, *mental clearness*—here are the inevitables. Again, Will—the realisation that Art is absolutely self-development. The knowledge that genius is dormant in every soul—that that very individuality which is at the root of our being is what matters so poignantly.

Here then is a little summary of what I need—power, wealth and freedom. It is the hopelessly insipid doctrine that love is the only thing in the world, taught, hammered into women, from generation to generation, which hampers us so cruelly. (*Journal*, pp. 36–37)

Clearly, Mansfield's male biographers have certain difficulties coming to terms with her feminism and with her youthful struggles for independence. Their discomfort is most apparent when they describe her first experiences as a woman alone in London after her arrival from New Zealand in 1908. Jeffrey Meyers writes:

Katherine's first adult year in Europe was a disastrous period of her life and confirmed all her father's fears. Her violent rebellion against Harold's values was an acknowledgement of his power and influence over her, the reluctant homage of disobedience to authority. Within ten months of her arrival she had had an unhappy love affair with one man, conceived his illegitimate child, married a second man and left him the next day, endured a period of drug addiction and suffered a miscarriage. Though Katherine was afraid of her uncontrollable feelings, she believed she had to 'experience' life before she could write about it. But her raw emotion was only thinly veiled by a pose of sophistication, and she abandoned herself to a destructive sexual extremism that expressed both her craving for and her repudiation of men.[11]

---

between Mansfield's description of harmony and "the gift of discrimination" as essential to artistic development, and the following passage from Gabriele D'Annunzio's *Il Fuoco* (*The Flame of Life*): "He had brought about in himself the intimate marriage of art with life, and he thus found in the depths of his own substance a spring of perennial harmonies. . . . He was gifted with an extraordinary facility of language that enabled him to instantly translate into words even his most complex modes of feeling with a precision so detached and vivid that they seemed at times to belong to him no longer, to have been made objective by the isolating power of style" (*The Flame of Life* [New York: Boni & Liveright, 1900], pp. 12–13).
[11]Meyers, *Katherine Mansfield: A Biography,* p. 36.

I wonder what Meyers would have said about a young *male* artist's sexual activity? Sexual experimentation by young men is usually seen as a sign of positive growth, but "destructive sexual extremism" becomes the label for a young woman's insistence on nonvirginity! ("Drug addiction," incidentally, turns out to be only a pathetic dependence on Veronal, prescribed for insomnia—a "treatment" frequently given to women at the turn of the century.)

Most revealing is Meyers's assumption that Mansfield's complex and serious-minded questioning of patriarchal standards of feminine behavior is "an acknowledgement of [her father's] power and influence over her." Instead of considering Mansfield's recognition of her own sexual needs, Meyers establishes the father's position as more important than the daughter's; hers is primarily reactive. In this way, female sexuality can be interpreted—yet again—as the passive response to male authority.

While Meyers entitles his chapter on Manfield's escape to London "Disorder and Early Sorrow," and Antony Alpers names his (in his first biography of Mansfield in 1954) "'Experience' and Its Price," Claire Tomalin, Mansfield's most recent biographer, situates those first days in England under the heading "London 1908: New Women."[12] This shift in emphasis makes a great difference. Tomalin recognizes that Mansfield's experience was not anomalous, that she "sailed towards London in the summer of 1908 in the joyous mood of the successful rebel," and that she was entering a society "in which the patterns of Victorian life were being thoroughly shaken about, and none more vigorously than the pattern of Victorian womanhood" (p. 46). Tomalin describes a London in which the women's movement for suffrage had reached its height, where newspapers and journals were filled with articles debating the changes in women's roles and opportunities and were taking up such issues as marriage reform, the sexual rights of women, and the question of compulsory motherhood. Mansfield's attempts to make a place for herself in the midst of the creative tumult of Edwardian England involved considerably more than a *personal* drive for sexual freedom. It is too easy to assume that it alone was the reason behind her decision, at the age of twenty, to leave New Zealand and attempt to live independently as a writer in London. Her early note-

[12]Tomalin, *Katherine Mansfield: A Secret Life*, p. 46.

books and letters make it clear that a strong feminist impulse guided an intense desire to become a creative artist. The predominant issue is one of power. From childhood on she struggled to keep her life under her own control. Not surprisingly, she developed an exaggerated concept of the artist as a source of power, and her avid reading in the avant-garde literature of the turn of the century confirmed that concept.

Most readers of Mansfield recognize a feminist thrust to many of her stories, but critics, until the recent resurgence of the women's movement, have tended to ignore or downplay its significance. Alpers's statement, quoted above, that she "was never an incipient feminist" typifies one kind of critical reaction. Others recognize at least an ambivalent attitude toward feminism in Mansfield's work, but they tend to attribute that ambivalence to strictly psychological causes: her bisexuality,[13] her unresolved relationships with her parents, or her need for personal comfort and security. While all of these factors are relevant to Mansfield's shifting attitudes, they need to be linked to the social factors: first, the history and politics of the women's movement itself during the years of her writing career, and second, the situation of the artist with regard to political questions in the period of early modernism. Without that grounding in social history, the discussion of "feminism" in Mansfield's life and work becomes deadlocked at the level of the personal.

Part of the problem remains that of an insufficiently theorized definition of "feminism." The word is used in some cases to refer strictly to support of the suffrage movement. In other cases, it refers more broadly to a defense of women against oppression by men. In yet others, it refers to a totalizing world view, an emphasis on the differences between men and women.[14] At different times Mans-

---

[13]Clare Hanson remarks that "an ambivalent attitude towards the opportunities afforded by feminism persisted throughout KM's life: like many of the characters in her fiction, she seems to have been torn between a desire to reject the conventional feminine role and a desire to accept it—to annihilate herself, as it were, by identifying completely with it. This ambivalence is clearly related to KM's bisexuality, itself a complex of forces and orientations which biography can only struggle to recover. What is important for her writing is that this sexual ambivalence produced a fiction which is stronger, in feminist terms, than that of Virginia Woolf, who was of course shocked (and frightened?) by KM's exposure of the emptiness behind stereotypical female role-playing in the story 'Bliss'" (Critical Writings, p. 19).

[14]For example, Hanson and Gurr point toward "what must be called a feminist awareness running throughout her writing, in the sense that there is always a strong

field seems to project each one of these definitions of feminism, but her emphases shift, her position regarding them alters. The term "feminism" itself was not a conscious attribution to her self-definition. Her earliest writing tends to subsume women's protest under the first definition: the struggle for the vote.[15] She refers to suffragists in a number of places, for example, in a letter to her sister in June 1908, a few weeks after the reference to Elizabeth Robins in her journal: ". . . and *do* read 'Come and Find Me' by Elizabeth Robins—that woman has genius—and I like to think she is only the first of a great never ending procession of splendid, strong woman writers—All this suffragist movement is *excellent* for our sex—kicked policemen or not kicked policemen" (*Letters* I, p. 47).

It is important to notice that Mansfield's writing career overlaps several stages of the women's movement. Her earliest writing, between 1906 and 1912, corresponds with a period of active debate in the public arena, debate in which the emotions were intense and the vocabulary of protest colorful and frequently inflammatory. In 1909, for example, the English feminist Cicely Hamilton published a book entitled *Marriage as a Trade*, and in 1907, Florence Farr, writing in *The New Age* (the journal Mansfield would later find to be the first home for her fiction), had defined marriage as "a profession in which the amateur commands a higher price than the skilled artist."[16]

Mansfield was an upper-middle-class young woman, and her feminism would not have been the same as that of working-class women, whose activism was related to their constricted environment of overburdened maternity and oppressive working conditions. Neither was it compatible with that of many nineteenth-century feminists who posited an absolute choice between marriage and career for women. By separating herself from the bourgeois world of her parents, she also left its style of efforts at social improvement: philanthropy, volunteer "social work," women's clubs,

---

feeling of division and discontinuity between male and female experiences of life" (*Katherine Mansfield*, pp. 13–14).

[15]Tomalin remarks that Mansfield "was, in general, on the side of the suffragettes, but had not the temperament for the dreary, necessary political work of meetings, discussions and fund-raising" (p. 59).

[16]Quoted in Wallace Martin, *"The New Age" under Orage* (New York: Barnes & Noble, 1967), p. 28.

and so on. Still, despite physical distance, she never separated herself entirely from the driving ideology of that bourgeois world. As the journal entry from May 1908 makes perfectly apparent, Mansfield accepted wholeheartedly many of the tenets of late-nineteenth-century capitalistic individualism. Her references to "independence, resolve, firm purpose. . . . Will . . . self-development" reveal how much she had incorporated of the ideology she professed to reject. And when she insists that what she needs is "power, wealth and freedom," it is with the purpose of absolute "self-development" that she confronts the quandary of feminist aspirations.

Mansfield's emancipation was to be through her efforts as an artist (and she had not yet escaped from the flamboyant extrava-gances of Wilde, nor from D'Annunzio's exaggerated descriptions of genius), but such efforts to become an accepted member of the special "tribe" of artists (as she later referred to them) precluded political interaction with middle-class social groups. Her feminism, therefore, focused on the area of her greatest personal knowledge: sexuality and women's experience of it. In some ways, this entry into feminist concerns allowed her to dissolve some class distinc-tions, for she recognized that *all* women are subject to oppression from men at some level and are subject to victimization as sexual objects through rape, unwanted pregnancy, venereal disease, aban-donment by male partners, economic dependency on men. These consequences of women's physical vulnerability moved her deeply, the agitation for the vote not so much so. Nevertheless, we should not take her comments to Garnet Trowell about the suffragettes, quoted below, as her last words on the issue, for those comments were written *before* her experiences of pregnancy, miscarriage, and abandonment. Besides, she was a very young woman in love and still hopeful that she might escape the constricted life of her nineteenth-century female forebears.

An interesting feature of this letter to Garnet Trowell, written in September 1908, only a few weeks after she had arrived in London from New Zealand, is its precise description of the atmosphere of a suffrage meeting, conveyed in Mansfield's characteristically concise and witty manner:

This evening I ended with going to report on a Suffrage Meeting at 8 o'clock in Baker Street. It was my first experience. Immediately I entered the hall two women who looked like very badly upholstered chairs pounced upon me, and begged me to become a voluntary worker. There were over two hundred present—all strange looking, in deadly earnest—all looking, especially the older ones, particularly "run to seed". And they got up and talked and argued until they were hoarse, and thumped on the floor and applauded—The room grew hot and in the air some spirit of agitation of revolt, stirred & grew. It was over at 10.30. I ran into the street—cool air and starlight—I had not eaten any dinner, so bought a 2d sandwitch at a fearful looking café, jumped into a hansom, & drove home here, eating my sandwitch all the way . . . & decided I could not be a suffragette—the world was too full of laughter. Oh, I feel that I could remedy the evils of this world so much more easily—don't you? Starlight and a glad heart and hunger and beef in hansoms, and the complexities of life vanish like cobwebs before a giant's broom. But I must needs look at life differently to others—wonderful and life giving miracle—*you are alive*—nothing else matters. (*Letters* I, p. 60)

Again, Mansfield's characteristic sentence rhythms reveal connections between one level of response and another. The sentence "Oh, I feel that I could remedy the evils of this world so much more easily—don't you?" resembles the section of an earlier letter to Sylvia Payne of April 1906, in which she says: "O, how many times I have felt just the same. I just long for power over circumstances—& always feel as though I could do such a great more good than is done—& give such a lot of pleasure—" (*Letters* I, p. 18). But there, the context is in direct opposition to her longing to merge with Garnet Trowell. Instead, in the earlier letter she says, a few sentences before the one quoted above, "I am so keen upon all women having a *definite* future—are not you? The idea of sitting still and waiting for a husband is absolutely revolting—and it really is the attitude of a great many girls." The letter concludes with her question to Sylvia: "Would you not like to try *all* sorts of lives—one is so very small—but that is the satisfaction of writing—one can impersonate so many people" (p. 19). It is almost as if in the later letter to Garnet Trowell, she is "impersonating" the opposite role: the woman in love who distinguishes herself from the suffragettes and imagines them to lead sexless lives. Here, also, she is in a transitional period of feminist ideology. Unlike some of the nineteenth-century theorists and activists who advocated celibacy as a political stance, a necessary withdrawal from men to a women-centered community, in what Martha Vicinus has termed "the empowering nature of freely chosen chastity,"[17] Mansfield insisted on being actively sexual from an early age. That overt sexuality would have been in opposition to the stance of some of the militant feminists she encountered who seemed to her asexual, or at the least, sadly repressed.[18]

There may be an unconscious connection between Mansfield's description of the suffragists, which contains such strong elements of revulsion converted to humor, and the following remarks from a curious source, a possible (even if suppressed) influence on her work:

> It is natures like these, with a minus of sexual life and therefore a surplus of bitterness and self-righteousness, which for some decades have held themselves up as the standard of "sound relations" in public life, in literature, art, science, and political economy, and have played the leading roles in the woman movements through the world—when these are not combined with free love, and sometimes even then![19]

The quotation comes from Laura Marholm's *Studies in the Psychology of Woman*, a book Mansfield apparently read in New Zealand in 1907–8.[20] As we know from Mansfield's reading notes in her jour-

---

[17]Martha Vicinus, *Independent Women: Work and Community for Single Women, 1850–1920* (Chicago: University of Chicago Press, 1985), p. 289.

[18]Nineteenth-century feminist discourse on sexuality is far more complex and contradictory than the stereotype of women's sexual repression tends to suggest. See Ellen Carol DuBois and Linda Gordon, "Seeking Ecstasy on the Battlefield: Danger and Pleasure in Nineteenth Century Feminist Sexual Thought," in *Pleasure and Danger: Exploring Female Sexuality*, ed. Carole S. Vance (Boston: Routledge & Kegan Paul, 1984), pp. 31–49. DuBois and Gordon recognize that two traditions regarding sexuality derive from nineteenth-century feminist theory: "The strongest tradition, virtually unchallenged in the mainstream women's rights movement of the nineteenth century, addressed primarily the dangers and few of the possibilities of sex. Another perspective, much less developed despite some eloquent spokeswomen by the early twentieth century, encouraged women to leap, adventurous and carefree, into sexual liaisons, but it failed to offer a critique of the male construction of the sexual experience available to most women" (p. 31). A good overview of middle-class British women's reactions to and participation in the women's movement, especially in relation to issues of sexuality, is Jane Lewis, *Women in England: 1870–1950* (Bloomington: Indiana University Press, 1984), pp. 75–141.

[19]Laura Marholm, *Studies in the Psychology of Woman*, trans. Georgia A. Etchison (New York: Duffield, 1906), pp. 183–84.

[20]By studying borrowing records, Guy Scholefield determined which books

nal, she tended to jot down reactions to books that affected her conceptualization of the role of artist. The notes on Oscar Wilde, George Eliot, and the prose writers of the late nineteenth century are copious. But she also tended to omit references to material she found disturbing or threatening to her pursuit of a writing career (as I indicated earlier in terms of her response to Symons's treatment of Balzac). What interested me in the case of her reading of Laura Marholm was why she never referred to Marholm's book in her notebooks or letters. Not that Mansfield wrote about every book she encountered (Guy Scholefield's study of library borrowing records reveals that she read voraciously); most of her reactions remained unrecorded. But Marholm's is the only book written by a woman on Scholefield's list, and Mansfield's silence about it is in contradiction to her enthusiastic writing about Elizabeth Robins, as well as Marie Bashkirtseff, whom she also read during this same period.[21] This silence is even more puzzling when we consider that not only is it a book by a woman, it is a book *about* women.

Laura Marholm, although German, wrote in Swedish. She was married to the Swedish writer Ola Hansson, and the couple were active in the avant-garde in Berlin in the '90s. Hansson was one of the critics who promoted Nietzsche and encouraged German interest in experimental writers such as Huysmans and Strindberg.[22] But Marholm's concept of "woman" was far from "advanced." Under the guise of the improvement of women's condition, she wrote with a virulent antifeminism (and an increasingly apparent anti-Semit-

---

Mansfield checked out of the library in Wellington during 1907–8; Marholm's *Studies* was one of them. See Scholefield, "Katherine Mansfield," in Sir Harold Beauchamp, *Reminiscences and Recollections* (New Plymouth, N.Z.: Thomas Avery & Sons, 1937), p. 194.

[21]Marie Bashkirtseff, *The Journal of a Young Artist: 1860–1884*, trans. Mary J. Serrano (New York: Cassell, 1889). Bashkirtseff's journal was one of Mansfield's favorite books, and she identified closely with the tragic struggle of the talented aspiring artist who died at the age of twenty-four of tuberculosis.

[22]James McFarlane, "Berlin and the Rise of Modernism: 1886–96," in *Modernism*, ed. Malcolm Bradbury and James McFarlane, pp. 106, 114–17. Laura Marholm's Nietzschean affinities become increasingly apparent in *Studies in the Psychology of Woman*. Since Mansfield was actively reading Nietzsche's *Dawn of Day* at about the same time, she must have recognized a connection between Marholm and Nietzschean philosophy. Mansfield expressed no disapproval of Nietzsche, and in fact, must have been excited about some of his ideas, as her references in the journal to "Will" and self-development seem to indicate.

ism, I might add). Put crudely, Marholm's thesis is that because of industrialism and its resulting social changes, men have become demasculinized, diminished in power, and correspondingly, women have been forced to emancipate themselves since they no longer can rely on the strength of men. Marholm links this development with evolutionary trends (in keeping with late-nineteenth-century manifestations of social Darwinism) and sees a movement toward "an intermediate form, a third sex, which certainly may have the qualifications of competition with man, and of stamping the human spirit with the sterility of hermaphroditism" (p. 119). The women's movement is thus a symptom of a degenerate age, marked by widespread physical debilitation, female illnesses, and the like. Marholm insists that "man must first obtain a firm hold upon the soil again, before woman can take root in him, according to her nature" (p. 128). The distinction between men and women is innate, biologically determined, according to this theory:

> We must impress one fact upon our minds; man is, what we women never are, a supra-sensuous being. He is never satisfied in any way nor at any point with what really exists,—precisely because through his mental and physical constitution he is the creative organism; whereas woman is the bearing organism. As soon as man ceases to be creative, ceases, that is, to consider the world and us also as his material,—he begins to resemble woman. But thereupon he ceases to be man; it is his declaration of bankruptcy.
>
> Therefore I do not hesitate to say that the men who teach and advocate the equality and the similar position of man and woman, always produce rather the impression of physical or mental bankrupts,—be they scholars, poets, or simply train-bearers to the ladies. (Pp. 105–6)

One of Marholm's most antifeminist pronouncements links the woman's movement with the displacement of women's sexual energy: "The same emotional necessity which impelled women three hundred years ago to denounce each other as witches, and avow themselves as such, now drives them into the movement for the emancipation of women. Both phenomena are the result of emotional cravings misplaced and diverted from their natural channels" (p. 145).

Surely Mansfield must have been angered, or at the least troubled,

by Marholm's analysis of the decline of western civilization symbolized by the rise of independent women. (It is interesting to note
that Mansfield's close friend D. H. Lawrence later began to formu-
late theories that correspond with many of Marholm's. His, like
those of several other male modernists, were more probably derived
from reading Otto Weininger's *Sex and Character* [1904], which
draws from a similar collection of antifeminist, frequently protofas-
cist works.) Especially troubling to her must have been Marholm's
attack on the prevalence of authorship among young women,
which, like the women's movement, is to be interpreted as a displacement of the "natural" roles of women:

> They all write,—these intelligent young women—either openly or
> in secret. They write in order to feign to themselves a contentment;
> whereas the man who writes does so in order to unburden himself of a
> contentment, real or fancied. The young woman who writes and the
> young man who writes are alike dissatisfied; but the woman writes in
> order to have something, the young man in order to be relieved of
> something. Gradually the scribbling woman grows to interpret her
> lack as a virtue. She was desirous of love; now she is desirous of
> knowledge. She begins to read; she gains for herself an outward con-
> tent since she cannot gain an inward one, and the longing of the
> woman in her begins to grow silent and die away. (P. 73)

Despite the attribution of "lack" to women—a symptom of Marholm's entrapment in the dominant ideology—Marholm recognizes
that women writers are of value, if only in demonstrating the crisis
of civilization that her book defines: "The woman writer affords
excellent material for the psychological study of woman; she cannot
help betraying that process of becoming woman—or non-woman,
whichever it may be—always concealed by other women and difficult to discover" (p. 74).

Mansfield might well have seen herself in the extended portrait of
the struggling young woman writer which Marholm creates. She
would have seen her drive for artistic success defined by Marholm as
"woman's demand for life, which in maiden fashion, unclear and
vague and cautious, is generally formulated as the demand of the
artist-nature for the exercise of her art" (p. 75).

It is not surprising that Marholm concludes her book with a
discussion of "woman's productive work," which gets defined as

work best suited to women's "nature": "The best work which the woman can create, and in which her productivity is complete, undiminished and enduring,—is the child" (p. 328). It is no wonder that Mansfield's imaginative interaction with her female precursors was ambivalent. What might seem like antifeminism in her writing at times (that is, negative portrayals or criticism of women's behavior) was frequently frustration and anger over many women's refusal to overcome their conditioned acceptance of women's role. When she saw such conditioned behavior rationalized as "natural" by intellectual women like Marholm, apologists for the defense of reactionary principles, her disappointment must have been extreme.

Katherine Mansfield may have set Marholm's book aside, but it left its mark on her style, nonetheless. For in spite of its seeming antifeminism, it contained the germ of a different approach to the exploration of women's lives. I suppose one could call it a very early example (or late, if it is considered a manifestation of the nineteenth-century defense of separate spheres) of "cultural feminism": the defense of "female" values, the belief in the special dimensions of women's creativity, ethics, and modes of consciousness.[23] What might have impressed itself on Mansfield was Marholm's method of analysis and her narrative technique. Presenting itself as "the first attempt at a Psychological Study of Woman which has been laid before the public by a woman" (p. 7), the book unfolds in a very different manner from the traditional psychological treatise. It begins very much like a novel: "She sat upon her handsome puffed divan, surrounded by many soft embroidered cushions, busily engaged in embroidering one more" (p. 13). What follows is a vignette, a character study of a frustrated "modern" woman. The "analysis" of her situation follows the lively description, and is conveyed through the thoughts of the narrator, the "I" who watches and records.

This first-person narrator is the constantly critical eye, the speaker who only intrudes in the narrative as a questioner and—most pertinent to Mansfield—a passive, ironic consciousness interposed between the characters and the reader. The voice is quite similar to that

[23]For a discussion of the recent history of "cultural feminism" and a critique of its political implications, see Alice Echols, "The New Feminism of Yin and Yang," in *Powers of Desire: The Politics of Sexuality,* ed. Ann Snitow, Christine Stansell, and Sharon Thompson (New York: Monthly Review, 1983), pp. 439–59.

of the narrator in the stories Mansfield published in *The New Age* in 1910–11, which were collected for her first book, *In a German Pension* (1911). This narrator is a woman, writing about other women—questioning them, observing them, at times identifying herself with them, but more often establishing her differences from them. Here is a good example from Marholm, describing some guests at an ocean resort:

> Suddenly a sharp feminine laugh came sounding up from the beach, then a buzz of women's voices, then a ceaseless concert of laughter. I sat up and looked over the cliff. Below were my neighbors of the hotel where I had taken my abode, hard at work in a very singular occupation. Half a dozen ladies assisted a young wife to bury her husband in the sand. . . . With hands and feet and spades a hill was scraped and shoveled over him; the man vanished; only the points of his toes and his nose still showed. When he lay so fixed that he could not move, the wife jumped up, caught the hand of a twenty-year-old youth who had stood pensively by, and sprang with him across the mock grave and back, amid jubilant shouts; the others standing about accompanied the symbolical act with silly laughter.
>
> All at once, by some reflex association beneath the threshold of consciousness, the "old specter," the renowned creator of the question of "Woman's Emancipation" in the North, stood visibly there below near this strange new wife; the figures of that very intellectual woman and of this very ordinary, narrow-minded teacher-wife blended for a moment into one, and it wore an expression of aversion—of sharp aversion for the man. (Pp. 29–30)

The focus on a symbolic moment is similar to Mansfield's, as is the choice of an odd and arresting image: the points of the nose and the toes. Marholm *uses* the vignette in the old-fashioned, allegorical method of the sermon or political tract; Mansfield makes her own vignettes elaborately suggestive, makes them radiate numerous meanings, psychological and cultural. A symbolic moment like the one at the beach might become the nucleus of a short story, complete in itself without analytical statement. Of course, Marholm's purpose in setting down the vignette was entirely different. Yet Mansfield might have appreciated its visual detail and its intensity of focus.

In contrast to Marholm's antifeminist emphasis, Mansfield's *In a*

*German Pension* contains vivid portraits of women who are trapped by their sexuality and dominated by men, creatures bound to the earth and their own bodies. These stories reflect Mansfield's own experiences of consciousness within a woman's body: pregnancy and labor, fears of rape, disgust with female submission. In "At Lehmann's," for example, Frau Lehmann's young servant, Sabina, does not know the facts of childbirth, let alone sexuality:

> Frau Lehmann's bad time was approaching. Anna and her friends referred to it as her 'journey to Rome,' and Sabina longed to ask questions, yet, being ashamed of her ignorance, was silent, trying to puzzle it out for herself. She knew practically nothing except that the Frau had a baby inside her, which had to come out—very painful indeed. One could not have one without a husband—that she also realized. But what had the man got to do with it? (Pp. 73–4)

What indeed! All Sabina knows is that the impulses of her own body confuse her. Ambivalence characterizes all of her responses: "If she herself should one day look like that—feel like that! Yet it would be very sweet to have a little baby to dress and jump up and down" (p. 74).

Mansfield then brings all of Sabina's ignorance, desire, and repugnance together in one startling scene. For at the same time as the Frau is giving birth upstairs, a young man attempts to seduce Sabina. The insistence of his pressing, pushing body simultaneously arouses and frightens her:

> "Look here," he said roughly, "are you a child, or are you playing at being one?" . . .
> He pulled her closer still and kissed her mouth.
> "Na, what are you doing?" she whispered.
> He let go her hands, he placed his on her breasts, and the room seemed to swim round Sabina. Suddenly, from the room above, a frightful, tearing shriek.
> She wrenched herself away, tightened herself, drew herself up.
> "Who did that—who made that noise?"
>
> In the silence the thin wailing of a baby.
> "Achk!" shrieked Sabina, rushing from the room. (P. 78)

*137*

Here is a very early example of a device that Mansfield developed and brought to perfection: scenic simultaneity. She links action occurring in two places at exactly the same point in time: the baby's wail, Sabina's shriek—and the young man's hands.

"At Lehmann's" is more advanced technically than many of the other stories in the collection, which are loosely linked together, like the vignettes in Marholm's *Psychology*, by the first-person, female narrator, a guest at the pension who distances herself from the behavior of the Germans through her critical, ironic tone. "The Modern Soul," for example, attacks the pretensions of female modernity. And here Mansfield attacks as sharply as had Marholm. Fraulein Sonia, in contrast to the aloof, independent narrator, expresses herself—like many of the Germans in the book—histrionically. She presents herself as a new woman longing for freedom, but trapped by the necessity to take care of her mother. This "modern soul" declaims to the narrator:

> "Do you know that poem of Sappho about her hands in the stars?... I am furiously sapphic. And this is so remarkable—not only am I sapphic, I find in all the works of the greatest writers, especially in their unedited letters, some touch, some sign of myself—some resemblance, some part of myself, like a thousand reflections of my own hands in a dark mirror." (P. 69)

(The narrator responds abruptly to this rhapsody with "But what a bother," a symptomatic denial on Mansfield's part of her own lesbian experiences.) The "modern soul" reveals to the narrator that she longs for greatness and individual autonomy, but the narrator's responses make it clear that Fraulein Sonia is in reality sex-starved, apologetic, and ready to sell herself into the protection of a bourgeois marriage.

Mansfield is even more astringent in "The Advanced Lady." One of the Germans is amazed to discover a female author at the pension, and remarks to her: "I personally [have never] known a woman who was writing a book. How do you manage to find enough to write down?" (p. 104). But Mansfield portrays this "advanced lady," who is writing a novel "upon the Modern Woman," as self-centered, rationalizing her cruelty to her husband and child as a sign of her independence of mind and forward thinking. (This is an early version of Mansfield's growing suspicion of the fashions of modernism; it prefigures such stories as "Bliss" and "Marriage à la Mode.") But in spite of her apparent dislike for this type of woman, her scorn for the conventional self-satisfaction of bourgeois women is even greater. Frau Fischer, in the story of the same name, sentimentally suggests to the narrator that "every wife ought to feel that her place is by her husband's side—sleeping or waking. It is plain to see that the strongest tie of all does not yet bind you. Wait until a little pair of hands stretches across the water—wait until he comes into harbour and sees you with the child at your breast." But the narrator simply responds with: "But I consider child-bearing the most ignominious of all professions" (p. 55).

The most disturbing story in the collection is "Frau Brechenmacher Attends a Wedding." A German woman, oppressed by household chores, rushes to get ready for a village wedding. Her husband is rude, thoughtless, and in the excitement and crush of the celebration, "so far forgot his rights as a husband as to beg his wife's pardon for jostling her against the banisters" (p. 58). The omnipresent, culturally sanctioned disdain for women extends to the innkeeper who "voiced his superiority by bullying the waitresses" (p. 58). The wedding celebration itself has a grim atmosphere. First, there is the bride with her dress and ribbons, "giving her the appearance of an iced cake all ready to be cut and served in neat little pieces to the bridegroom beside her" (p. 58). The bride has a child already, and that provides the company with more ammunition for criticism: "That's what I call a sin against the Church for a free-born child to attend its mother's wedding." As Frau Brechenmacher looks on at the crude hilarity of the crowd and realizes that she has "no hope of being asked to dance," she watches the couples swirling around her and for a moment she "forgot her five babies and her man and felt almost like a girl again" (p. 61). This woman might feel a fleeting pleasure as she sways to the music of the wedding dance, but her five babies have disfigured her body, left her to be pushed aside, treated rudely, disregarded. Life itself has become one dreadful round of heavy labor.

Throughout the evening, disillusionment and an ironic sense of a mystery despoiled affect her mood. By the time she returns with her husband to their small house, she questions, "Na, what is it all for?" The ending of the story encapsulates the woman's entrapment and despair in an image brilliantly characteristic of Mansfield's grounding in symbolist technique: "She lay down on the bed and put her arm across her face like a child who expected to be hurt as Herr Brechenmacher lurched in" (p. 62).

Clearly, this group of stories contains sufficient evidence of Mansfield's anger over both women's sexual oppression and their cultural definition as childbearers. As Kate Fullbrook observes, Mansfield's "early fiction is both more overtly aggressive and more obviously politically embattled than the later work" (p. 35). Yet Mansfield's male biographers tend to underestimate or distort the importance of these stories and the significance of her most overtly feminist writing phase. Alpers assures us that Mansfield was under "some sort of mental domination" by Beatrice Hastings, who worked with Orage on *The New Age* and who had befriended her when she first began to publish there. (Meyers calls Hastings a "rabid feminist" [p. 58].) Alpers describes Mansfield's sophisticated, powerful story "At Lehmann's" as "a crude protest against the horrors of childbirth, and this was a special department of Beatrice Hastings' polemics."[24] Hastings had written an article in *The New Age* in which she described childbirth as "the ugliest fact in human life." But surely, Katherine Mansfield—who had only recently suffered a miscarriage alone in Germany—did not need Beatrice Hastings to tell her about women's anger over the male advantage in sexual life. Mansfield—living in an age before reliable contraception—learned very quickly that women are punished for their attempts to live out the sexual freedom of men.

This is not to underestimate the importance of Beatrice Hastings to Katherine Mansfield's career, however. As I have previously suggested, Mansfield's imaginative interactions with her female precursors were problematic. Her interactions with her female contemporaries could be especially so. Undoubtedly, the emergence of a feminist consciousness in her was related to both literary and experiential influences. She had numerous close, sometimes intense, friendships with women. In addition to friendships of adolescence—such as those with Vere Bartrick-Baker, her cousin Sylvia Payne, Edith Bendall, Martha Grace Mahupuku ("Maata"), and Ida Baker (who was her most devoted, if sometimes unappreciated, friend, as

[24]Alpers, *Katherine Mansfield: A Biography*, p. 134.

well as her nurse and companion through most of the stages of her fatal illness)—Mansfield had significant adult friendships with women who notably affected her range of ideas, her emotions, and her aspirations as a writer: Frieda Lawrence and Beatrice Campbell (Lady Glenavy); visual artists such as Dorothy Brett and Anne Estelle Rice; patrons of the arts such as Lady Ottoline Morrell and Violet Schiff.

Only two major friendships were with women writers. Virginia Woolf, of course, was the most famous woman writer of Mansfield's acquaintance (and I consider their relationship in the next chapter); but the woman writer with the most power to affect the development of Mansfield's writing was—unquestionably—Beatrice Hastings.

Like other women who seem to be erased from the history of literary modernism, Beatrice Hastings played a crucial role in initiating, encouraging, criticizing, and eventually countervailing the dominant thrusts of the modernist movement.[25] Yet she is usually referred to slightingly as Orage's "mistress." Hastings's voluminous writings have disappeared from the critical record. Her books so long out of print that they are virtually inaccessible, her essays, short fictions, satires, and sketches in *The New Age* so often printed under a variety of pseudonyms (as were many of Mansfield's, by the way) that their attribution still remains unclear, her reputation so inextricably meshed with the notoriety of her sexual life (her relationship with Modigliani, for example), Beatrice Hastings appears only as a footnote, an aside, in the narrative of modernism's evolution.[26]

Beatrice Hastings was nearly a decade older than Katherine Mansfield, but she had come from a similar background. Like Mansfield, she was the child of upwardly mobile, newly rich colonialists. She was born in Port Elizabeth, Cape Colony, in 1879, but left home— and Africa—by the time she was twenty. Thus, Mansfield surely saw her as an example of the kind of liberated woman of talent whom she envisioned herself to be. Hastings became her mentor,

[25]For a discussion of the roles of similarly situated and similarly neglected— though influential—expatriate women in Paris during this same period, see Benstock, *Women of the Left Bank*.

[26]For the most detailed and sympathetic discussion of Hastings's role in literary history, see Carswell, *Lives and Letters*.

encouraging her first publications for the journal. She edited her writing, criticized it, helped Mansfield to see where it needed shaping and emphasis. For example, she reviewed pseudonymously *In a German Pension* (even though most of the stories had originally appeared in *The New Age*) with an eye toward improving Mansfield's style: "When Miss Mansfield gets quite clear of the lachrymose sentimentality that so often goes with the satirical gift, she will be a very amusing and refreshing writer."[27] Hastings and Mansfield wrote several pieces collaboratively for the journal, including parodies of contemporary authors. Hastings helped the younger woman immerse herself in the intellectual currents of the day, which were debated with intensity in *The New Age* in articles about contemporary art (on Epstein, Gaudier-Brzeska, Wyndham Lewis, Picasso), philosophy (on Bergson and Nietzsche), politics (on socialism, Fabianism, the suffrage movement), and psychoanalysis (M. D. Eder, one of the first followers of Freud in England, was a contributor).[28]

Beatrice Hastings's contributions to *The New Age* were frequently on subjects of feminist concern: women's victimization in marriage, the mistreatment of imprisoned suffragettes, the limitations of women's access to higher education, and so on. She moved away from support of the suffragettes, however, as the war approached, because she recognized the class bias inherent in their single-issue focus on the vote. As John Carswell explains,

> she denounced the suffragettes as middle-class exploiters of their own sex and no better than the men whose equals they claimed to be. They neither understood nor sympathised with the real problems women had to face, or the real claims they had in society. There were no bounds to her indignation when Mrs. Pankhurst said she would willingly serve a term in prison, but would feel herself demeaned by serving it along with common female criminals in Holloway.[29]

[27]Quoted by Alpers, *Life*, p. 129.

[28]The centrality of *The New Age* to Modernism is not always significantly appreciated. From its beginnings in 1907, under the sponsorship of George Bernard Shaw, its editor, A. R. Orage, brought a large number of the major new writers of the day into the journal. Shaw, Edward Carpenter, H. G. Wells, Arnold Bennett, F. S. Flint, Ezra Pound, T. E. Hulme, Richard Aldington, Edwin Muir, Herbert Read, and many other writers were contributors. See Wallace Martin, "*The New Age*" *under Orage,* for the fullest account of the journal's history and significance.

[29]Carswell, p. 80.

John Carswell believes that Hastings was more talented than Katherine Mansfield, that her "literary gifts were more abundant and her ambitions ranged wider, but failure of discipline and contempt for obstacles denied her success or even a single first-class piece of work."[30] Whether or not lack of discipline led to Hastings's failure to achieve fame, her career certainly took a downward turn after she broke finally with Orage and *The New Age.*

Katherine Mansfield's friendship with Beatrice Hastings occurred at a fruitful stage in her career as she moved from her earlier preoccupation with '90s aesthetic doctrine to more socially aware, realistic treatments of contemporary life. It encouraged the further development of her gift for satire and parody, her impulse to "try *all* sorts of lives" (*Letters* I, p. 19). Most of all, the friendship—and the whole involvement with the production of *The New Age*—centered her apprenticeship as a writer in a milieu in which feminism and modernism were interconnected. In *The New Age,* arguments about impressionism, Bergsonism, and psychoanalysis appeared in the same issues with articles about the women's movement and sexual freedom.[31]

Mansfield became disillusioned with Hastings as the years passed because of her friend's alcoholism and increasingly irrational behavior (see *Letters* I, pp. 164–65). Although the influence of Beatrice Hastings eventually dissipated, it left a curious footnote. To describe it requires returning to the same letter to Murry of November 1, 1920, in which Mansfield described her dream about Oscar Wilde. The Wilde dream is actually the second dream described in that letter. The first is about Beatrice Hastings, and it begins similarly with a reference to a return to the familial past: "I was living at home again in the room with the fire escape. It was night: Father and Mother in bed." But this dream is far more frightening than the one about Wilde, for in it Hastings leads a group of drunk, "vile" people into Mansfield's room and screams at her:

---

[30]Ibid., p. 273.
[31]Beatrice Hastings and A. R. Orage gave Mansfield an entry into a literary world quite unlike that of Bloomsbury, and especially unlike that of Virginia Woolf herself. Woolf once referred to Mansfield and Murry as members of the "underworld," and Alpers believes that Woolf would have defined *The New Age* in this way as well (*Life,* p. 109). Virginia Woolf and T. S. Eliot were not contributors to the journal; Ezra Pound was.

'You dont take me in old dear' said she. 'Youve played the Lady once too often, Miss——coming it over me.' And she shouted, screamed *Femme marqué* and banged the table.

The dream continues in a surrealistic landscape, first of "a costume play of the Restoration," and then of Piccadilly Circus, "black with people," filled with an ominous sense of apocalypse:

> Then I realised that *our* earth had come to an end. I looked up. The sky was ashy-green; six livid quarters swam in it. A very fine soft ash began to fall. The crowd parted. A cart drawn by two small black horses appeared. Inside there were salvation army women doling tracts out of huge marked boxes. They gave me one! 'Are you Corrupted?' It got very dark and quiet and the ash fell faster. Nobody moved.[32]

Thus Beatrice Hastings returns as accuser, as the one who sees through Mansfield's disguise. The feminist imperative represented by Hastings seems to have merged with the forces of disorder and disruption. Yet who knows what feelings of guilt or dishonesty the dream suggests? In her state of dissolution, Hastings intrudes herself into the dreamer's psyche, calling for self-revelation, forecasting death and destruction.

[32] *Selected Letters*, p. 184.

# 9

# Mansfield and Woolf: The Question of Feminist Aesthetics

April 16, 1919: Virginia Woolf and Katherine Mansfield at tea. They long to talk, each with the other. But they are not to be left alone; their husbands stay on, watching over them. Mansfield's husband, John Middleton Murry, makes Virginia Woolf especially uncomfortable, and writing about the tea in her diary the following day she is able to register the source of her displeasure:

> The male atmosphere is disconcerting to me. Do they distrust one? despise one? & if so why do they sit on the whole length of one's visit? The truth is that when Murry says the orthodox masculine thing about Eliot for example, belittling my solicitude to know what he said of me, I dont knuckle under; I think what an abrupt precipice cleaves asunder the male intelligence, & how they pride themselves upon a point of view which much resembles stupidity. I find it much easier to talk to Katherine; she gives & resists as I expect her to; we cover more ground in much less time.[1]

Virginia Woolf and Katherine Mansfield know how separate they are from "the orthodox masculine thing," the given assumptions of traditional phallocentric criticism. But since they have the power to see through those assumptions, they may achieve a method of communication that will take advantage of their similarities as women. They will not use the old rules of discourse; they will not debate,

---

[1]Virginia Woolf, *The Diary of Virginia Woolf*, vol. I: 1915–1919 (New York: Harcourt Brace Jovanovich, 1977), p. 265.

contest each other. Communication will not become a means of scoring points. Each one accepts the fact that she does not know the outcome of their relationship at the beginning of their conversation. Since neither assumes that she speaks with the authoritative stamp of revealed truth, she realizes how much she needs to experiment in order to discover the way to where she senses she is going. And as each one is a writer of a new kind of fiction and a woman who will soon take her place as a central figure in the literature of modernism, I think we may safely assume that both Woolf and Mansfield recognize that they may be heading for the same place.

Yet, as with Mansfield's imaginative reworking and silencing of earlier women's voices in her texts, and as with her volatile apprenticeship with Beatrice Hastings, her relationship with Virginia Woolf—the only woman in her circle of friends who was a serious writer—was fraught with ambiguities.[2] The same can be said about Virginia Woolf's feelings. Woolf might complain that one of her friend's stories "was so brilliant,—so hard, and so shallow, and so sentimental that I had to rush to the bookcase for something to drink,"[3] or remark after Mansfield's death: "and I was jealous of her writing—the only writing I have ever been jealous of,"[4] but it would be too easy to overemphasize their competition and thus play into the stereotype of women as enemies, conspiring against each other for the favors of men—be they lovers or critics.[5] What is more to our purpose is to explore the creative consequences of their interaction.

[2]See Tomalin, *Katherine Mansfield: A Secret Life,* pp. 48–50, 160–62, 197–205, for an excellent overview of the friendship between Mansfield and Woolf; see also Alpers, *Life,* pp. 247–61; Meyers, *Katherine Mansfield: A Biography,* pp. 137–48. Two illuminating studies on the effect of the relationship on the writing of both authors are by Ann L. McLaughlin. See "The Same Job: Notes on the Relationship between Virginia Woolf and Katherine Mansfield," *Virginia Woolf Miscellany* 9 (Winter 1977), 11–12; and "The Same Job: The Shared Writing Aims of Katherine Mansfield and Virginia Woolf," *Modern Fiction Studies* 24 (Autumn 1978), 369–82. A useful discussion of Mansfield's impact on Woolf's writing is Louise A. DeSalvo, "Katherine Mansfield and Virginia Woolf's Revisions of *The Voyage Out,*" *Virginia Woolf Miscellany* 11 (Fall 1978), 5–6.

[3]*Letters of Virginia Woolf,* vol. II, p. 515.

[4]Quoted from Virginia Woolf's unpublished diaries by Leonard Woolf, *Beginning Again* (London: Hogarth, 1964), p. 207.

[5]An imaginative, perceptive reading of the alternation of envy and respect in the relationship between Mansfield and Woolf is Louise Bernikow, *Among Women* (New York: Harmony, 1980), pp. 126–41.

Katherine Mansfield became acquainted with Virginia Woolf through their mutual association with Lady Ottoline Morrell and the group gathered around her at Garsington. Lytton Strachey had arranged for their first meeting and by early 1917, Mansfield and Woolf were tentatively developing a friendship. As we have seen, in April 1917 Woolf asked Mansfield for a story she might produce on her newly acquired printing press at Hogarth House. That request spurred Mansfield's resolution to revise *The Aloe*, which the Woolfs then published in July 1918 as "Prelude." They continued to meet, with numerous interruptions (when Mansfield spent long periods abroad), until the end of 1920, when their meetings and correspondence apparently ceased. Mansfield's last letter to Woolf was the one that included the phrase "You are the only woman with whom I long to talk *work*."[6]

In an earlier letter (June 1917), Mansfield tells Woolf that she is "a bit 'haunted'" by her (*Letters* I, p. 313). That letter contains a passage that encapsulates the two women's similarity of vision in the same kind of elastic sentence "capable of stretching to the extreme, of suspending the frailest particles, of enveloping the vaguest shapes" which Woolf later described—in relation to Dorothy Richardson—as "the psychological sentence of the feminine gender."[7] Here is Mansfield's sentence:

> The memory of that last evening is so curious: your voice & Vanessa's voice in the dark, as it were—white rings of plates floating in the air— a smell of strawberries & coffee—Murry telling Woolf that you worked it with a handle & it had a cylinder & then M. and W. disappearing—and a feeling that outside the window floated a deep dark stream full of a silent rushing of little eels with pointed ears going to Norway & coming back.

In this rendering of a multileveled, richly metaphoric atmosphere charged with libidinal energy, Mansfield participates in an erotics of

---

[6]"Fifteen Letters from Katherine Mansfield to Virginia Woolf," *Adam International Review* nos. 370–75 (1972–73), 24.

[7]Virginia Woolf, "Romance and the Heart," *Contemporary Writers* (New York: Harcourt Brace Jovanovich, 1965), p. 124. This review of Dorothy Richardson's *Revolving Lights* appeared on May 19, 1923, only a few months after Mansfield's death.

writing, conveying that quality that Woolf later described in *Mrs. Dalloway*, of "something central which permeated; something warm which broke up surfaces and rippled the cold contact of man and woman, or of women together."[8]

What follows in Mansfield's letter continues that curious sexual quality:

> My God I love to think of you, Virginia, as my friend. Dont cry me an ardent creature or say, with your head a little on one side, smiling as though you knew some enchanting secret: "Well, Katherine, we shall see"... But pray consider how rare is it to find some one with the same passion for writing that you have, who desires to be scrupulously truthful with you—and to give you the freedom of the city without any reserves at all.

We have already seen how frequently Mansfield encoded sexuality in language, especially in the *rhythms* of language, so it is not difficult to recognize the level of sexual invitation in this letter—even if it is not overt. The transformation of the word "passion"—after the remark about being "ardent"—into the "same passion for writing" is a similar transformation to the one Mansfield effected in the journal passages cited in Chapter 2, on Mansfield and Wilde. A similar sense of an undercurrent of sexually charged intimacy occurs in the scene between Bertha and Pearl by the pear tree in "Bliss."

> And the two women stood side by side looking at the slender, flowering tree. Although it was so still it seemed, like the flame of a candle, to stretch up, to point, to quiver in the bright air, to grow taller and taller as they gazed—almost to touch the rim of the round silver moon.
>
> How long did they stand there? Both, as it were, caught in that circle of unearthly light, understanding each other perfectly, creatures of another world, and wondering what they were to do in this one with all this blissful treasure that burned in their bosoms and dropped, in silver flowers, from their hair and hands?
>
> For ever—for a moment? And did Miss Fulton murmur: "Yes. Just *that*." Or did Bertha dream it? (P. 347)

Woolf did not like "Bliss," by the way. It was the story that she complained about in the letter quoted above, the story she called

8Virginia Woolf, *Mrs. Dalloway* (New York: Harcourt, Brace, 1925), p. 46.

"brilliant" but "so shallow, and so sentimental." It should also be noted in this context that Woolf frequently expressed discomfort over Mansfield's "past," at what she took as intimations of the younger woman's promiscuity. Mansfield's sexual impulsivity might have insinuated itself disturbingly into Woolf's consciousness. (Only years later, after Mansfield's death, would Woolf express her own lesbian impulses.) It seems that Mansfield's New Zealand upbringing had given her more physical freedom than Woolf's.[9] She had actively pursued sexual fulfillment during the same stages of adolescence when Woolf was undergoing withdrawal and mental breakdown.[10]

Undoubtedly, there is much we can never know about the relationship between these two women. Influence—especially influence of contemporaries on each other—is so intangible. Aside from the meager written record, it is nearly impossible to reconstruct those mutual currents of thought continually retranslated, repeated, and repossessed. Those long afternoons talking about writing must have affected both of them. Did Mansfield tell Woolf, for instance, about her interest in "shape" and its relation to the structure of a novel? We know that she had described it to Murry (in a letter on March 25, 1915, predating her friendship with Woolf), when she envisioned the shape of *The Aloe* as a boat: "Not big, almost 'grotesque' in shape I mean perhaps *heavy*——with people rather dark and seen strangely as they move in the sharp light and shadow and I want bright shivering lights in it and the sound of water" (*Letters* I, p. 168). Many years later, in *A Room of One's Own* (1929), Virginia Woolf remarked that "a book is not made of sentences laid end to end, but of sentences built, if an image helps, into arcades or domes."[11] In her diaries she referred to the force of images in suggesting the shape and internal structure of her novels, as in this remark in 1926: "One sees a fin passing far out. What image can I

---

[9]See Mansfield's *The Urewera Notebook* for her accounts of her camping trip into the remote regions of the North Island with a group of men and women during 1907.

[10]Another significant difference between Mansfield's and Woolf's adolescent sexual development was the secretly incestuous atmosphere of the Stephen household. See Louise DeSalvo, *Virginia Woolf: The Impact of Childhood Sexual Abuse on Her Life and Work* (Boston: Beacon, 1989).

[11]Virginia Woolf, *A Room of One's Own* (New York: Harcourt Brace & World, 1929), p. 80.

reach to convey what I mean?"—her first insight in a long process culminating in *The Waves*.[12]

Oblique, metaphoric, associational patterns are characteristic of Mansfield's written communication with Woolf. There is always the sense of a more powerful, silent subtext, sometimes erotic, sometimes hostile. When Mansfield reviewed Woolf's *Kew Gardens*, she employed a sexual analogy to describe what is unique about Woolf's story. Mentioning how young writers often mistake their notebook contents for finished pieces, Mansfield complains that "they shall be regarded as of the first importance, read with a deadly seriousness and acclaimed as a kind of new Art—the art of not taking pains, of never wondering why it was one fell in love with this or that, but contenting oneself with the public's dreary interest in promiscuity." In contrast, for Mansfield, Woolf's *Kew Gardens* "belongs to another age. It is so far removed from the note-book literature of our day, so exquisite an example of love at second sight."[13]

In this public form of discourse, the erotic is reduced to a conventional trope: falling in love. Woolf is praised cautiously, judiciously, for her restraint. Hers is a passion under control, not to be expressed until its various components can be composed, perfected, *understood*. The tendency toward abstraction, toward intellectualization, which Mansfield attributed to Woolf and later criticized in her review of *Night and Day*,[14] is, in the case of *Kew Gardens*, still an attractive tendency. Mansfield's hesitation about its ultimate value in conveying "life" is held at bay. In homage to Woolf, then, Mansfield's review of *Kew Gardens* repeats, in its own structure, the movement of Woolf's story. Her last paragraph describes the end of Woolf's narrative: "Fascinated and credulous, we believe these things are all

[12]*The Diary of Virginia Woolf*, vol. III (New York: Harcourt Brace Jovanovich, 1980), p. 113.

[13]Mansfield, *Novels and Novelists*, ed. J. Middleton Murry (New York: Knopf, 1930), p. 39.

[14]Much of the later tension between Woolf and Mansfield relates to Mansfield's negative criticism of *Night and Day*. The review, published in *The Athenaeum* in November 1919, is reprinted in Mansfield's *Novels and Novelists*, pp. 112–15. In this review Mansfield faulted the novel for its lack of a sense of the new postwar consciousness: "If the novel dies it will be to give way to some new form of expression; if it lives it must accept the fact of a new world" (p. 112). Mansfield was more directly hostile about Woolf's novel in her private correspondence. In a letter to Murry she complained: "Talk about intellectual snobbery—her book *reeks* of it. (But I can't say so.)" *Letters to John Middleton Murry*, p. 388.

her concern until suddenly with a gesture she shows us the flower-bed, growing, expanding in the heat and light, filling a whole world" (p. 40). The review ends here with Mansfield's discovery of Woolf's epiphanic moment. That "gesture" takes the reader as well through the double experience of Woolf's epiphany and Mansfield's own in trying to recreate it.

Mansfield clearly appreciated Woolf's efforts toward a new kind of prose, but it seems that she believed that Woolf still held on to an older form of phrasing and diction. Compared with Virginia Woolf's earlier novels—such as *The Voyage Out* and *Night and Day* —everything Katherine Mansfield wrote seems crisp, pointed, bright, bold in outline like the following description of Bertha's dinner table in "Bliss":

> There were tangerines and apples stained with strawberry pink. Some yellow pears, smooth as silk, some white grapes covered with a silver bloom and a big cluster of purple ones. These last she had bought to tone in with the new dining-room carpet. Yes, that did sound rather far-fetched and absurd, but it was really why she had bought them. She had thought in the shop: "I must have some purple ones to bring the carpet up to the table." And it had seemed quite sense at the time. (P. 338)

The direct, simple, seemingly objective description quickly reveals itself as Bertha's own observation, but we are able to discern Mansfield's ironic light shining through Bertha's quite serious decision to "have some purple ones to bring the carpet up to the table."

My own reaction to Katherine Mansfield's style resembles the remark of Virginia Woolf's that I quoted at the beginning of this chapter: "she gives and resists as I expect her to." It is really that sense of expectation fulfilled, rather than some pseudomystical notion of the "essentially feminine," which marks Mansfield's style as that of a writer seeking to develop a means to reveal a woman's experience of reality. When I read Mansfield's stories I have no need for a defensive straining or anticipation. And what is more, again in Virginia Woolf's words, "we cover more ground in much less time." I notice that Woolf uses the word "we." She concentrates on the *relationship* between the two of them. Similarly, Mansfield's readers (and I suspect her female readers in particular) very likely sense themselves to be in such a special relationship with her stories. After all, we do fill in her ellipses; who else cries Ma Parker's unshed tears? The characteristic effects of a Mansfield story—indirection, implicit suggestion, shifts in tone, juxtaposition of incongruities— we know, don't we, these very same devices as well as we know our own unsaid speeches, our quick anger at a barbed word, a phony gesture, a plate snatched from our place just a moment before we've finished, a masculine voice interrupting a leisurely flow of associations? And how well Virginia Woolf understood the last— remember how Peter Walsh cut into Clarissa Dalloway's high moment following Sally Seton's kiss with "musing among the vegetables" (p. 4)? And Mansfield captures the sense of outside intrusion at the moment of intimacy between women in the scene I quoted above from "Bliss." After "Or did Bertha dream it?" she writes: "Then the light was snapped on. . . ." Mansfield also preceded Woolf in the treatment of male intrusion in "A Dill Pickle" (1917):

> But she was thinking how well she remembered that trick of his—the trick of interrupting her—and of how it used to exasperate her six years ago. She used to feel then as though he, quite suddenly, in the middle of what she was saying, put his hand over her lips, turned from her, attended to something different, and then took his hand away, and with just the same slightly too broad smile, gave her his attention again. (P. 331)

Mansfield prefigures the dichotomy between Clarissa and Peter in yet another way in the same story. Clarissa remembers that "however beautiful the day might be, and the trees and the grass, and the little girl in pink—Peter never saw a thing of all that. He would put on his spectacles, if she told him to; he would look" (*Mrs. Dalloway*, p. 9). Mansfield's corresponding male figure in "A Dill Pickle" remarks:

> "Do you remember that first afternoon we spent together at Kew Gardens?
>     You were so surprised because I did not know the names of any flowers. I am still just as ignorant for all your telling me. But whenever it is very fine and warm, and I see some bright colours—it's awfully strange—I hear your voice saying: 'Geranium, marigold and verbena.'" (Pp. 331–32)[15]

[15]The reference to "Kew Gardens" hints at other connections. "A Dill Pickle" was

Woolf's comment that "Peter never saw a thing of all that" is also prefigured in Mansfield's "Psychology" (1920), with a woman's observation of a man's leave-taking, following an evening of failed communication: "She saw the beautiful fall of the steps, the dark garden ringed with glittering ivy, on the other side of the road the huge bare willows and above them the sky big and bright with stars. But of course he would see nothing of all this. He was superior to it all. He—with his wonderful "spiritual" vision!" (p. 319).

Another place where Mansfield's technique seems implicated in Woolf's fiction is the section of *Mrs. Dalloway* where Peter visits Clarissa after an absence of years. Their discourse takes up many pages of Woolf's text, but their spoken dialogue consists of only a few sentences. The discourse is one consisting of several levels of communication: body gestures, internal monologues by each character attempting to surmise the reality of the other, symbolic actions (Peter opening and closing his pocket knife, Clarissa cutting with her scissors).[16] Mansfield's "Psychology" is an entire story based on a similar encounter of two people who cannot speak their feelings for each other, but communicate unintended emotions through their differing responses to the same stimuli, through their delicately shifting moods seemingly out of keeping with the ordinary details of living: pouring tea, warming hands at a fireplace. Peter and Clarissa's interaction on that quiet afternoon before her party replicates the movement of an armed battle: the diminutive weapons (knife and scissors), the charging of emotions:

> "Well, and what's happened to you?" she said. So before a battle begins, the horses paw the ground; toss their heads; the light shines on their flanks; their necks curve. So Peter Walsh and Clarissa, sitting side

---

published in *The New Age* on October 4, 1917, but its dates of composition are not clear. It may have followed the interchange of letters among Mansfield, Lady Ottoline Morrell, and Virginia Woolf about Lady Morrell's garden in August 1917. Antony Alpers suggests that Woolf's story "Kew Gardens" was the culminating product of the exchange (*Life*, pp. 249–52). That Mansfield had read that story is clear from her letter to Woolf on August 23, 1917, in which she remarks: "your Flower Bed is *very* good" (the same letter, incidently, where Mansfield says she and Woolf are "after so very nearly the same thing"). See *Letters* I, p. 327.

[16]Incidentally, in Mansfield's "Prelude," Stanley Burnell is "comforted for the hundredth time, and taking a pearl pen-knife out of his pocket he began to pare his nails" (p. 233).

by side on the blue sofa, challenged each other. His powers chafed and tossed in him. He assembled from different quarters all sorts of things; praise; his career at Oxford; his marriage, which she knew nothing whatever about; how he had loved; and altogether done his job. (P. 66)

In "Psychology," Mansfield writes:

For the special thrilling quality of their friendship was in their complete surrender. Like two open cities in the midst of some vast plain their two minds lay open to each other. And it wasn't as if he rode into hers like a conqueror, armed to the eyebrows and seeing nothing but a gay silken flutter—nor did she enter his like a queen walking soft on petals. No, they were eager, serious travellers, absorbed in understanding what was to be seen and discovering what was hidden— making the most of this extraordinary absolute chance which made it possible for him to be truthful to her and for her to be utterly sincere with him. (Pp. 315–16)

The major difference between the two scenes is that in Woolf's, Clarissa and Peter recognize that what they are engaged in is a battle raging internally. The two characters rehearse their failures and triumphs, their capitulations to forces of egotism and social striving, but they break through to each other in surprising ways: Peter bursts into tears; Clarissa takes his hand and kisses him. Their internal turmoil has moments of catharsis (even if those moments cannot resolve the conflicts of two lifetimes). On the contrary, Mansfield's man and woman assume their own transparency, their minds "open to each other," yet Mansfield knows they are deluding themselves. Unstated sexual desire remains suppressed: "And the best of it was they were both of them old enough to enjoy their adventure to the full without any stupid emotional complication. Passion would have ruined everything; they quite saw that." But not to recognize its power makes the repressed return with a vengeance. As a consequence, their anticipated evening together dissipates into conventionalities and misunderstood gestures, such as the man's admiration of the marble head of a little boy, his nearly whispered comment, "I love that little boy," and later, her hushed comment, "It's raining." Instead of expressing their sexual desire, they hurriedly escape to the security of intellectual discussion, to the question of whether "psychology *qua* psychology has got anything to do with literature at all" (p. 318).

> On the talk went. And now it seemed they really had succeeded. She turned in her chair to look at him while she answered. Her smile said: "We have won." And he smiled back, confident: "Absolutely."
>
> But the smile undid them. It lasted too long; it became a grin. They saw themselves as two little grinning puppets jigging away in nothingness.
>
> "What have we been talking about?" thought he. He was so utterly bored he almost groaned.
>
> "What a spectacle we have made of ourselves," thought she. And she saw him laboriously—oh laboriously—laying out the grounds and herself running after, putting here a tree and there a flowery shrub and here a handful of glittering fish in a pool. They were silent this time from sheer dismay. (Pp. 318–19)

It is hard for a reader to ignore that seamless quality to Mansfield's prose, that dense apprehension of a multileveled reality characteristic of her style whether she is describing a character's behavior, portraying the natural setting, or propounding a critical opinion. That illusion of seamlessness (and it is an illusion no less than hierarchical discreteness is an illusion—or to put it more precisely, the quality of seamlessness results from artifice: the artificial that appears natural, a lesson she learned from Pater) allows her to link all kinds of associations and absorb the intellectual along with the emotional. A fine example is in the letter to Virginia Woolf of April 10, 1919. Mansfield had just read Woolf's essay "Modern Novels" in *The Times Literary Supplement*, that ground-breaking essay, that literary manifesto so crucial to an understanding of Woolf's revolutionary stance on the possibilities of fiction.[17]

> Virginia, I have read your article on Modern Novels. You write so *damned* well, so *devilish* well. There are these little others, you know, dodging & stumbling along, taking a sniff here and a stare there—& there is your mind so accustomed to take the air in the 'grand

---

[17]"Modern Novels" was later collected in *The Common Reader* under the title "Modern Fiction." Its first appearance in *TLS* was on April 10, 1919.

manner'—To tell you the truth—I am *proud* of your writing. I read &
I think '*How* she beats them—.' (*Letters* II, p. 311)

There is no discussion in the letter of Woolf's argument in the essay.
Mansfield does not take up the question of literary conventions (to
which, Woolf had argued, the modern writer needed to negotiate a
different relationship). The reference to Woolf's essay centers on her
own personal connection with Woolf, her identification with the
other woman as a writer, the pride in Woolf's achievement. The
unsaid, the submerged recognition is the pride that the essay was
written by a woman: "*How* she beats them—."

Mansfield's entire letter can be read as a demonstration of her own
straining to convey what Woolf calls in her essay that "transparent
envelope." It is as well Mansfield's display of her own ability to
"examine for a moment an ordinary mind on an ordinary day."[18]
Consequently, the whole letter, and not just the section referring
directly to "Modern Novels," is a response to Woolf's essay. Mansfield begins the letter with a reference to her illness, her "Left Lung"
and "the Germs & the Toxins—two families I detest," but moves
rapidly into her appreciation of the freshness of spring. Then she
launches into the passage I quoted in Chapter 5, a description of the
urban dwellers tentatively coming out into the open again in the
new season:

> But what I chiefly love, Virginia, is to watch the people. Will you laugh
> at me?—It wrings my heart to see the people coming into the open
> again, timid, airing themselves; they idle, their voices change & their
> gestures. A most unexpected old man passes with a paper of flowers
> (for whom?), a soldier lies on the grass hiding his face; a young girl *flies*
> down a side street on the—positive—*wing* of a boy— (*Letters* II, p. 310)

The details confirm the strength of Woolf's assertion in the essay:
"Let us not take it for granted that life exists more fully in what is
commonly thought big than in what is commonly thought small."

The entire letter coheres through Mansfield's ability to connect
seemingly disparate elements that later reverberate through repetition in a different context: "Lung"—with its intimations of illness
and debilitation—slides into "*wing*" (a word Mansfield used fre-

---

[18]Virginia Woolf, "Modern Fiction," *The Common Reader,* p. 154.

quently to refer to her lung in letters to Murry). But now "wing" is a connection, a support, "the—positive—," an approach to love, to intimacy. And to complete the intricate associational patterns of the letter, Mansfield includes a description of the birth of a kitten and the flowering of a daffodil. She slides easily from the image of the newborn kitten to the following remark: "Would a baby be more enchanting? I could get on without a baby—but Murry? I should like to give him one—but then I should like that he should be denied *nothing*... Love's very strange" (p. 311). Immediately following this reference to maternity appears the remark about Woolf's article on fiction. The movement from illness to springtime to birthing to *writing* connects them all as part of a creative continuum, in which writing subsumes the attractions, limitations, and prohibitions of all the others. Woolf would have understood Mansfield's emphasis very well, and she would have appreciated Mansfield's honesty in admitting that she "could get on without a baby"; it was similar to her own.

Although both women may have had regrets about their childlessness, they also recognized that their freedom from the demands of rearing children had given them time and space for their writing. Mansfield's admission to Woolf is in startling contrast to her expressed longings for a child in her letters to Murry, where they are implicated in a different kind of discourse: a dialogue of alternating emotions of desire and anger. There, the wish for a baby needs to be read in the context of her complaint against Murry's failures as a husband, her desperate denial of the seriousness of her illness, and her refusal to admit that it was nearly impossible for her to conceive.[19]

Mansfield's letter to Woolf about "Modern Novels" partakes in a critical dialogue that provides us with illuminating contrasts be-

---

[19]The question of maternity and its relation to creative production is one that has preoccupied a number of critical studies of women writers. For examples of such approaches to Mansfield, with which I am not completely in agreement, see Susan Gubar, "The Birth of the Artist as Heroine: (Re)production, the *Künstlerroman* Tradition, and the Fiction of Katherine Mansfield," in *The Representation of Women in Fiction*, ed. Carolyn G. Heilbrun and Margaret R. Higonnet (Baltimore: Johns Hopkins University Press, 1983), pp. 19–59; and Mary Burgan, "Childbirth Trauma in Katherine Mansfield's Early Stories," *Modern Fiction Studies* 24 (Autumn 1978), 395–412. See Tomalin, pp. 75–78, on Mansfield's (mis)treatment for gonorrhea and its result in almost certain infertility.

tween the two writers' theory and practice, and it puts to rest any simplistic definition of a feminist aesthetics, especially one deriving from biological essentialism. I recognize the temptation to valorize the maternal metaphor implicit in the matrix of flowering, generativity, and writing in the letter to Woolf. I am not denying the fact that Mansfield's style lends itself to the label of *écriture féminine*. It is fairly easy to locate the gaps, silences, sexual encodings, pre-oedipal rhythms, the fluidity and multiplicity in a given text. These are undoubtedly apparent in the letter's interweaving of daily contingencies, relationships, and personalities with an implicit critical theory. It is in this interweaving, this insinuation of identity and response rather than declarative statement, that one senses the persistence of the "feminine," that is, as the term has been used recently in relation to women's language, body consciousness, and rejection of phallocentricity.

On this subject, I tread cautiously. It is too easy to slide into retrograde definitions of the feminine, even under the guise of feminism. I have struggled with this dilemma for many years. In *Feminine Consciousness in the Modern British Novel* (1975), I was concerned with demonstrating how a few women writers incorporated traditional notions of male and female thought processes into their constructions of the internal life of female characters. I did not believe then, nor do I believe now, that what these writers constructed was evidence for an essential "feminine" nature or psyche, and I continue to argue that such constructions are implicated in a culturally bound, historically defined situation, which is, in the case of such writers as Woolf, Richardson, and Sinclair, that of the altered relations of men and women in the midst of the suffrage struggle. The resurgence in our own time of essentialistic definitions of either "woman," "the female," or "the feminine" may relate to both the second wave of feminism and the complicated relations of women to hegemonic discourse within the academic disciplines.

It is possible to distinguish Mansfield's strategy from the valorization of the feminine implicit in the assault on patriarchal structures in Dorothy Richardson's writing, as well as from its more cautious, qualified articulation in Woolf's *A Room of One's Own* and other essays. Mansfield's practice—if not her theoretical explanation of it—is deconstructive, in that it insists on interpreting all *constructions* as finally arbitrary, not as representations of the real. Thus the presence of certain features in her writing which might be coded "feminine" is not evidence of an underlying, essential female nature, but the result of a writing practice that is conscious, deliberate, and "artificial."

Woolf later attempts to describe the features of feminine style in terms of sentence structure, diction, and pattern, but she does so to promote the acceptance of such differences from masculine modes as a component of feminist desires for change. She defines in order to elevate the feminine. In contrast, Mansfield frequently takes the culturally defined characteristics of "feminine" style as the object of satire. Mansfield *sees through* the stylistic devices to their origins in women's oppression or self-delusion. It is interesting to see how so many of the earlier critics of Mansfield are unable to discern her deconstruction of the "feminine;" rather, they define her as its apotheosis. André Maurois, for example, called her technique "*feminine impressionism*" and noted that in her fiction "we know these things as women know them, without having it clearly stated, without any logical structure being built up."[20] In his popular history of the short story, H. E. Bates describes Mansfield's style as "essentially feminine; she delights in making her characters show their thoughts by a kind of mental soliloquy, fluttering, gossipy, breathless with question and answer."[21] For Bates there is a danger to this style: "the voice of the narrator may become confused, even though wrongly, with the voice of the character; and one feels in certain of Katherine Mansfield's stories that this has happened, and that the girlish, chattering voice is the voice of the writer thinly disguised." As Bates continues, his stereotyped assumptions about the "essentially feminine" become even more obvious: "as the method is repeated, it tends to give even very different characters a touch of sameness, until they are all chattering overgrown schoolgirls busy asking and answering breathless facile questions about love and life and happiness" (p. 130).

It is really Bates, the critic, who is repetitious. The tendency to mistake narrator for character is his own. And it also sounds to me like an unconscious declaration that all women are basically the same. The merging of Mansfield's Laura, Kezia, Linda, Bertha into

[20]André Maurois's definition of Mansfield's style as "*feminine* impressionism" appears in *Prophets and Poets*, trans. Hamish Miles (New York: Harper & Bros., 1935), p. 337. The term "feminine impressionist" is used by Nariman Horjasji in *Katherine Mansfield: An Appraisal* (London: Collins, 1967), p. 83.

[21]H. E. Bates, *The Modern Short Story* (Boston: The Writer, Inc., 1941), p. 130.

"all chattering overgrown schoolgirls" disallows any realization of Mansfield's careful delineation of each one and her own *distance* from all of them. The young adolescent in "Her First Ball" quite appropriately questions: "Why didn't happiness last for ever? For ever wasn't a bit too long" (p. 517). But her "girlish" voice is similar on only one level to Bertha's in "Bliss." Rather than blurring narrator and character, Mansfield is very deftly satirizing Bertha's rhapsodic mental soliloquies:

> Really—really—she had everything. She was young. Harry and she were as much in love as ever, and they got on together splendidly and were really good pals. She had an adorable baby. They didn't have to worry about money. They had this absolutely satisfactory house and garden. And friends—modern, thrilling friends, writers and painters and poets or people keen on social questions—just the kind of friends they wanted. And then there were books, and there was music, and she had found a wonderful little dressmaker, and they were going abroad in the summer, and their new cook made the most superb omelettes....
>
> "I'm absurd. Absurd!" She sat up; but she felt quite dizzy, quite drunk. It must have been the spring.
>
> Yes, it was the spring. Now she was so tired she could not drag herself upstairs to dress. (P. 342)

The rapid piling-up of details begins to collapse along with Bertha's happiness, for Mansfield juxtaposes Bertha's ecstasy and her immediately reactive sense of fatigue. What is more, the sentence structure itself provides us with clues to Mansfield's attitude toward Bertha's mental style. Simply by using the conjunction "and" so many times she coordinates all the details of Bertha's "bliss" on the same level; "adorable baby," "books," and "dressmaker" come to mean the same thing. A remark of Katherine Mansfield's about Dorothy Richardson's style might be read as her own ironic commentary on any view of life similar to Bertha's: "Darting through life, quivering, hovering, exulting in the familiarity and the strangeness of all that comes within her tiny circle, she leaves us feeling, as before, that everything being of equal importance to her, it is impossible that everything should not be of equal unimportance."[22]

Mansfield's letter and Woolf's essay on "Modern Novels" are

[22]*Novels and Novelists*, p. 140.

dated April 1919, the same month that Mansfield began writing book reviews for *The Athenaeum*, after Murry was appointed its editor. During the course of Mansfield's career as a reviewer (which was relatively short, ending in December 1920), she wrote about many of the same books that Woolf was also reviewing for other periodicals.[23] This critical duet serves to demonstrate how the similarities between Mansfield and Woolf only intensify their differences as women and as writers.

In comparing Mansfield's and Woolf's criticism, one needs to remember that reviewing contemporary writers was only one area of Woolf's critical inquiry. Woolf's reviewing was of long duration, a continuing occupation for most of her adult life. Her critical writing also included numerous essays on historical figures in the literary canon, especially portraits of women writers.[24] In October 1918, for example, in a review of *The Women Novelists* by R. Brimly Johnson, Woolf expressed, in incipient form, many of the ideas about women writers which surfaced later in *A Room of One's Own*.[25] Some of her most incisive critical writing was concerned with precursors. Gilbert and Gubar explain how Woolf's criticism "from 1904 on" was involved in "a complex process of looking at and for a matrilineal inheritance."[26] Mansfield's relatively short time as a reviewer did not allow her to complete a similar body of critical writing of this type, although it is possible to construct a general overview of her critical approach through a study of her notebooks and letters as well as book reviews.[27] This body of miscellaneous writings records, albeit in an

[23]Following is a list of books reviewed by both Woolf and Mansfield:
Dorothy Richardson, *The Tunnel*: V.W., Feb. 13, 1919; K.M., April 4, 1919.
Joseph Hergesheimer, *Java Head*: V.W., May 29, 1919; K.M., June 13, 1919.
Frank Swinnerton, *September*: V.W., Sept. 25, 1919; K.M., Oct. 10, 1919.
Joseph Hergesheimer, *Gold and Iron*: V.W., Dec. 25, 1919; K.M., Feb. 6, 1920.
J. D. Beresford, *An Imperfect Mother*: V.W., March 25, 1920; K.M., April 9, 1920.
Joseph Hergesheimer, *Linda Condon*: V.W., July 8, 1920; K.M., July 23, 1920.
George Moore, *Esther Waters*: V.W., July 29, 1920; K.M., August 6, 1920.
D. H. Lawrence, *The Lost Girl*: V.W., Dec. 2, 1920; K.M. reviewed it only in letters, to Murry, Dec. 1920, and to the Schiffs, Dec. 3, 1921.
[24]For a useful discussion of Woolf's critical essays on women authors, including an incisive consideration of Woolf's relationship with Mansfield, see Michele Barrett, "Introduction" to Virginia Woolf, *Women and Writing* (San Diego: Harcourt Brace Jovanovich, 1979), pp. 1–39.
[25]Woolf, "Women Novelists," *Contemporary Writers*, pp. 24–27.
[26]Gilbert and Gubar, *No Man's Land,* vol. I, p. 200.
[27]Many of these notes, letters, and reviews are now accessible to students in the collection beautifully edited by Clare Hanson, *The Critical Writings of Katherine*

unsystematic fashion, Mansfield's varied and voluminous reading, her enthusiasms and disappointments.

Typical of the type of novel both women reviewed is Joseph Hergesheimer's *Java Head*, one of those many books that become popular with a mass readership and shortly thereafter are forgotten. Woolf's review appeared May 29, 1919, and Mansfield's on June 13, 1919. Woolf's review is more cognizant of the novel's historical context and even of its possible political dimension, in that its plot involves the tragic effects of a marriage between a Chinese woman and an American man. Woolf notes: "Somehow, too, it is not merely jealousy that has killed the Chinese woman, but America, with its 'unfamiliar circumstances, tradition, emotions.'"[28] For Woolf, the historical details, "the presence of a scaffolding of this sort," gives the book "its sobriety and distinction." She recognizes that Hergesheimer's weaknesses show when he "has to describe not what people wear but what they feel." Yet she apologizes for being critical, for her "fault-finding," because she believes that this novel "is one of the smaller number of novels which appear to be written by an adult; and therefore we make Mr Hergesheimer responsible for our disappointment instead of saying nothing about it, because it is useless to point out the immaturity of a child."

Mansfield had no patience with the "scaffolding" that Woolf felt gave the book its "sobriety"—that is, its historical/political dimension. Instead, she remarks that

> for all the author's inside information and professional way in handling a ship, we are never quite sure that the sea is real sea or that these curious perfumed chests and jars are really full. While we read we are fascinated, but our fascination is conscious and almost assumed, as at a spectacle—something arranged and specially 'set' for a performance.[29]

Mansfield never mentions the Chinese woman's alienation in America, nor does she discuss the captain's sense of alienation because of new technology, a subject Woolf takes up with interest. But she does highlight the way the suffering of the Chinese woman is a

---

*Mansfield*. See Hanson's "Introduction" and editorial notes for an incisive discussion of Mansfield's concerns, methods, and insights as a critic.

[28]*Contemporary Writers*, p. 109.

[29]*Novels and Novelists*, p. 41.

function of her being a woman, an example of the universal victimization of women, of their entrapment. Characteristically, her critical approach involves the use of highly figurative language, such as her reference to the woman who:

> was pining away, like some fabulous exquisite bird in a cage in Shanghai until he rescued her and brought her into a bigger cage, with heavier bolts and clumsier bars, and stupid unpainted faces to stare through and wonder at her. Her appearance, her clothes, her appointments, they are game indeed for the greedy light to play with, but, absorbed in them, it penetrates no further than to give us just a glimpse of her superhuman calm, of the tragedy it was for her that this calm should be broken by . . . a low wretch whose mind has been poisoned by opium and who realises in his fiendish dreaming way how she suffers. (P. 42)

For Mansfield, the most successful part of the book is the section describing the "growing anxiety of the household" over the return of the hero from the sea: "Here, at least, it is hardly possible to avoid a sense of progression, and the members of the family, gathered together under the shadowy wing of disaster are more nearly seen in relation to one another" (p. 42). Typically, for Mansfield, unity and coherence are the primary values. The other predominant issue is that of depth: "We are excited; our curiosity is roused as to what lies beneath these strange rich surfaces" (p. 43).

However, it is in their respective reviews of Dorothy Richardson's *The Tunnel* that Mansfield's and Woolf's differing positions become most noticeable. Woolf is immediately sympathetic with Richardson's frustration over the restrictions of the conventions of fiction. She recognizes that Richardson's method "represents a genuine conviction of the discrepancy between what she has to say and the form provided by tradition for her to say it in. She is one of the rare novelists who believe that the novel is so much alive that it actually grows."[30] Woolf is also immediately attracted to her feminism and sees the connection between her critique of patriarchal society and her experimental method. Thus, Woolf singles out a quotation from *The Tunnel* which makes that connection clear: ". . . but if books were written like that, sitting down and doing it

---

[30]*Contemporary Writers*, p. 120.

cleverly and knowing just what you were doing and just how somebody else had done it, there was something wrong, some mannish
cleverness that was only half right. To write books knowing all
about style would be to become like a man" (p. 120).

Woolf's understanding of Richardson's innovations must have
influenced her own ideas about narrative conventions, ideas expressed in the "Modern Novels" essay, which appeared only two
months later. Thus Woolf explains that with *The Tunnel*, instead of

> the old deliberate business: the chapters that lead up and the chapters
> that lead down; the characters who are always characteristic; the
> scenes that are passionate and the scenes that are humorous; the elabo-
> rate construction of reality; the conception that shapes and surrounds
> the whole. All these things are cast away, and there is left, denuded,
> unsheltered, unbegun and unfinished, the consciousness of Miriam
> Henderson, the small sensitive lump of matter, half transparent and
> half opaque, which endlessly reflects and distorts the variegated pro-
> cession, and is, we are bidden to believe, the source beneath the sur-
> face, the very oyster within the shell.
>     The critic is thus absolved from the necessity of picking out the
> themes of the story. The reader is not provided with a story; he is
> invited to embed himself in Miriam Henderson's consciousness, to
> register one after another, and one on top of another . . . impressions
> as they flicker through Miriam's mind. . . . Here we are thinking,
> word by word, as Miriam thinks. The method, if triumphant, should
> make us feel ourselves seated at the centre of another mind, and,
> according to the artistic gift of the writer, we should perceive in the
> helter-skelter of flying fragments some unity, significance, or design.
> (P. 121)

Woolf's disappointment is finally not with Richardson's theory but
with its application. She remarks that in spite of the originality of
the method, "we still find ourselves distressingly near the surface.
Things look much the same as ever." Nonetheless, Woolf respects
the intensity of Richardson's effort: "We want to be rid of realism,
to penetrate without its help into the regions beneath it, and further
require that Miss Richardson shall fashion this new material into
something which has the shapeliness of the old accepted forms. We
are asking too much; but the extent of our asking proves that *The
Tunnel* is better in its failure than most books in their success" (p.
122).

On the contrary, Mansfield's review of *The Tunnel*, published nearly two months later, is much less appreciative.

> Miss Richardson has a passion for registering every single thing that happens in the clear, shadowless country of her mind. One cannot imagine her appealing to the reader or planning out her novel; her concern is primarily, and perhaps ultimately, with herself. 'What cannot I do with this mind of mine!' one can fancy her saying. . . . There are times when she seems deliberately to set it a task, just for the joy of realizing again how brilliant a machine it is, and we, too, share her admiration for its power of absorbing. . . . This is a rare and interesting gift, but we should hesitate before saying it was a great one.[31]

Mansfield describes this book about Miriam Henderson, like the others in the series that would eventually become *Pilgrimage*, as being

> composed of bits, fragments, flashing glimpses, half scenes and whole scenes, all of them quite distinct and separate, and all of them of equal importance. There is no plot, no beginning, middle or end. Things just 'happen' one after another with incredible rapidity and at breakneck speed. There is Miss Richardson, holding out her mind, as it were, and there is Life hurling objects into it as fast as she can throw. . . .
> There is one who could not live in so tempestuous an environment as her mind—and he is Memory. She has no memory. . . . If we are to be truly alive there are large pauses in which we creep away into our caves of contemplation. And then it is, in the silence, that Memory mounts his throne and judges all that is in our minds—appointing each his separate place, high or low, rejecting this, selecting that— putting this one to shine in the light and throwing that one into the darkness. (P. 6)

Mansfield insists, therefore, that "until these things are judged and given each its appointed place in the whole scheme, they have no meaning in the world of art."

It is important to notice that Mansfield does not concern herself with Richardson's theoretical position or the feminist impulse behind her revolt against literary conventions. Unlike Woolf, Mans-

---

[31] *Novels and Novelists*, pp. 5–6.

field does not focus on Richardson's concern with the processes of a *woman's* mind. It appears that Mansfield misunderstood the novelist's revolutionary critique of phallocentricity in language and the conventions of fiction. Clare Hanson suggests that Mansfield's negative reactions to Richardson (and to May Sinclair as well) "were defensive rather than offensive, and that her wariness of their fiction stems from the fact that it pointed to a whole area which was problematic and unresolved for her."[32] Hanson believes that Mansfield "saw in feminine prose possibilities of exposure and subsequent retributive attack, rather than freedom. We might read KM's strictures on the undifferentiated worlds/words of Richardson and Sinclair as over-reaction against something recognised and repressed in herself" (p. 18). Yet there are reasons besides those of personal psychology for Mansfield's negative reaction to Richardson. It is important to restate here that Mansfield refused to establish *difference* as the center of her poetics or her (implied) politics. As with her distaste for Lawrence's obsessive categorizing of all things as either male or female, she must have bristled over Richardson's similar obsession, even if it was used in the service of promoting the superiority of women. Moreover, Mansfield's objections to Richardson involve a much larger issue, which I take up in the next chapter: the problem of subjectivity itself in artistic production. Mansfield fears that Richardson's method is a function of an underlying egoism: "Her concern is primarily, and perhaps ultimately, with herself." Woolf expressed a similar uneasiness when she remarked in her diary some months later: "I suppose the danger is the damned egotistical self; which ruins Joyce and Richardson to my mind."[33]

In her reviews of Richardson, Mansfield seems closest to Woolf in her insistence on the need to have a plan, or design—but she does not use the word "design" as Woolf did. Mansfield emphasizes judgment, and that is where she diverges the most from Woolf. Whereas Woolf values depth over surface, Mansfield is concerned with hierarchies of value: "separate place, high or low, rejecting this, selecting that." Also noteworthy is Mansfield's use of Memory as masculine, Life as feminine. As Clare Hanson says: "KM here seems to privilege male authority, and clarity, over feminine 'confu-

[32]Hanson, "Introduction," *Critical Writings of Katherine Mansfield*, p. 17.
[33]Virginia Woolf, *A Writer's Diary*, ed. Leonard Woolf (New York: Harcourt Brace Jovanovich, 1954), p. 22.

sion.'"[34] Thus, as Mansfield begins her brief reviewing career, she bows to patriarchal authority through elevating the role of judgment over experience, contemplation over discovery.

Consequently, in comparing Mansfield's and Woolf's reviews of the same books, one finds that Katherine Mansfield is more impatient, demanding, and sardonic; she values the ineffable, the realization of an intangible sense of the text coming alive. Woolf, on the other hand, remains more tentative, more cautious. Yet Woolf, in the final analysis, is more sympathetic to the authors' intentions. She ventures out into the new, questions it, respects the attempt to experiment, and tries to understand it. She values the breaking of tradition, the plunge into the unknown. Not so impatient, she realizes that she has time left for discovery. On the contrary, Mansfield seems to be grasping for what is completed, for what may contain the answer.

Such contrasts, of course, have much to do with each woman's sense of achievement at the time she wrote these reviews. Although Woolf was older than Mansfield, she was still in the midst of working out her personal aesthetics. She had not yet written her major novels and had only just begun to experiment with narrative techniques. Mansfield, quite the opposite, was in the midst of her most fully matured stage as a writer. She had already worked out her method, which flowered in "Prelude," and was now approaching the period of the great, late stories: "At the Bay," "The Garden-Party," and "The Daughters of the Late Colonel." She was reaching the culmination rather than the formulation of her personal aesthetic theory. Besides, the press of mortality made her restive, made her reach for perfection, finish, durability.

Mansfield searched for methods to convey the interconnectedness of individuals' sense of reality as well as the pressures of the "moment," the sudden breakthroughs into deeper levels of consciousness. In this way her work was simultaneously "romantic" and "modernist," yet her emphasis on "wholeness," organic unity, and the like is open to the charge that it is counterfeminist, according to some definitions of feminist aesthetics. That is, a theory positing open-endedness, refusal of closure, and the definition of "the feminine" as a kind of undifferentiated pre-oedipal apprehension of real-

[34]Hanson, "Introduction," p. 19.

ity has difficulty including Mansfield's insistence on *discrimination* within its paradigm. While the critic may find numerous instances of multiplicity and open-endedness in particular texts by Mansfield, she will not find them articulated—as feminist theory—in Mansfield's critical writing, as she may with Woolf. There are places where Mansfield's critical theory serves almost to contradict her own practice, or perhaps it serves to demonstrate the gaps in her conscious awareness of her own practice.

# ❧ 10

# Impersonation / Impersonality

Katherine Mansfield's aesthetics are grounded in a pre-
cocious recognition of the self as many selves—male/female being
only one of several possible polarities. She had a very early experience of *multiplicity* (and I want to stress the use of this term rather
than *fragmentation*, which suggests the end of a process, the breaking
apart of something that was once whole; multiplicity, implying an
original complexity that continues to cohere, has an ontological
status quite different from the linearity connoted by "fragmentation"). Such a recognition of multiplicity also allowed Mansfield to
realize how easily *anyone* might live a secret life—that any human
being is not what she appears on the surface. Other people become
objects of endless fascination, therefore, and to observe them and
imagine their secret lives are activities of redoubled pleasure. She
retained a vision of herself as a young, "innocent" girl living in her
father and mother's house—reading, writing, attending parties, enduring dinner-table conversations, arguments, petty gossiping—
and at the same time, beneath the bones of her skull was going on
the most remarkable life. What would Father have thought of Kathleen's lesbian revelations in her diary? What would Mother have
thought of Kathleen's descriptions of herself as a sexual being?

Here Mansfield saw her own duplicity (in the sense of doubleness,
rather than evil), and at first, she was disturbed by it. She experienced it initially as sexual ambiguity, then as a dualistic "changing of
the tide," as she expressed it in her notebook in 1907: "This is
madness—I know—but it is too real for sanity—it is too swiftly

incredible to be doubted—Once again I must bear this changing of the tide—my life is a Rosary of Fierce combats for Two—each bound together with the powerful—magnetic chain of sex—and at the end—does the emblem of the crucified—hang—surely—."[1] Mansfield's adolescent awakening to her own bisexuality provided the impetus for newer, more elastic definitions of self. But in the initial stages of that awakening, as the passage above so crudely reveals, her imagination remained culturally bound, limited by the dualism of Christian tradition. (That tradition ironically provided her with one method for self-aggrandizement: martyrdom.) This "combat for Two" implied as well a binary opposition of good and bad, which is equally apparent in the notebook entries about Maata quoted in Chapter 3. But she would be able to break out of that restrictive dualism—if only for brief expansive and experimental periods—when she asserted herself through impersonation, through trying on *all* sorts of lives" (*Letters* I, p. 19).

Impersonation gave her a sense of freedom, but only when she could make clear to herself that she was playing a role, that no one could mistake the role for her essential self. But not knowing who that self was—and even worse, not being sure that it was not *essentially* divided—made her uneasy in spite of her defiance. At times she tried to resolve her uneasiness by casting out or denying the existence of the other in herself. Thus she would search for moments when her sense of division ceased. She increasingly defined these as "natural"—moments when she felt herself part of nature (and, significantly, not *unnatural*), even ordinary—for the "ordinary" was an achievement for someone who had always felt herself to be outside the conventional ideal. A good example of such a moment is expressed in a love letter to Garnet Trowell, in October 1908:

> Sunlight was drenching the trees, but the road was in shadow. I was so happy that I felt I must fling myself down on the warm grass—feel *one* with the whole great scheme of things. You know the sun filled world seemed a revelation—I felt as tho' Nature said to me "now that you have found your true self—now that you are at peace with the world accepting instead of doubting—now that you love—you can

[1]Quoted from Mansfield Notebook 39, Alexander Turnbull Library, by Vincent O'Sullivan in "The Magnetic Chain," p. 117.

see". Beloved half the world is blind, as you say—I cannot understand how they pass their days, but, since you have held and dominated my life, I feel the last veil between me and the heart of things has been swept away— (*Letters* I, pp. 72–73)

Such sentiments are not unusual at twenty, but Mansfield's seem to be heavy with relief: she now can rest, freed from the "combat of two." The "true self" somehow is connected "with the world accepting instead of doubting." Love has made her feel one with nature; nature approves of her newfound heterosexuality. But *that*, as this excerpt makes perfectly clear, involves a giving up of the autonomy she had been seeking; for now, "since you have held and dominated my life," she has accepted what she once had feared: the feminine role. Of course, as the conventional sentimentality of Mansfield's style here reveals, this is not her final revelation. It may be no more than another impersonation, and one that will involve her in as much—if not more—pain, doubt, and disillusionment as her earlier entrapment in duality.

The question of the relation of life to art, personal experience to completed literary object, becomes especially complicated in the case of a woman writer, for it is at the center of the problematic critical response to women's writing in general, in that everything a woman writes has usually been assumed to be a function of her autobiographical impulse, either confession or wish fulfillment. Mansfield's stylistic development, if seen from the perspective of the modernist debate over impersonality, individualism, subjectivity, and tradition, is related to a whole range of interrelated issues including the question of authorship itself, the role of biographical criticism, the status of confessional literature, and the limits of realism.[2]

Accordingly, one of the recurring critical discussions concerns Mansfield as a "confessional" writer. The critical debate about Mansfield's confessional impulse appears to have originated as a reaction to J. Middleton Murry's excessive idealization of Mansfield

[2]I realize that even to suggest such a relationship of necessity assumes the existence of an "author" and puts me into the embattled camp of defenders of the Author rather than of the Reader. This is not the place to argue this issue. I recommend, in this regard, Lawrence Lipking's illuminating essay "Life, Death, and Other Theories," in *Historical Studies and Literary Criticism*, ed. Jerome J. McGann (Madison: University of Wisconsin Press, 1985), pp. 180–98.

after her death, which was abetted by his selective ordering of her diary notebooks in his editing of the *Journal*. Dubious about Murry's emphasis on Mansfield's life as a spiritual quest, critics enlarged the issue into an interrogation of subjectivity in Mansfield's work. For example, James Justus discusses "the problem of autobiography in Katherine Mansfield's career: the extent, that is, to which the art is transposed life, and the nature of that transposition." Justus considers how the autobiographical issues enmeshed in that transposition have stylistic manifestations, which account "for not only the basically egoistic character of the stories, but also their control, the hard disinterestedness, which prevents the infections of her life from invading her art."[3] C. A. Hankin goes further in suggesting that for Mansfield, artistic self-expression, from adolescence on, became a way to confess the hidden, unacceptable inner life. Confession, although strategically structured to reveal and not to reveal, could bring her love and acceptance.[4]

At the farthest remove from these sophisticated analyses is a remark made in 1946 by a religious writer, Cecil Johnson Eustace, who must have been so taken in by Murry's rendering of Mansfield's quest that he insists that "her work is characterized by its almost complete avoidance of emphasis on sex, and by its preoccupation with what we might call the spiritual nature of Nature."[5] One can never account for some readers' inability to see what is in front of them, but Eustace's naiveté may be very useful to our purposes. Katherine Mansfield's writing partakes in a *hidden* dis-

[3]James H. Justus, "Katherine Mansfield: The Triumph of Egoism," *Mosaic* 6 (1973), 19.

[4]C. A. Hankin is the foremost proponent of the confessional position. She describes Mansfield as one of "a long line of confessional writers stretching from Rousseau to Proust. Her achievement was to carry the confessional tradition forward into the twentieth century, examining the inner life in a manner which places her among the major psychological writers of her age. Confession, albeit under the guise of fiction, was an inseparable part of Katherine Mansfield's lifelong quest for psychological understanding. Relentlessly, she probed her own conflict-ridden personality, the personalities of her parents—and, by extension, human nature" (*Katherine Mansfield and Her Confessional Stories*, p. ix). An opposing position is taken by Kate Fullbrook, who insists that "one can, of course, only speculate about Katherine Mansfield's motives, but here it is more useful to turn to her literary development than to the details of her life" (*Katherine Mansfield*, p. 53).

[5]Cecil Johnson Eustace, *An Infinity of Questions: A Study of the Religion of Art, and of the Art of Religion in the Lives of Five Women* (1946; repr. Freeport, N.Y.: Books for Libraries Press, 1969), p. 54.

course, in which her personal revolt against the family as the model of bourgeois repression and stagnation coincided with a more general assault on those same values by most of the other emerging modernists. Their views correlate with Michel Foucault's observation that "this discourse on modern sexual repression holds up well, owing no doubt to how easy it is to uphold."[6] Foucault unveils the relation between the defiance of repression and the *power* of the one who *speaks* that defiance:

> If sex is repressed, that is, condemned to prohibition, nonexistence and silence, then the mere fact that one is speaking about it has the appearance of a deliberate transgression. A person who holds forth in such language places himself to a certain extent outside the reach of power; he upsets established law; he somehow anticipates the coming freedom. (P. 6)

Mansfield's assertions of sexual freedom are a function of her belief in the superiority of the artist, a superiority based on the *power* of the artist to live more fully and *speak about* experiences ordinary people fear to pursue. Her personal discoveries and the techniques she evolved to express them conform to Foucault's awareness of "the existence in our era of a discourse in which sex, the revelation of truth, the overturning of global laws, the proclamation of a new day to come, and the promise of a certain felicity are linked together" (p. 7).

Mansfield's need to recount her "adventures" in her diaries is a sign of the impulse for confession, for "the task of passing everything having to do with sex through the endless mill of speech" (Foucault, p. 21). In this way, Mansfield is linked with a major, ongoing movement in the modern period, what Foucault calls "the great process of transforming sex into discourse" (p. 22).

Eustace's overt statement of Mansfield's avoidance of the discourse of sexuality is, therefore, a transparent admission of his own seeking for that discourse and relief at not having to defend it. But Mansfield herself may have given him permission for such misreading. Her expression of sexuality is so highly encoded, so diffuse and symbolic, that a reader can willfully ignore it. Again, Foucault is

[6]Michel Foucault, *The History of Sexuality,* vol. I: *An Introduction,* trans. Robert Hurley (New York: Vintage, 1980), p. 5.

helpful: "Silence itself—the things one declines to say, or is forbidden to name, the discretion that is required between different speakers—is less the absolute limit of discourse, the other side from which it is separated by a strict boundary, than an element that functions alongside the things said, with them and in relation to them within over-all strategies. There is no binary division to be made between what one says and what one does not say."[7]

Mansfield's confessional impulse, however, cannot be explained simply by her individual psychological history, her unique set of so-called neuroses. Freudian critics, in particular, have tended to ignore the power of *social* forces in the construction of individual responses and strategies. It used to be almost compulsory among Freudian critics to insist on a neurotic impulse behind art, thus making every artistic expression a confessional one as well. It should be noted that "confession" carries with it connotative baggage of several sorts and sizes: traditional religious exhortations, the command for submission to a higher authority, a sense of inherent sinfulness or badness, a desire to give over the control of personal impulses to someone or something with more knowledge, goodness, vision, strength, and authority. Authority is the central theme. But confession is doublesided. While it expresses a longing to put oneself in the hands of a power outside the self, it also insists that there is a self important enough to give up. It assumes something central in the one who confesses: an essential nature, a "true" self, a "secret" center. Confession in this respect takes back power from the confessor—the priest, the psychoanalyst, the reading public. It elevates the self; it focuses all attention on that self.

[7]Foucault, p. 27. Of course Foucault's discourse involves silences of his own about the particular forms the discourse on sexuality takes when it is used by women. Gender is not a predominant category of analysis in his work. He is silent, for example, on the perceptions of the little girl in the story about the simpleminded farm hand persecuted by the authorities because "he had obtained a few caresses from a little girl" (p. 31). To Foucault, the issue was not the girl's powerlessness in relation to this event (which surely would have been Mansfield's focus should she have told this story). Instead, Foucault remarks: "What is the significant thing about this story? The pettiness of it all; the fact that this everyday occurrence in the life of village sexuality, these inconsequential bucolic pleasures, could become, from a certain time, the object not only of a collective intolerance but of a judicial action, a medical intervention, a careful clinical examination, and an entire theoretical elaboration" (p. 31). Foucault's "inconsequential bucolic pleasures" shield an unconscious assertion of masculine privilege which women writers like Mansfield have struggled to illuminate.

As Mansfield grew older she became dubious about such attention. In January 1920, she wrote in her journal about her "philosophy—the defeat of the personal" (*Journal*, p. 195), and in a letter the next month she complained about her contemporaries: "People today are simply cursed by what I call the *personal.*"[8] Her criticism of Dorothy Richardson's "confessional novel," as discussed in the previous chapter, was related to a similar impulse. Such rejection of egoism also surfaces in Mansfield's attitude toward the writing of those close to her, including Murry, as when she criticized his self-absorption:

> I feel (forgive fanciful me) that when certain winds blow across your soul they bring the smell from that dark pit & the uneasy sound from those hollow caverns—& you long to lean over the dark driving danger & just not fall in—But letting us all see meanwhile how low you lean—
>
> Even your style of writing changes then—little short sentences—a hand lifted above the waves—the toss of a curly head above the swirling tumble—Its a terrible thing to be alone—yes it is—it is—but dont lower your mask until you have another mask prepared beneath—As terrible as you like—but a *mask.*[9]

A similar attitude marks her review of Virginia Woolf's *Night and Day*, where she notes that the novel "is extremely cultivated, distinguished and brilliant, but above all—deliberate. There is not a chapter where one is unconscious of the writer, of her personality, her point of view and her control of the situation."[10]

If Katherine Mansfield insisted on the primacy of the loss of self in art, it might well have been because her own assertions of autonomy always involved her in so much personal chaos. She must have had the doubts of the pioneer about her discoveries. She needed to create surfaces she could hide beneath. Woolf's comment in her diary that Mansfield's "hard composure is much on the surface"[11] tells us as much about Mansfield's style as a writer as it does about her personality as a woman. As a means of avoiding personal confrontation

[8]*Letters of Katherine Mansfield*, p. 294.

[9]*Letters* I, p. 318. On Mansfield's use of the symbolist theory of the mask, see Fullbrook, pp. 16–17.

[10]Mansfield, *Novels and Novelists*, p. 108.

[11]*The Diary of Virginia Woolf*, vol. I, p. 265.

Mansfield would make the object itself significant, not herself as its creator. She needed to develop strategies for distancing. She would strive to separate her personal feelings about what she had experienced from her fictional re-creations of those experiences. She would eliminate the voice of the transparent "I" that dominated most of the stories in her first book, *In a German Pension* (1911). And she would make certain that the reader could not mistake an individual character's anger for that of the author herself. Above all, her stories must not appear confessional.

Accordingly, confession and impersonation are opposing forces in Mansfield's writing. The relative weight of each may depend on an individual reader's response to conflicting cultural imperatives, as is apparent in the critical record.[12] For example, C. A. Hankin de-emphasizes Mansfield's use of impersonation by calling it "a defense which would protect her vulnerable, inner self from exposure and condemnation" (p. 16). In this way, impersonation becomes merely disguised confession. Yet it seems to me that it plays a far larger role for Mansfield as a means of assertion rather than reaction. Two years before she moved to London in 1908, she wrote to her cousin, Sylvia Payne: "I just long for power over circumstances and always feel as though I could do such a great deal more good than is done— and give such a lot of pleasure—." In the same letter she concludes that becoming a writer might provide her with that power: "Would you not like to try *all* sorts of lives—one is so very small—but that is the satisfaction of writing—one can impersonate so many people" (*Letters* I, pp. 18–19).

In his first biography of Mansfield, Antony Alpers mentions her unique talent for impersonation, for capturing the subtle nuances of voice and gesture that unmistakably reflect an individual's sense of self, way of being in the world, one's personal style.[13] Mansfield transferred that unerring actor's talent to her writing until that economy of the visually perceived gesture, the telling phrase, the perti-

---

[12]That critical record has reflected numerous fashions during the last half-century. As an example, see Jack Garlington, "Katherine Mansfield: The Critical Trend," *Twentieth Century Literature* 2 (July 1956), 51–62. Garlington mentions that critics of the late 1930s and '40s criticized Mansfield for sentimentality, preferred her most bitter stories, and attacked the lack of sociological insight in her work. Of course that was all followed largely by numerous New Critical "readings" of Mansfield's work, and then by psychoanalytic interpretations of her "problems."

[13]Antony Alpers, *Katherine Mansfield: A Biography*, p. 88.

nent object that grows into symbol became the hallmark of her style as a writer of fiction.[14]

It is important to remember that as Mansfield's letter about "power over circumstances" suggests, impersonation—role-playing, in the jargon of our own times—gives a sense of power. It may finally be illusory power—especially if it cannot be transformed into action in the real world—but for a young woman feeling desperately trapped by her sex, family, and country, it would be at least a first step in a long battle for genuine autonomy.

Later in her life Mansfield would understand much more about the multiple dimensions of self-making. In April 1920, she would write in her journal under the heading "The Flowering of the Self":

> True to oneself! which self? Which of my many—well really, that's what it looks like coming to—hundreds of selves? For what with complexes and supressions[15] and reactions and vibrations and reflections, there are moments when I feel I am nothing but the small clerk of some hotel without a proprietor, who has all his work cut out to enter the names and hand the keys to the wilful guests.
>
> Nevertheless, there are signs that we are intent as never before on trying to puzzle out, to live by, our own particular self. . . . Is it not possible that the rage for confession, autobiography, especially for memories of earliest childhood, is explained by our persistent yet mysterious belief in a self which is continuous and permanent; which, untouched by all we acquire and all we shed, pushes a green spear through the dead leaves and through the mould, thrusts a scaled bud through years of darkness until, one day, the light discovers it and shakes the flower free and—we are alive—we are flowering for our moment upon the earth? This is the moment which, after all, we live for,—the moment of direct feeling when we are most ourselves and least personal. (*Journal*, p. 205)

This passage contains several indications of Mansfield's uncertainties about the validity of her own experience of multiplicity, as well as her recognition that her discovery of it was one of the precondi-

---

[14]One of the best discussions of Mansfield's talent for impersonation appears in a review by Claude Rawson of Claire Tomalin's biography; see "The Mimic Art," *Times Literary Supplement,* January 8–14, 1988, pp. 27–28.

[15]Murry's edition of the *Journal* prints "repressions" here, but my own reading of the manuscript (MS Papers 119, Alexander Turnbull Library) leads me to believe that Mansfield wrote "supressions" instead.

tions of modernism. She had begun the piece with a reminiscence about the days "when autograph albums were the fashion" (*Journal*, p. 205) and about the easy assumptions of "*l'âge d'innocence!*" which were apparent in the trite repetition of the phrase "To thine own self be true" in so many of the autographs. That was a time in obvious contrast to her own, in which the predominance of psychoanalytic interpretations, the "complexes and suppressions and reactions," made her feel powerless: "the small clerk of some hotel without a proprietor." Struck with the seeming impossibility of recognizing which self—out of hundreds—could be the true one, Mansfield responds with the longing for an essential self, a revelatory recognition of one. Her response suggests the persistence of romantic conceptions in the modernist period: the organic metaphor, the insistence on the innate ability to recognize "the moment," the elevation of "direct feeling."

Mansfield counters this nearly nostalgic explosion of belief with her ironic tone in the first paragraph, where she ruefully depicts the contemporary response. That final elevation of tone, equivalent to the "flowering" it describes, demonstrates her refusal to relinquish the *energy* produced by the nineteenth century's construction of the artist as visionary. As Ronald Bush has so well expressed it (in relation to T. S. Eliot, but of no less significance to Katherine Mansfield), "and yet, at the bottom of all this sophistication, the literature of early modernism continues to reflect a belief in what Arnold called 'the buried life'—the seat of 'what we really are and feel' and the perpetual antagonist of our conventional selves. This belief is one of the major supports of Eliot's famous assertion of impersonality."[16]

Bush also explores the development of modernist concepts about the self:

> Although in the beginning of their careers the modernists disavow a belief in the old stable ego of character, they do not despair of discovering something analogous. In this first phase of modernism's revolution of the self, sincerity resides not in disowning but in finding indirect ways to imply this invisible "tougher self," this "individuating rhythm," this "real, vital, potential self." (P. 198)

[16]Ronald Bush, "Modern/Postmodern: Eliot, Perse, Mallarmé, and the Future of the Barbarians," in *Modernism Reconsidered*, ed. Robert Kiely (Cambridge: Harvard University Press, 1983), pp. 197–98.

Kate Fullbrook, however, notes the contradictions in Mansfield's attraction to the notion of an underlying unified self: "While she is attracted to the possibility of a unified self, even if knowable only in infinitesimal moments, there is a final hanging back. And it is this hesitation, this honest uncertainty in the face of desire and need, that finally makes Katherine Mansfield, at times, one of the toughest and darkest of the modernists."[17]

The organicism implicit in the trope of "flowering" partakes in a discourse of self-finding rather than self-making. But these two reactions to multiplicity are in dynamic interaction throughout Mansfield's career. Let us not forget how strongly she was influenced by Pater, for whom, in Perry Meisel's words, "personality is . . . something fashioned, something aesthetic from the start."[18] The nostalgia for an essential, original self alternates with a defiant—and at times triumphant—admission of self-generation. Although Mansfield's conclusion to the journal entry "The Flowering of the Self" reiterates a predominant modernist concern about impersonality, for her, as for other women writers, the whole question of impersonality is problematic because of women's long-standing need to assert themselves after centuries of suppression. Mansfield had to situate herself uncomfortably within the modernist debate over subjectivity, authorial control, and reactions against egoism.[19]

Such issues have become increasingly complicated since their original articulation by the major modernists because of the dominating influence of poststructuralist theory. The deconstruction of the "subject," whether through discourse, grammar, or psychoanalysis, goes much further than Mansfield did in rejecting subjectivity—that is, subjectivity as it is assumed to be constructed by humanist discourse. But as a number of feminist theorists have pointed out, poststructuralism poses particular problems for women.[20] If subjectivity is to be completely deconstructed, if "identity"

[17]Fullbrook, p. 19.

[18]Perry Meisel, *The Myth of the Modern: A Study in British Literature and Criticism after 1850* (New Haven: Yale University Press, 1987), p. 72.

[19]The parameters of this debate as well as its chronological development are perceptively described by Michael Levenson in *A Genealogy of Modernism*.

[20]The body of feminist theory in which poststructuralism is questioned continues to grow. See, for example, Linda Alcoff, "Cultural Feminism versus Post-Structuralism: The Identity Crisis in Feminist Theory," *Signs: Journal of Women in Culture and Society* 13 (Spring 1988), 405–36. For an excellent brief discussion of the

is to be understood totally as social construction, women's political stance in favor of women's self-assertion can be similarly deconstructed. Even the recognition given to women writers for achieving autonomy can be put under suspicion as a liberal-humanist elevation of the "individual." "Authorship" itself becomes a problematic term. There is always the danger of "seeing through" so far that all material problems disappear: "women" as entities disappear since they are merely socially constructed; "women authors" disappear since both "women" and "authors" are equally suspect constructions. The experiences and contributions of actual women, like Katherine Mansfield, dissolve into invisibility once again.

Consequently, it should be noted that Mansfield's concept of the artist's impersonality differs in significant ways from that of her male contemporaries. It should not be confused with Joyce's vision of a god considering his creation, paring his fingernails.[21] It should not be confused with Eliot's reification of hierarchical tradition by impersonality achieved through the use of the "objective correlative." Mansfield's concept of impersonality comes closer to that of Murry, who remarked in an essay of April 1920 that the great artist is one "whose work manifests an incessant growth from a merely personal immediacy to a coherent and all-comprehending attitude to life."[22] These are Murry's words, but it is reasonable to infer that his view of the growth of the artist was based on his close observation of the artistic process of his most intimate companion. It should be noted that Murry is not calling for objectivity here. Objectivity, by its nature as something *other* than the subjective, cannot contain it. Although objectivity may be something achieved, its adherents must erase the process of that achievement. Murry retains the organicism of the romantics in his insistence on the growth process. He speaks of a movement from the "merely personal" to the all-comprehending. The personal, of course, is not repressed or destroyed; it remains as a function of the "all-comprehending," be-

difficulties of poststructuralism for feminist literary criticism in relation to Katherine Mansfield, see Fullbrook, pp. xi–xv.

[21]That really is not Joyce's position either; it belongs to Stephen as a stage in *his* artistic evolution. But it has become popularly identified with Joyce.

[22]J. Middleton Murry, "The Function of Criticism," in *Aspects of Literature* (New York: Knopf, 1920), pp. 13–14.

cause it contained, originally, the germ of the coherence of the whole.

By moving toward the impersonal, Mansfield aligned herself with many of the other artists associated with modernism, a movement where theories about the necessary impersonality of the artist abounded. There was T. S. Eliot's "objective correlative," for example. Or the program of the Imagists, under the influence of T. E. Hulme, who insisted on dryness, hardness, and avoidance of direct expression of emotion—especially in language now suspect: the language of feeling. Associating that language with the dying Victorians, the exaggerated jingoism of misplaced patriotism and the glories of empire, the modernists preferred the kind of understatement we now tend to identify with the Hemingway style, or with Pound's exposition of the tenets of Imagism—that urge toward simplicity, clean lines, sharpness, and again that dryness which Virginia Woolf later characterized in *Orlando* as the 1920s antidote to the damp, overly cozy, rampant fertility of the later nineteenth century.

Such attitudes and marks of style cannot be disassociated from Mansfield's desire to refine the shape of fiction. But she had to guard herself against absorbing the masculinist ideology behind them, for there is another side to this careful reshaping, this whittling down, this avoidance of direct emotion: a curious version of antifeminism. On the one hand it is a rejection of the old "feminine" style of popular fiction. But on the other it speaks to a rejection, equally strong, of the female body—so damp and so fertile, and considered so dangerous by those male artists longing to escape from what they imagined as its powers to entrap them. How much a part of the Futurists' manifesto, for example, was the call for the destruction of feminism and the glorification of "masculine" energy and the power of the industrial machine![23]

[23]The Italian Futurists were one of a number of modernist groups to issue a literary manifesto. Some pertinent statements reveal their antifeminist bias: "We want to sing the man who holds the steering wheel, whose ideal stem pierces the Earth, itself launched on the circuit of its orbit. . . . There is no more beauty except in struggle. No masterpiece without an aggressive character. Poetry must be a violent attack against the unknown forces, summoning them to lie down before man. . . . We want to glorify war—the only hygiene of the world—militarism, patriotism, the anarchist's destructive gesture, the fine ideas that kill, and the scorn of woman. . . . We want to demolish museums, libraries, fight against moralism,

# Katherine Mansfield

What Mansfield struggled to achieve was a transformed subjectivity. She tried to express it in a letter to a friend, the painter Dorothy Brett:

> It seems to me so extraordinarily right that you should be painting Still Lives just now. What can one do, faced with this wonderful tumble of round bright fruits, but gather them and play with them—and *become them*, as it were. When I pass the apple stalls I cannot help stopping and staring until I feel that I, myself, am changing into an apple, too—and that at any moment I may produce an apple, miraculously, out of my own being like the conjuror produces the egg. When you paint apples do you feel that your breasts and your knees become apples too? . . . But that is why I believe in technique, . . . just because I don't see how art is going to make that divine *spring* into the bounding outlines of things if it hasn't passed through the process of trying to *become* these things before recreating them. (*Letters* I, p. 330)

To *become* the thing is to take the direction away from self. While it may appear as a movement toward objectivity, Mansfield's statement really is about a merging of self and object, distancing without losing the intensity of the original identification with the emotion. In a way, she is reformulating her much earlier use of impersonation, but bringing to it a more sophisticated awareness of modernist aesthetics. Her emphasis on "changing into an apple" depends on a belief in the possibility of intuition—intuition in the Bergsonian sense, as when Bergson calls it "the kind of *intellectual sympathy* by which one places oneself within an object in order to coincide with what is unique in it and consequently inexpressible."[24]

Clearly, Mansfield is not describing any purely scientific attempt to see the object in itself:

> What it comes to is that we believe that emotion is essential to a work of art; it is that which makes a work of art a unity. Without emotion writing is dead; it becomes a record instead of a revelation, for the sense of revelation comes from that emotional reaction which the

---

feminism, and all opportunistic and utilitarian cowardices" ("A Manifesto of Italian Futurism" [1909], in *Literary Modernism*, ed. Irving Howe [Greenwich, Conn.: Fawcett, 1967], pp. 169–72).

[24]Henri Bergson, *An Introduction to Metaphysics*, trans. T. E. Hulme (New York: G. P. Putnam's Sons, 1912), p. 7.

artist felt and was impelled to communicate. To contemplate the object, to let it make its own impression . . . is not enough. There must
be an initial emotion felt by the writer, and all that he sees is saturated
in that emotional quality. It alone can give incidence and sequence,
character and background, a close and intimate unity.[25]

But when Mansfield refers to emotion here it is necessary to remember that she is not speaking of the idiosyncratic personal emotion.
Although she struggled to distance her personal emotions from her
writing, she wanted her fiction to be infused with emotion just the
same. In a practical way, without jargon, Mansfield's aesthetics
resemble those of Roger Fry and Clive Bell. She has a belief in
"significant form," which Bell described as "form behind which we
catch a sense of ultimate reality."[26]

If Mansfield's fiction begins to swerve from personal revelation,
her awareness of the multiplicity of sexual desire and the arbitrari-
ness of gender role continues throughout her career and is reflected
in the subtleties of her treatment of human relationships. Although
she aimed for distance and impersonality, most readers are aware of
the ways in which her personality actually dominates her fiction.
Her very act of diffusing herself through those multiple roles establishes her own consciousness as the real center of the work. With
her, and with most writers, consciously articulated intention often
works to quite a different final effect. When she wrote to Brett
about her ideal of becoming the object under attention, she assumed
a corresponding loss of ego during the process. She might feel herself "changing into an apple," but the apple should not become
Katherine Mansfield! She continued to worry about contemplation
that finally became mere contemplation of the egotistical self.

Consequently, in "Je ne parle pas français" (1918), Mansfield di-
rects her critical attack against the dangers of narcissism to the artist.
Raoul Duquette, the story's narrator and central consciousness, provides Mansfield with a suitable vehicle for parodying the self-
centeredness of some of her modernist contemporaries. She lets
Duquette spend nearly five pages spinning associations based on his

[25]*Novels and Novelists*, p. 236.
[26]Clive Bell, *Art* (New York: Stokes, 1923), p. 54. Bell also uses a phrase similar
in spirit to Katherine Mansfield's when he refers to an artist speaking about "a
passionate apprehension of form" (pp. 51–52).

observations of his favorite cafe in Paris before he introduces himself by name, and in a brief paragraph dismisses the usual biographical data: "My name is Raoul Duquette. I am twenty-six years old and a Parisian, a true Parisian. About my family—it really doesn't matter. I have no family; I don't want any. I never think about my childhood. I've forgotten it" (p. 355).

There is no need for Mansfield, as author, to describe the characteristics of early modernist subject matter; Raoul Duquette reels them off as glibly as if they were his own inventions: first of all, the death of god and the triumph of contingency—

> I don't believe in the human soul. I never have. I believe that people are like portmanteaux—packed with certain things, started going, thrown about, tossed away, dumped down, lost and found, half emptied suddenly, or squeezed fatter than ever, until finally the Ultimate Porter swings them on to the Ultimate Train and away they rattle. (Pp. 350–51)

Second, the ugliness of modern, urban life and its absurdity—

> And then there is the waiter. Not pathetic—decidedly not comic. Never making one of those perfectly insignificant remarks which amaze you so coming from a waiter. . . . When he is not smearing over the table or flicking at a dead fly or two, he stands with one hand on the back of a chair, in his far too long apron, and over his other arm the three-cornered dip of dirty napkin, waiting to be photographed in connection with some wretched murder. "Interior of Café where Body was Found." You've seen him hundreds of times. (Pp. 351–52)

And finally, the degeneration of "culture" through the influence of the popular media—

> Query: Why am I so bitter against Life? And why do I see her as a rag-picker on the American cinema, shuffling along wrapped in a filthy shawl with her old claws crooked over a stick?
>
> Answer: The direct result of the American cinema acting upon a weak mind. (P. 352)

It is Raoul Duquette's self-conscious awareness of his own *performance* as he entertains himself by spinning out these allusions that makes Mansfield's irony apparent. He keeps letting the reader know that he's not quite up to form with most of these. After the elaborate trope of the portmanteaux, Duquette remarks: "But before I started that long and rather far-fetched and not frightfully original digression, what I meant to say quite simply was that there are no portmanteaux to be examined here because the clientele of this café, ladies and gentlemen, does not sit down. No, it stands at the counter . . ." (p. 351). He undercuts himself through his final fall into triviality, his descent into insignificance. Or, he draws attention to the literary clichés floating in his own head by underscoring them: "Anyhow, the 'short winter afternoon was drawing to a close,' as they say, and I was drifting along, either going home or not going home, when I found myself in here, walking over to this seat in the corner" (p. 352).

As Duquette keeps on drawing attention to his use of various devices as intentional, he simultaneously brings to the foreground his own talents, his cleverness, his ability to see through his own encapsulation in triviality. He makes himself the center by continually attempting to outdo himself with more and more elaborate and farfetched figurative digressions:

> The waiter disappeared and reappeared with an armful of straw. He strewed it over the floor from the door to the counter and round about the stove with humble, almost adoring gestures. One would not have been surprised if the door had opened and the Virgin Mary had come in, riding upon an ass, her meek hands folded over her big belly....
> That's rather nice, don't you think, that bit about the Virgin? It comes from the pen so gently; it has such a "dying fall." I thought so at the time and decided to make a note of it. One never knows when a little tag like that may come in useful to round off a paragraph. (P. 353)

Mansfield thus allows Duquette to undo himself through his love of his own voice even before she demonstrates his moral failure in the story he tells about his involvement with Dick Harmon and Mouse. Her most brutal dissection of his narcissism comes through in her repeated contrasting of Duquette's self-admiration with his lack of recognition of his moral failure. In no scene is this more brilliantly depicted than in Duquette's experience of the "moment."

After he realizes that he should write down his "little tag" about the Virgin Mary, he finds a "a morsel of pink blotting-paper, incredibly soft and limp and almost moist, like the tongue of a little dead kitten" on the next table: "I sat—but always underneath, in this state of expectation, rolling the little dead kitten's tongue round my finger and rolling the soft phrase round my mind while my eyes took in the girls' names and dirty jokes and drawings of bottles and cups that would not sit in the saucers, scattered over the writing pad" (p. 353). (This sentence is in itself a parody of a particular kind of modernist sentence, in which discordant and disassociated—even obscene—elements are strewn together to give an "impression" of urban depravity.) But then he suddenly notices "that stupid, stale little phrase: *Je ne parle pas français*" written in green ink at the bottom of the pink blotting paper:[27]

> There! it had come—the moment—the *geste*! And although I was so ready, it caught me, it tumbled me over; I was simply overwhelmed. And the physical feeling was so curious, so particular. It was as if all of me, except my head and arms, all of me that was under the table, had simply dissolved, melted, turned into water. Just my head remained and two sticks of arms pressing on to the table. But, ah! the agony of that moment! How can I describe it? I didn't think of anything. I didn't even cry out to myself. Just for one moment I was not. I was Agony, Agony, Agony. (Pp. 353–54)

Although "the moment" contains many of the features of epiphanic revelation, Mansfield makes sure that we do not mistake it for genuine enlightenment. Duquette must be forced to undercut his authenticity with self-aggrandizement:

> Then it passed, and the very second after I was thinking: "Good God! Am I capable of feeling as strongly as that? But I was absolutely unconscious! I hadn't a phrase to meet it with! I was overcome! I was swept off my feet! I didn't even try, in the dimmest way, to put it down!"

[27]When Duquette sees the phrase in the midst of dirty jokes and drawings on the blotting pad, his epiphanic moment is reminiscent of Stephen Dedalus's in Joyce's *Portrait of the Artist as a Young Man*, when Stephen sees the obscenity carved in his father's old schoolroom desk. It is possible that Mansfield was deliberately parodying Joyce, although I have no proof of that assertion.

And up I puffed and puffed, blowing off finally with: "After all I must be first-rate. No second-rate mind could have experienced such an intensity of feeling so... purely. (P. 354)

Mansfield's critique is as much about herself as it is about Duquette and the pseudo-avant-garde he represents. Her own tendency to watch herself, to admire her revelatory discoveries, is parodied here with a ruthless thrust. Duquette's allegorical "Ultimate Porter" has more than surface similarities with Mansfield's own "clerk of some hotel without a proprietor." She recognized also how closely his self-absorption matched her own. The difference was her determination to overcome it. A journal entry more than two years later, in October 1921, shows her continuing struggle:

I wonder why it should be so difficult to be humble. . . . And yet, when I have finished a story and before I have begun another, I catch myself *preening* my feathers. . . . There seems to be some bad old pride in my heart; a root of it that puts out a thick shoot on the slightest provocation.... This interferes very much with work. One can't be calm, clear, good as one must be, while it goes on. I look at the mountains, I try to pray and I think of something *clever*. (*Journal*, p. 269)

# ঙ II

## Katherine Mansfield's
## "Passion for Technique"

The early modernist claims for the preeminence of subjectivity (for example in Dorothy Richardson and May Sinclair) are tempered by Mansfield's (and Woolf's) suspicions about their grounding in egoism. A recognition of interconnections, of the ways subjectivity is informed by social and cultural imperatives—especially as they are inculcated in family structure—remains a distinctive feature of Mansfield's epistemology. Mansfield's questioning of subjectivity occurs despite the seeming multiplicity and fluidity of the treatment of consciousness in her fiction. That questioning becomes apparent in two ways: through the satirical tone that emerges as the result of juxtaposition and selection, and through her efforts to achieve a *transformed* subjectivity, to *become* the object through an intuitive, Bergsonian "sympathy" with its internal structure. The latter tends to work by seeming to re-infiltrate a semblance of "objectivity" into the text.

Yet we know that for Mansfield, "objectivity" is as suspect a term as its opposite. She actually creates an *illusion* of objectivity in her fiction, an illusion whose source is the mastery of technique. The hidden author herself, insisting on her own access to truth, on the authenticity of her interpretation of reality, shows a mastery that she will not relinquish. She expresses it as a concern for "craft," for a precision in the use of details:

It's a very queer thing how *craft* comes into writing. I mean down to details. *Par example*. In *Miss Brill* I choose not only the length of every sentence, but even the sound of every sentence. I choose the rise and fall of every paragraph to fit her, and to fit her on that day at that very moment. After I'd written it I read it aloud—numbers of times—just as one would *play over* a musical composition—trying to get it nearer and nearer to the expression of Miss Brill—until it fitted her. . . . If a thing has really come off it seems to me there mustn't be one single word out of place, or one word that could be taken out.[1]

This technical "mastery," as is apparent in the encoded masculine in the word itself, might be interpreted (although I do not do so) as a kind of "masculinist" behavior, a recapture by the patriarchy, or, in orthodox Freudian terms, evidence of penis envy, masculine identification, and so forth. The problem for assertive, energetic, intelligent women is often this one: the cultural inscription of the masculine on all *active* creative endeavor.[2]

Mansfield does not accede to the assumed dominance of male authority and control. She takes an activist feminist position (and I am defining "activist" here not in terms of specific political actions, but as direct protest against injustice) when she insists on her authority to speak, to argue that one course of behavior is better than another. Rather than succumb to uncertainty, to never-knowingness, she takes up an ethical stance, what she calls her "cry against corruption," which is evident in the late story "The Fly" (1922), where she demonstrates how power corrupts, how patriarchal dominance victimizes. In this instance the small and powerless victim is a fly that struggles to escape from the inkwell of a businessman, who mindlessly lifts and submerges it with his pen. Because of the man's refusal to relinquish control, the fly ultimately is drowned. Although Mansfield allows the reader to understand that this man's sadistic behavior is a reaction to his despair over the death of his son, she does not condone it. The man is wrong, no matter how much he has suffered. Nothing justifies his mistreatment of the "other" (and

---

[1]*Letters of Katherine Mansfield*, pp. 360–61.

[2]A notorious example of an attack on Mansfield generated by this type of cultural inscription is that of the short-story writer Frank O'Connor, who complains of Mansfield's "assertiveness," and considers her search for experience as "a typical expedient of the woman with a homosexual streak who envies men and attributes their imaginary superiority to the greater freedom with which they are supposed to be able to satisfy their sexual appetite. It is the fallacy of Virginia Woolf's *A Room of One's Own*" (*The Lonely Voice* [Cleveland: World, 1963], p. 130).

certainly, "other" here brings with it a full realization of how the man has projected his own vulnerability into another creature).

In some ways Mansfield appears to be in agreement with other modernists about the alienation and decay of the postwar world, but that does not mean that she would ever have taken the same political direction as her friend D. H. Lawrence, for example, let alone that of T. S. Eliot or Ezra Pound. Mansfield's deepest suspicions were aroused by authoritarianism in any form, as her lifelong critique of male dominance gives clear evidence.[3] In this respect she resembles some of the other female modernists, particularly Woolf and H. D., whose writings evidence strong opposition to authoritarianism. But Mansfield's growing personal isolation—although caused by her increasingly debilitating illness—reflects as well her disassociation from politics and from efforts for social change, a severance that may have resulted from her association with Murry and her exclusion from the dominant centers of cultural power. Despite her sense of alienation from political life, however, she was far more ambivalent about the notion of modern civilization as the "waste land" than some of her male contemporaries.[4] She expressed an alternating (or perhaps simultaneous) awareness of "joy" and "hopelessness," and both of these were bound up with her self-definition as a writer. In an often quoted letter to Murry which bears repeating here, Mansfield explains:

> Ive two 'kick offs' in the writing game. *One* is joy—real joy—the thing that made me write when we lived at Pauline, and that sort of writing I could only do in just that state of being in some perfectly blissful way *at peace*. Then something delicate and lovely seems to open before my eyes, like a flower without thought of a frost or a cold breath—knowing that all about it is warm and tender and 'steady'. And *that* I try, ever so humbly to express.

[3]Modernism's links with incipient fascism and right-wing political theories have been discussed by many critics, especially in relation to Pound, Eliot, Lawrence, and Wyndham Lewis. Shari Benstock takes up this subject (as well as the emergence of anti-Semitism among some of the women modernists in Paris). See, in particular, her discussion of Natalie Barney in *Women of the Left Bank*, pp. 412–15.

[4]Gilbert and Gubar recognize the relationship between the male focus on the "waste land" and the male reaction to the emergence of important women writers. They note: "Indeed, the acute sense of disgrace we associate with such a waste land may arise from the fact that, as much as the industrial revolution and the fall of God, the rise of the female imagination was a central problem for the twentieth-century male imagination" (*No Man's Land*, vol. I, pp. 155–56).

The other 'kick off' is my old original one, and (had I not known love) it would have been my all. Not hate or destruction (both are beneath contempt as real motives) but an *extremely* deep sense of hopelessness—of everything doomed to disaster—almost wilfully, stupidly—like the almond tree and 'pas de nougat pour le noël'— There! as I took out a cigarette paper I got it exactly—*a cry against corruption* that is *absolutely* the nail on the head. Not a protest—a *cry*, and I mean corruption in the widest sense of the word, of course—(*Letters*, II, p. 54)

This letter, written before the end of the war, reveals Mansfield gradually shifting her focus of concern as a writer. I say "gradually" because I do not think it is possible to see any sharp break between stages of her work, and as her early letters and fiction suggest, there is a consistency of style and substance throughout her career. Yet the contrast between the youthful hope and enthusiasm over the "new" in her letters of 1906–8 and the suffering and disgust expressed in letters but a decade later is startling and unsettling. A letter to Ottoline Morrell on May 24, 1918, is even bleaker than the one to Murry:

But the ugliness—the ugliness of life—the intolerable corruption of it all—Ottoline. How is it to be borne? Today for the first time since I arrived, I went for a walk—Anne Rice has been telling me of the beauty of the spring—all the hedges one great flower, of the beauty of these little 'solid' white houses set in their blazing gardens—and the lovely hale old fishermen. But—the sea stank—great grey crabs scuttled over the rocks—all the little private paths and nooks had been fouled by human cattle—there were rags of newspaper in the hedges—the village is paved with *concrete* and as you passed the 'tiny solid white houses' a female voice yells: "you stop it or Ill lay a rope end across eë." (*Letters* II, p. 192)

During the last months of the war, but especially during the first years after its conclusion, Mansfield's long-standing emphasis on women's victimization was subsumed into a larger concern with oppression and victimization on a global scale. If one considers the works of other modernists who have been considered "major" writers in the canon—Lawrence, Pound, Woolf, Eliot, Stein—only Mansfield centers her work so deeply on the victimization of individuals. Joyce certainly was sensitive to such victimization in his earlier book, *Dubliners*, which shares with Mansfield's short fiction an emphasis on the epiphanic moment; but Mansfield's late work does not move away from this primary focus on human suffering. "The Garden-Party," "The Doll's House," "Life of Ma Parker," "The Fly," "Miss Brill," "Revelations," "The Canary" are "cries against corruption," expressions of outrage against a society in which privilege is so marked by indifference to the misery of others that it must demean or ignore any unmediated reaction to injustice, such as Laura's recognition that "we can't possibly have a garden-party with a man dead just outside the front gate" ("The Garden-Party," p. 542).

Mansfield's artistic vision never loses its grounding in a nineteenth-century, *ethical* conception of literature's purpose.[5] And it is here that her intense and long-standing fascination with the great Russian writers is most apparent. Mansfield was not alone in her devotion to the Russians; their influence was felt by twentieth-century writers ranging from Shaw to Joyce.[6] Her devotion most certainly was abetted by Murry's nearly obsessive study of Dostoevsky during the period when she was writing "Prelude."[7] Virginia Woolf also felt the Russians' overpowering influence. In the essay "Modern Fiction," she had insisted: "The most elementary remarks upon modern English fiction can hardly avoid some mention of the Russian influence, and if the Russians are mentioned one runs the risk of feeling that to write of any fiction save theirs is waste of time. If we want understanding of the soul and heart where else shall we find it of comparable profundity?"[8]

For Mansfield, the connection with the Russians also signified her own personal identification with their portrayals of human suffering, and, in the case of Chekhov, a sense of like identity, a realization that she and he were condemned to death by the same disease.

[5]See Hanson's discussion of the "ethical dimension" to Mansfield's aesthetics, in *Critical Writings of Katherine Mansfield*, pp. 10–11.

[6]For an informative general survey of the impact of Russian fiction on English and American writers see Gilbert Phelps, *The Russian Novel in English Fiction* (London: Hutchinson's University Library, 1956).

[7]J. Middleton Murry, *Fyodor Dostoevsky: A Critical Study* (London: Secker, 1916).

[8]Woolf, *The Common Reader*, first series, p. 157. See also Woolf's essay in the same volume "The Russian Point of View," pp. 177–87. For a concise and informative study of Dostoevsky's influence on Woolf see Bill Handley, "Virginia Woolf and Fyodor Dostoevsky: Can Modernism Have 'Soul'?" *Virginia Woolf Miscellany* 31 (Fall 1988), 3–4.

A preoccupation with the relentless course of that disease forms the persistent undercurrent of Mansfield's later writing. It helps to explain her seeming disgust with some of the male modernists' outspokenness about sex and other bodily processes. Such attitudes about sexuality are in great contrast with her youthful experimental posture toward the subject and hint at a kind of latent prudishness which is often the other side of promiscuity. Her biographers relate these later attitudes to a sense of guilt about her youthful sexual adventures, but I am not entirely convinced by that argument. More important, it seems to me, is the fact of her dying, the overriding reality to all her later discourse on sexuality. A remark in her journal in 1918 gives an unnerving glimpse of her recognition that Murry was withdrawing from her as a sexual partner: "Do you remember when you put your handkerchief to your lips and turned away from me—In that instant you were utterly, utterly apart from me—and I have never felt quite the same since" (*Journal*, p. 134).

One finds a certain body consciousness permeating all facets of Mansfield's writing, but its locus now shifts from sexuality to disease; its depiction is distorted by the reality of what Elaine Scarry calls "the inexpressibility of physical pain."[9] There are only brief glimpses of that pain in Mansfield's letters and journals, and it is noteworthy how often its attempted expression quickly swerves to concentrate on her relation to Murry. A journal entry of August 12, 1920, is illustrative:

> I cough and cough and at each breath a dragging, boiling, bubbling sound is heard. I feel that my whole chest is boiling. I sip water, spit, sip, spit. I feel I must break my heart. And I can't expand my chest; it's as though the chest had collapsed. Life is—getting a new breath: nothing else counts. And J. is silent, hangs his head, hides his face with his fingers *as though* it were unendurable. 'This is what she is doing to me! Every fresh sound makes *my* nerves wince.' I know he can't help these feelings. But, oh God! how wrong they are. If he could only for a minute, serve me, help me, give *himself* up. I can so imagine an account by him of a 'calamity'. 'I could do nothing all day, *my* hands trembled, I had a sensation of *utter* cold. At times I felt the strain

[9]Elaine Scarry, *The Body in Pain: The Making and Unmaking of the World* (New York: Oxford University Press, 1985), p. 3. Scarry's meditation on physical pain has particular relevance to Katherine Mansfield, whose fiction both suggests and denies the physical suffering of its author.

would be unbearable, at others a *merciful numbness...*' and so on. What
a fate to be self-imprisoned! (*Journal*, p. 207)

Mansfield's attitude about this physical suffering is suffused with a
sense of the impossibility of its being shared, of its alienating effect.

In her stories, too, the sufferer is nearly always placed in conjunction with another person who is emotionally incapable of responding to her pain. Such a juxtaposition occurs in "The Man without a
Temperament," which is closely based on Mansfield's relationship
with Murry and her disappointment over his behavior during her
illness. It also occurs in "Life of Ma Parker" (1920), where the
horror of Ma Parker's husband's death from consumption is treated
at a slant, through the irony of the "literary gentleman's" sentimentalized attitudes about the working class:

> "A baker, Mrs. Parker!" the literary gentleman would say. For
> occasionally he laid aside his tomes and lent an ear, at least, to this
> product called Life. "It must be rather nice to be married to a baker!"
> Mrs. Parker didn't look so sure.
> "Such a clean trade," said the gentleman.
> Mrs. Parker didn't look convinced.
> "And didn't you like handing the new loaves to the customers?" (P.
> 487)

Ma Parker counters the sentimentalized portrait of the "clean trade"
with her memories of endless work, bearing thirteen children and
losing seven of them, and then the death of her husband: "It was
flour on the lungs, the doctor told her at the time." The image of
flour, of "white powder," "a great fan of white dust," works to
undercut the superficial hypocrisy of the literary gentleman's supposed sympathy. He does not allow himself to be aware of the pain
behind her description of her losses; rather, he moves back into
complacency: "shuddering, and taking up his pen again." Thus he
consigns Ma Parker to the helpless silence in which she finds herself
at the end of the story, alone, on the street, questioning: "wasn't
there anywhere in the world where she could have her cry out—at
last?" (p. 490).

Pain can also be filtered through the words of others, through
Keats, for example. And Mansfield quotes from his letters: "'Noth-

ing is so bad as want of health—it makes one envy scavengers and cinder-sifters.' (*August* 23, 1820)" (*Journal*, p. 225).[10] Chekhov, Keats, and Mansfield become, in this context of bodily suffering from tuberculosis, a triad of initiates to the secrets of pain, to a higher state of consciousness known only to those who have undergone its rituals. By identifying herself with these two others, she shares in their "genius" as well. And this was very much the point for Murry when, after Mansfield's death, he began to create his portrait of the suffering, spiritual Katherine Mansfield. Clearly, Murry encouraged her identification with Keats and Chekhov. In a letter of March 10, 1918, for instance, he urged her to change the name of a character in "Bliss" because he felt the name tended toward caricature: "It is a Dickens touch & you're not Dickens— you're Tchehov—more than Tchehov."[11] Or, "You are as classic as Tchehov in your way."[12]

Murry once called Chekhov "the only great modern artist in prose,"[13] and many of the terms he used to express his admiration for the Russian author he also used elsewhere to praise the writing of Katherine Mansfield. That Murry saw her as England's answer to Chekhov is clear by implication. Murry tells us that Chekhov's attitude "is complete, not partial. His comprehension radiates from a steady centre," and that as a writer he "had slowly shifted his angle of vision until he could discern a unity in multiplicity."[14] Murry believed that Chekhov had much to teach the modernists:

> Tchehov is . . . a good many phases in advance of all that is habitually described as modern in the art of literature. The artistic problem

[10]Jeffrey Meyers gives parallel examples from Keats's and Mansfield's letters to show how "her letters to Murry quite consciously echoed Keats's last letters to Fanny Brawne" (*Katherine Mansfield*, p. 179). Meyers also links Mansfield's identification with Chekhov with her earlier interest in that other Russian, Marie Bashkirtseff, who also died of tuberculosis. He notes that Mansfield's "attraction to Gurdjieff was the fatal culmination of her life-long passion for the Russians" (p. 242).

[11]*Letters of John Middleton Murry*, p. 135.

[12]Ibid., p. 276.

[13]Murry, "Thoughts on Tchehov," *Aspects of Literature*, p. 82.

[14]Ibid., pp. 76–77. In his introduction to Mansfield's collected stories, Murry remarks that Mansfield's "suffering and her delight were never partial" and that "she accepted life completely, and she had the right to accept it, for she had endured in herself all the suffering which life can lavish upon a single soul" (*Stories*, p. xi).

which he faced and solved is one that is, at most, partially present to the consciousness of the modern writer—to reconcile the greatest possible diversity of content with the greatest possible unity of aesthetic impression. Diversity of content we are beginning to find in profusion—Miss May Sinclair's latest experiment shows how this need is beginning to trouble a writer with a settled manner and a fixed reputation—but how rarely do we see even a glimmering recognition of the necessity of a unified aesthetic impression! The modern method is to assume that all that is, or has been, present to consciousness is *ipso facto* unified aesthetically. The result of such an assumption is an obvious disintegration both of language and artistic effort, a mere retrogression from the classical method.[15]

Murry's analysis of Chekhov's importance to modernism takes up many of the same aesthetic concerns that Mansfield was also expressing—at the same time (August 1919)—in her reviews for *The Athenaeum*. Less than two months before Murry's remarks about Chekhov were published, Mansfield reviewed May Sinclair's stream-of-consciousness novel *Mary Olivier*: "For the difference between the new way of writing and the old way is not a difference of degree but of kind. Its aim, as we understand it, is to represent things and persons as separate, as distinct, as apart as possible." And Mansfield complains, in a manner similar to her criticism of Dorothy Richardson, that Sinclair's method prevents her from seeing how "one thing is to be related to another thing." In fact, Mansfield suggests that "it is too late in the day for this new form, and Miss Sinclair's skilful handling of it serves but to make its failure the more apparent."[16]

I have held off bringing in the subject of Mansfield's imaginative relation to Chekhov until nearly the end of this book for a reason. For many years Mansfield's reputation was bound up with a continuing critical discussion of Chekhov's influence on her work. While this focus undoubtedly was abetted by Murry's valorization of the Mansfield-Chekhov link, Mansfield herself encouraged such discussion.[17] Her letters and notebooks contain many references to Chek-

[15]Ibid., p. 79.

[16]*Novels and Novelists*, pp. 43–45.

[17]In her study of Murry, Sharron Greer Cassavant notices the interchangeability of Mansfield's and Murry's critical concepts: "It is impossible to say who sponsored which idea, for they constantly echoed one another's phrases and judgements,

hov. For example, in a letter of 1919 to S. S. Koteliansky, with whom she worked on translating Chekhov's letters for *The Athenaeum*, she remarked:

> I wonder if you have read Joyce and Eliot and these ultra-modern men? It is so strange that they should write as they do *after* Tchekhov. For Tchekhov has said the last word that has been said, so far, and more than that he has given us a sign of the way we should go. They not only ignore it: they think Tchekhov's stories are almost as good as the 'specimen cases' in Freud. (*Letters* II, p. 345)

Typical of the standard critical discussion of Mansfield's indebtedness to Chekhov is that of Gilbert Phelps, in 1956. He remarks:

> There were undoubtedly elements in her own temperament and sensibility that found a genuine stimulus in Chekhov. It came naturally to her to develop her stories by the gradual accumulation of impressionistic scenes, to use random details, casual incidents, unconscious gestures and remarks, making them suddenly responsible for the whole emotional content of a tale, as a small lever launches an unexpected weight, and to choose themes of melancholy, frustration, indifference.
>   In this sense Chekhov's influence acted mainly as a confirmation of personal preferences and a stimulus to their expression. . . .
>   And of course Katherine Mansfield does not possess Chekhov's comprehensive vision of the relation of man to his social background, and to the vaster backgrounds of Nature. She does not possess his fundamental sanity, or his objectivity, or his self-discipline. And though she learned a good deal from him it was certainly not from him that she derived the sentimentality, the parochialism, the coyness and preciosity which mar so much of her work.[18]

Phelps repeats some of the typical complaints of critics in the '40s and '50s about the Chekhov-Mansfield connection, complaints that

---

shared the same heroes and enemies, and assured one another that they alone were concerned with fostering a literature morally adequate to their time. They constructed an ideology together" (*John Middleton Murry: The Critic as Moralist* [University: University of Alabama Press, 1982], p. 82).

[18]Gilbert Phelps, *The Russian Novel in English Fiction*, pp. 189–90.

unconsciously register a criticism of the feminine. Phelps considers Mansfield's use of devices similar to Chekhov's as something that "came naturally to her" rather than the result of intellectual effort and craftsmanship. Phelps's contrast of the "natural" to the "objective," the "comprehensive" to the "parochial," reiterates the pattern of exclusion which phallocentric criticism has used to trivialize the achievements of women. The choice of the words "sentimentality," "coyness," and "preciosity" in the last sentence encodes the conventional negative description of the feminine as well.

Critics like Phelps frequently mark the difference between Chekhov and Mansfield in terms of scope and breadth.[19] That Chekhov's view of the world was broader, more comprehensive, and that the range of his experience was larger, are obvious and commonplace conclusions by now. What is important is to remember that Chekhov's breadth resulted from the knowledge of the world allowed him as a man: a man with a profession that gave him the freedom to mingle with all types of people, protected by his professional role as a physician but also enabled by it to learn about those people in quite intimate ways. He had the kind of freedom belonging to men which Woolf described in *A Room of One's Own*. Although Mansfield's attempt at independence brought her more experience than many women of her generation, she was not allowed or expected to have the same range of experience as men. As we have seen, her pursuit of experience continually brought her back to the contingencies of women's vulnerability in a male-dominated society.

Mansfield has been called everything from a mere "follower" of Chekhov to a blatant plagiarizer of one of his stories. The reader

[19]It is noteworthy that even in the 1940s, another woman writer complained about a description in a college textbook of Mansfield's work as lacking "depth and range." Marjorie Kinnan Rawlings replied: "This is of course nonsense. If there are 'deeper' stories than 'The Man Without a Temperament' or 'The Stranger,' in both of which lives are seen collapsing quietly before one's eyes, I do not know them. The very quiet is perhaps the snare. She works her wonders so subtly that the shallow-minded no doubt read no more than the actual words. As to range, call Poe 'limited' if you must, but not the writer who could move from 'Life of Ma Parker' to 'Poison.'. . . The college tome that so irked me gave a full page to identifying her as a disciple of Chekhov. If the author of nearly a hundred published stories, all exquisite, some of them acknowledged classics, was a 'disciple,' she was more faithful than Peter or Paul" ("Introduction," in Katherine Mansfield, *Stories: A Selection Made by J. Middleton Murry* [Cleveland: World, 1946], p. 11).

who wishes to trace the connections between Mansfield's fiction and Chekhov's has ready material at hand. Yet I believe that this line of inquiry—much overworked—is fruitless unless it is accompanied by attention to gender difference. I believe that the critical fixation on Mansfield's debt to Chekhov obscures the complexity of her development as a modernist, pushing one line of influence into the foreground while other, less critically acceptable lines are hidden in the background.[20]

In some sense, Chekhov was the foil to Wilde—at least in the Bloomian sense of "anxiety of influence." The opposition is clearest if we play with the notion of Mansfield having two literary "fathers," Wilde and Chekhov. Wilde as father, as we have seen, is connected in Mansfield's development with aestheticism, but also with her lesbianism. The emotional/intellectual complex related to Wilde is thus bound up with secrecy, posing, sexual guilt, and repression. Wilde's influence makes itself felt in her writing through experimentation and *impersonation*. Its finale is spectacular, tragic death linked with public shame. Chekhov is in some ways an escape from Wilde to a more socially acceptable model. His influence is connected with realism but also with heterosexuality, and it is bound up with a drive toward achievement and approval, maturity of vision, and *impersonality*. Its finale is private rather than spectacular: early death through tuberculosis, suffering linked with that of humanity in general. But this "mature" father also suggests the hidden, the secret, in another sense than Wilde. Although Mansfield's role as "daughter" to Chekhov signals a partial reconciliation with the patriarchy, her absorption in him also contains an element of secrecy and guilt. Rather than the pose or mask associated with the Wilde influence, Chekhov's is associated with expropriation— even with plagiarism.[21]

[20]Hanson and Gurr de-emphasize the Chekhov influence, seeing more a "relationship between her fiction and the plotless story of the nineties" than with Chekhov's fiction: "She modelled her early stories on those of the Yellow Book writers, and it is from them, not Chekhov, that she would have learnt the techniques of stylised interior monologue, flashback and daydream which became so important in her work. By 1909, which was when she probably first read Chekhov, his techniques must have seemed distinctly old-fashioned by comparison with much English fiction" (*Katherine Mansfield*, p. 19).

[21]Claire Tomalin argues a strong case supporting the allegations that Mansfield plagiarized. She even believes that Mansfield was blackmailed by an earlier lover

## Katherine Mansfield

In an early Burnell story, "The Little Girl," published in *Rhythm* in October 1912, Kezia inadvertently uses the manuscript of a speech her father has written as the stuffing for a pincushion she is making for his birthday present. He punishes her severely with the blows of a ruler against her hands. "You must be taught once and for all not to touch what does not belong to you"(p. 141). But the "theft" from the father is followed by a retreat to the maternal when Kezia turns for comfort to her grandmother and sits cuddled on her lap, venting her anger at masculine authority: "What did Jesus make fathers for?" This story's encoded suggestion of daughterly revolt against the prerogatives of patriarchal authority in language may be connected with this whole issue of Mansfield's alleged plagiarism of Chekhov. For while the child endures punishment over the destruction of her father's words, by the end of the story she has gained his love. The anger against the unjust punishment (she had protested: "But it was for your b-b-birthday") is suppressed, and later, when both her grandmother and mother are away, it returns in the form of fear unleashed through the dream-state: "The butcher with a knife and a rope . . . grew nearer and nearer, smiling that dreadful smile, while she could not move, could only stand still, crying out, 'Grandma, Grandma!' She woke shivering, to see father beside her bed, a candle in his hand" (pp. 141–2). The father takes her into his own bed to comfort her:

> He lay down beside her. Half asleep still, still with the butcher's smile all about her, it seemed, she crept close to him, snuggled her head under his arm, held tightly to his pyjama jacket.
>     Then the dark did not matter; she lay still.
>     "Here, rub your feet against my legs and get them warm," said father.
>     Tired out, he slept before the little girl. A funny feeling came over her. Poor father! Not so big, after all—and with no one to look after him.... He was harder than the grandmother, but it was a nice hardness.... And every day he had to work. . . . She had torn up all his beautiful writing. . . .

because he knew she had read the Chekhov story "Sleepy" on which "The Child-Who-Was-Tired" was based. The evidence for this is highly circumstantial, however. I am not thoroughly convinced about the blackmail attempt. See Tomalin, *Katherine Mansfield: A Secret Life,* pp. 261–72, for a transcription of letters to the *Times Literary Supplement* in 1951 regarding the plagiarism controversy.

"What's the matter?" asked father. "Another dream?"

"Oh," said the little girl, "my head's on your heart; I can hear it going. What a big heart you've got, father dear." (P. 142)

There is both recapitulation and triumph in the end of this story. The child has established rapport with the father, as Kate Fullbrook has observed, by the "imagining of commonality with her father rather than on recognition of his superiority or his power."[22] She has defused the fear of difference by considering it "a nice hardness." But it is important to see at the same time how the last line, "What a big heart you've got, father dear," retains a level of the original fear of the male inculcated by his patriarchal authority, his will to punishment. For as C. A. Hankin notes in her excellent Freudian reading of the story, the phrase is an echo of Red Riding-Hood's refrain in the old nursery tale. "What big teeth you have, Grannie dear," she utters before the wolf leaps up to answer, "All the better to eat you with, my dear."[23] The last line of "The Little Girl" thus suggests a multiple reading, including accommodation, acceptance, fear, and a masochistic sexual desire. Hankin's emphasis on the story's repeated references "to the mouth," including the father's kiss, loud speaking voice, and most significantly, his "great speech," is illuminating, especially in the contrast of these examples of the father's oral prerogative with Kezia's stuttering, her own difficulty with speech. Hankin sees this stuttering as a sign "not just of fear but also of hostility. The same repressed hostility causes her apparently accidental destruction of his speech."[24]

Feminist theory brings additional complexity to this focus on speech. Using feminist revisions of Lacan, critics are paying attention to the various ways women writers have subverted the authority of phallocentric speech. A recent book, for example, is called *Stealing the Language,*[25] an important essay, "Still Practice, A/

---

[22]Fullbrook, *Katherine Mansfield,* p. 51.

[23]Hankin, *Katherine Mansfield and Her Confessional Stories,* p. 84. Hankin notes that Murry also had "published his own self-pitying story, 'The Little Boy', in the August 1912 issue of *Rhythm*" (p. 79). Hankin sees the two stories as part of the need of both writers to establish their similarity in terms of their mistreatment as children.

[24]Ibid., p. 84.

[25]Alicia Suskin Ostriker, *Stealing the Language: The Emergence of Women's Poetry in America* (Boston: Beacon, 1986).

Wrested Alphabet."[26] The trope of expropriation has become a convention of many feminist critical texts. Mansfield's alleged plagiarism of Chekhov's "Sleepy" in her story "The Child-Who-Was-Tired" (1909) takes on a different meaning when interpreted within this context of feminist revolt. A number of critics have taken the similarity of plot outline in the two stories as evidence of plagiarism, but Hanson and Gurr maintain there is a great difference between them. They see Chekhov's as "a restrained, pathological study, in which action is convincingly related to a specific social and psychological context" and Mansfield's as "a symbolic fable, in which certain elements of the original plot are exaggerated and key images repeated in order to express a general, rather than a specific truth: the harshness of woman's lot in life."[27] This emphasis on "woman's lot" allows us to bring the subject back within the scope of feminist analysis. Like much feminist writing, Mansfield's story is an attempt to deconstruct a phallocentric myth by retelling it. The basic plot to both stories concerns an overworked, mistreated child servant who is so driven to exhaustion by her cruel employers that she smothers their baby in order to finally get some sleep. It is revealing that Mansfield uses an image she will repeat, quite literally, years later in "Prelude." When the child covers the baby's face with the bolster, he struggles "like a duck with its head off, wriggling" (p. 99). The submerged anger at the male infant who must be nurtured at the cost of her own emotional life is released—if only momentarily—in the image of castration.

Mansfield's devotion to Chekhov is also related to the continuing preoccupation with the concept of the artist in her journal, letters, and critical writings. This preoccupation had its roots in the '90s valorization of art above experience—in Wilde's attachment to artifice—but it soon shifted to a belief in the artist's deeper understanding of experience rather than exception from it, a version of the romantic view of the artist as visionary and sufferer. By the time of her late fiction, Mansfield had enlarged this preoccupation to include the newer, postwar concern with authenticity, destruction of hypocrisy, and admiration for craft. Such concern is expressed in

[26]Jane Marcus, "Still Practice, A/Wrested Alphabet: Toward a Feminist Aesthetic," *Art & Anger: Reading Like a Woman* (Columbus: Ohio State University Press, 1988), pp. 215–49.

[27]Hanson and Gurr, p. 19. See also pp. 32–34 for an excellent discussion of the differences between the two stories.

the following letter written to her brother-in-law, Richard Murry, on February 3, 1921, during a time of personal and aesthetic consolidation, a time of coming to terms with both her impending death from tuberculosis and her decision to continue her struggle to live as a creative artist:

> Here is painting, and here is life. We can't separate them. Both of them have suffered an upheaval extraordinary in the last few years. There is a kind of tremendous agitation going on still, but so far anything that has come to the surface seems to have been experimental, or a fluke—a lucky accident. I believe the only way to *live* as artists under these new conditions in art and life is to put everything to the test for ourselves. We've got, in the long run, to be our own teachers. There's no getting away from that. We've got to win through by ourselves. Well, as I see it, the only way to do that honestly, dead truthfully, shirking nothing and leaving nothing out, is to put everything to the test. (Your desire for technical knowledge is a kind of profound *symbol.*) Not only to face things, but really to find out of what they are composed. How can we know where we are, otherwise? How can we prevent ourselves being weak in certain places? To be *thorough*, to be *honest*, I think if artists were really thorough & honest they would save the world. . . . Your generation & mine too, has been 'put off' with imitations of the real thing and we're bound to react violently if we're sincere. This takes so long to write & it sounds so heavy. Have I conveyed what I mean to even? You see I too have a passion for technique. I have a passion for making the thing into a *whole* if you know what I mean. Out of technique is born real style, I believe. There are no short cuts.[28]

The practice of "technique," that "passion for making the thing into a *whole*," had become a mission for Katherine Mansfield by 1921, a purpose in living;[29] but her dedication to it was not a sudden

[28] *Selected Letters*, pp. 197–98.

[29] Mansfield's seriousness about herself as an artist and about the artistic process itself was well known to her friends. Virginia Woolf wrote in her diary on March 22, 1919: "And again, as usual, I find with Katherine what I don't find with the other clever women a sense of ease and interest, which is, I suppose, due to her caring so genuinely if so differently from the way I care, about our precious art" (*Diary*, vol. I, p. 258). But by June 14, 1919, Woolf expressed some hesitation about Mansfield's defensiveness over her role as artist: "And then there's the question of Katherine's writing. Isn't she a little querulous and restless about that? Standing emphatically yet not quite firmly on her rights as an artist; as people do who must insist upon being one" (p. 281).

development. Her emphasis on craft relates to her long-standing appreciation for technical perfection, beginning with her adolescent immersion in the study of music, her continued practice and imitation of different literary styles in the years of her apprenticeship as a writer, and continuing in adulthood through her interest in painting encouraged by her close friendships with artists such as Dorothy Brett, Mark Gertler, and Anne Estelle Rice. Mansfield's and Murry's brief, tumultuous friendship with the sculptor Henri Gaudier-Brzeska[30] and Murry's knowledge of and involvement with continental avant-garde artists through his editorship of *Rhythm* were equally influential. Late in the same year of the letter to Richard Murry, on December 5, 1921, Mansfield wrote to Dorothy Brett about her recollections of the first Postimpressionist exhibit in 1910:

> Wasn't that Van Gogh shown at the Goupil ten years ago? Yellow flowers—brimming with sun in a pot? I wonder if it is the same. That picture seemed to reveal something that I hadn't realised before I saw it. It lived with me afterwards. It still does—that & another of a sea captain in a flat cap. They taught me something about writing, which was queer—a kind of freedom—or rather, a shaking free. When one has been working for a long stretch one begins to narrow ones vision a bit, to fine things down too much. And its only when something else breaks through, a picture, or something seen out of doors that one realises it. It is—literally—years since I have been to a picture show. I can smell them as I write.[31]

Mansfield's use of the expression "a shaking free" is reminiscent of her description of the revelatory moment in the journal passage "The Flowering of the Self," written more than a year earlier ("our persistent yet mysterious belief in a self which is continuous and permanent . . . [which] shakes the flower free and—we are alive—we are flowering for our moment upon the earth" [*Journal*, p. 205]). Thus it is clear that "shaking free" as an aesthetic issue is interwoven with a metaphysical shaking free as well.

Throughout her career, Mansfield recognized that one of her cen-

---

[30]For a vivid account of this brief friendship, see H. S. Ede, *Savage Messiah: Gaudier-Brzeska* (New York: Literary Guild, 1931), pp. 133–43.

[31]*Selected Letters*, p. 233. Clare Hanson notes that Mansfield was mistaken about the location of the exhibit; it was at the Grafton Galleries, not the Goupil. *Critical Writings of Katherine Mansfield*, p. 137.

tral strengths was her sensitivity to visual stimuli. From the "vignettes" of her youth to her most sophisticated longer works of fiction, Mansfield's descriptions convey a sense of being "composed." Often they seem like verbal equivalents of paintings. A good example is a fairly early one, from a narrative of 1915, "An Indiscreet Journey":

> A green room with a stove jutting out and tables on each side. On the counter, beautiful with coloured bottles, a woman leans, her breasts in her folded arms. Through an open door I can see a kitchen, and the cook in a white coat breaking eggs into a bowl, and tossing the shells into a corner. The blue and red coats of the men who are eating hang upon the walls. Their short swords and belts are piled upon chairs. (P. 186)

Although Mansfield was herself an experimenter and interested in experimentation in the arts in general, she kept up her guard against the temptations of innovation for its own sake—the lure of the mechanical trick, the flaunting of convention, the clever phrase. All departures from the traditional must have a foundation in the search for meaning. To merely record whatever impinges on the mind was never enough for Katherine Mansfield. As with her complaint about Dorothy Richardson, she would insist that "until these things are judged and given each its appointed place in the whole scheme, they have no meaning in the world of art."[32]

To proceed as if all objects and values are equal in significance prevents emphasis and shadowing. But most of all it might prevent "that divine *spring* into the bounding outline of things" Mansfield spoke of in her letter to Brett. For "how are we to appreciate the importance of one 'spiritual event' rather than another? What is to prevent each being unrelated—complete in itself—if the gradual unfolding in growing, gaining light is not to be followed by one blazing moment?"[33] And here, perhaps, we may realize the ultimate direction of Katherine Mansfield's "passion." In that "one blazing moment" she evokes epiphany, the movement of so many of her own stories to that moment of enlightenment, exposure, understanding—the instant when the walls come down.

[32]*Novels and Novelists*, p. 4.
[33]Ibid., p. 30.

# ɔ 12

## Conclusion: Modernism
## from Mansfield's Perspective

In retrospect, it seems that Mansfield's modernism is remarkably prefigured in a series of letters she wrote in 1908 to her lover, the musician Garnet Trowell. These letters, written during the first, romantic, not yet disillusioned stage of their affair—before her pregnancy, her marriage to George Bowden, and her miscarriage—contain the germ of many of the issues she would take up later in her fiction and criticism, and also bear the sign of nearly every innovation she would make as a writer. The issues range from the suffrage movement to the question of the "self," from the musical analogues of writing to the role of violence and masochism in art: what she phrased as "the subtle joy in pain—which is the supreme ecstacy of modern music" (*Letters* I, p. 59). When I say all this, however, I recognize that I am contributing to the fiction of the symbolic moment, the decisive turning point around which all that follows and all that precedes cohere. Such devices make our actions as critics seem logical and systematic, but it is essential that we not confuse them with "truth." There are many stories we can tell about the objects of our attention, and we tell one story one time and another the next.

By choosing 1908, I shape Mansfield's development in particular ways closest to the ends I strive to attain. Because my emphasis is on modernism, Mansfield's break with her bourgeois, family-centered past in 1908 is a convenient explanation for her literary advances, but it precludes as much as it clarifies. To use it requires an effort of willed affirmation of narrative authority, a gesture difficult for me to take seriously. Yet Mansfield's own depiction of this moment is bound up with her own such affirmation. The "reality" of her leap into the new, as well as her assault against the persuasions of parental caution and the codes of appropriate behavior for women, is known to us only through her efforts to transcend them through her struggle with the written word. The "Katherine Mansfield" who appears in the letters to Garnet Trowell is a creation of her author no less than the characters in her stories. The medium of the letter gave her a chance to express her opinions and to experiment with a wide variety of devices ranging from extended metaphors to impressionistic descriptions to internal monologues verging on stream of consciousness. And this medium also allowed her a totally accepting audience (even if it was only an audience of one) who reflected "this complete absorption of the one into the other" (*Letters* I, p. 67).

These letters reveal a refashioning of late romantic notions of art and the artist into a modernist idiom. Remnants of the older diction, such as the personification of "Dawn" in one letter, appear infrequently. Yet even there, although Mansfield begins the trope with its traditional connotations, she quickly transforms it through parody and self-reflexiveness:

> At last Dawn came—in the sky hung a pink banner of cloud. It grew and widened until at last it touched the houses & fields—peered into the mirror. Dawn sat up in bed with a pink fascinator round her head. At the station sleepy officials shouted French French French, & then St. Lazare at last—a great platform—cold with the coldness of more than Winter. (*Letters* I, p. 76)

This self-reflexiveness relates to the persistence of the Paterian valorization of artifice, which I discussed in Chapter 4. There is also the persistence in these letters of certain phrases, tropes, and other patterns notable in her notebooks and fiction of the same period. For example, "Beloved this silent, clockfilled room is waiting for you to come in" (*Letters* I, p. 69) is similar to the phrasing in the passage about Maata in the notebook many months earlier: "I alone in this silent clockfilled room have become powerfully—I want Maata—I want her as I have had her—terribly."[1] The slide from the lesbian to

---

[1]Quoted in Alpers, *Life,* p. 49, from Mansfield's Notebook 39, p. 17, Alexander Turnbull Library.

the heterosexual brings with it simultaneously a vocabulary and syntax enmeshed in its origins. Even the association of swimming and sexuality which Mansfield used in "Summer Idylle. 1906" makes its appearance in a letter to Trowell:

> I wonder if you have ever swum in a very rough sea. I have—You plunge into the breakers—the waves break right over you—but you shake the water out of your eyes and hair—and there is a sensation of extraordinary strength. Something gigantic has you in its power— you are laughing, intoxicated—half wild with laughter and excitement. So I feel when I am tossed upon the very sea of passionate bliss. (*Letters* I, pp. 64–70)

But now the analogy has become tired, and its transformation to the heterosexual brings with it a conventionality tied to the impulse to explain it, to add the trite transition "so I feel." Yet, the very same letter contains a description reminiscent of the earlier London sketches and is poised on the brink of a modernist conception of the "waste land":

> The sky was flushed with faint fires—hollowed into a perfect pearl. Dim men and women were clustering in broken groups round the doors of the public houses. From some of the bars came the sound of horrible laughter. And all the streets stretching out on every side like the black web of some monstrous spider. In the Edgeware Road we passed a great procession of the unemployed. They carried a scarlet banner. You cannot think of how horrible and sinister they looked— tramping along—hundreds of them—monotonously, insistently— like a grey procession of dead hours. (P. 70)

What is most remarkable about the letters is their powerful impressionism. A description of a journey across the channel is filled with precise detail—"black grapes in frilled white paper," "sailors in great coats and boots like Flying Dutchman mariners"—along with a sense of disruption and internal reshaping of the objects of perception: "a confused impression of rain." A woman knitting a stocking becomes archetypal as she is seen through a "wavering light": "All through the hours, half sleeping, half waking I would open my eyes and see this little bowed figure & the wavering light seemed to play fantastic tricks with her & the stocking in my fancy grew—

gigantic—enormous. It seemed almost symbolical—the sleeping figures and in the light the little quiet woman knitting an eternal stocking" (*Letters* I, p. 75). (Ten years later, Mansfield would write a satirical sentence that seems to repeat and to mock the self-consciousness of the last line, when in "Bliss," the avant-garde poet Eddie Warren declaims: "I saw myself *driving* through Eternity in a *timeless* taxi" [p. 343].)

Mansfield's emphasis on the subjectivity of perception extends to other associational patterns in these letters. Travel itself sets off chains of association which foreshadow her later use of these same patterns in fictional narratives. The story "The Voyage" (1921) is prefigured in the following description: "A rough sea journey is a strange conglomeration of sensations—I, in a moment, seem caught in a web of a thousand memories—am a child again, sitting on the deck in my Grandmother's lap, & me in a red riding hood cloak! And then going over to Picton & Nelson, to England for the first time and the second time" (*Letters* I, pp. 78–79). Mansfield's late style emerges at moments in these letters. One passage might have come straight out of "The Man without a Temperament" (1920)— that bitter story about a dying woman and her withdrawn, reluctant husband—except that in the letter emotion has not yet been tarnished by disillusionment:

> Indeed it is easy to realise what Paris means—And she is a city for – – – – you & I. The picturesque aspect of it all—the people—and at night from the top of a tram—the lighted interiors of the houses—you know the effect—people gathered round a lamp lighted table—a little, homely café—a laundry—a china shop—or at the corners the old chestnut sellers—the Italians selling statuettes of the Venus de Milo— & Napoléon encore Napoléon. I picture us with perhaps two small rooms high in the Quartier Latin—setting out at night—arm in arm— and seeing it all and because we were together—a thousand times more. I picture us coming home at night—and sitting over a wood fire—coffee and cigarets—the shutters closed—the lamp on the open table—like the sun on a green world—& *you* & *I*—the world shut out—and yet the world in our power—I love you too much to dare to fully realise all this— (*Letters* I, pp. 77–78)

In these early letters the future is continually being constructed through visual projection. The imagination seems cinematic, the possibilities open as far as she is capable of envisioning them. This same power later reverses itself into retrospection. In "The Man without a Temperament," Mansfield interjects fragmentary memories of happy moments in the past, such as the following quotation, into the sour reality of the couple's present situation, in which the husband withdraws emotionally from his dying wife:

> Just home in time for a bath and change before supper.... In the drawingroom; Jinnie is sitting pretty nearly in the fire. "Oh, Robert, I didn't hear you come in. Did you have a good time? How nice you smell! A present?" "Some bits of blackberry I picked for you. Pretty colour." "Oh, lovely, Robert! Dennis and Beaty are coming to supper." Supper—cold beef, potatoes in their jackets, claret, household bread. They are gay—everybody's laughing. "Oh, we all know Robert," says Dennis, breathing on his eye-glasses and polishing them. "By the way, Dennis, I picked up a very jolly little edition of..." (P. 420)

Mansfield's technical precocity is evident in a number of her apprentice efforts, "Summer Idylle," "Juliet," and "The Tiredness of Rosabel" among them. It is less apparent in the *German Pension* stories, but even there one can find her trying out a sophisticated type of ironic juxtaposition which foreshadows the use of similar techniques in the later works of the modernists, most noticeably in Eliot's *The Waste Land*. In "Frau Fischer" (1910), Mansfield's unnamed narrator says:

> I was reading the "Miracles of Lourdes," which a Catholic priest—fixing a gloomy eye upon my soul—had begged me to digest; but its wonders were completely routed by Frau Fischer's arrival. Not even the white roses upon the feet of the Virgin could flourish in that atmosphere.
>
> "... It was a simple shepherd-child who pastured her flocks upon the barren fields. . . ."
>
> Voices from the room above: "The washstand has, of course, been scrubbed over with soda."
>
> "...Poverty-stricken, her limbs with tattered rags half covered..."
>
> "Every stick of the furniture has been sunning in the garden for three days. And the carpet we made ourselves out of old clothes. There is a piece of that beautiful flannel petticoat you left us last summer."

"Deaf and dumb was the child; in fact, th'e population considered her half idiot..."

"Yes that is a new picture of the Kaiser. We have moved the thorn-crowned one of Jesus Christ out into the passage. It was not cheerful to sleep with. Dear Frau Fischer, won't you take your coffee out in the garden?"

"That is a very nice idea. But first I must remove my corsets and my boots. Ah, what a relief to wear sandals again. I am needing the 'cure' very badly this year. My nerves! I am a mass of them. During the entire journey I sat with my handkerchief over my head, even while the guard collected the tickets. Exhausted!" (P. 51)

This jumble of associations contains, in miniature, in a totally casual, unpretentious manner, many of the devices and themes of modernist discourse. Mansfield juxtaposes the emotionally wrought prose of the book about Lourdes (the narrator is simultaneously appalled by its sentimental, stereotypical phrases and aware of its reference to serious, spiritual matters) with the mundane, superficial conversation filtering down from the room upstairs. That conversation reflects the general emptiness and malaise of Europeans before the war. There is the replacement of Jesus by the Kaiser (religion and politics become as trivial as decoration: "It was not cheerful to sleep with"). There is the abiding neurasthenia: "I am needing the 'cure' very badly this year. My nerves!" And the narrator herself is scornful, distanced, and emotionally cool.

As Mansfield entered the last phase of her writing career, she recognized that she needed to situate herself in relation to the other writers who were achieving prominence within a modernist movement that was in itself reaching its apex. (The last year of her life coincided with the publication of *Ulysses* and *The Waste Land*.) This last phase was deeply marked by the war and its aftermath and by her sense of urgency and personal and collective crisis.

Although Mansfield's awareness was sharpened by the horrors of the war and by her own personal situation—her failing marriage, her worsening illness, her knowledge of impending death—her letters and journal reflect also a preoccupation with both distinguishing herself from other modernists and defining her own methodology, as in the following letter in July 1919 to Lady Ottoline Morrell:

I am infinitely grateful to you for these chapters of Ulysses. Heaven send the drain that will soon receive them. I think they are loathsome

& if that is Art—never shall I drink to it again. But it IS not Art; it is not even a new thing. Why these young men should lean and lean over the decomposing vapours of poor Jules Laforgue is inexplicable—but there they do. In Joyce there is a peculiar *male* arrogance that revolts me more than I can say—it sickens me. I dislike his method equally with his mind & *cannot* see his power of writing. Power? That beautiful quality that makes one feel a man is at ease among all these difficult and simple & intricate and moving words—and knows their perfect place and meaning—but Joyce gapes before an immensely great rubbish heap & digs in it for his swollen dogs & ---No, I can't mention the stuff. Then I glanced at that unspeakable Ezra Pound and the rest of em—

It only makes one feel how one adores English prose—how to be a writer—is *everything*. I *do* believe that the time has come for a "new word" but I imagine the new word will not be spoken easily. People have never explored the lovely medium of prose. It is a hidden country still—I feel that so profoundly.[2]

Mansfield's opposition of "peculiar *male* arrogance" to the "hidden country" "never explored" of "the lovely medium of prose" suggests a masculine/feminine dichotomy. "Prose" in this sense is linked through metaphorical association with the feminine. Language—as it is still constituted—has no terminology to express what she is straining toward. There is yet no "new word." By implication, evident only through tone, Mansfield suggests that she and Lady Ottoline share some kind of subtle understanding of this "hidden country," and this understanding marks their difference from "these young men." (A similar assumption marks Mansfield's comment to Woolf the next year about Eliot's poems being "unspeakably dreary," and there she enlarges her complaint to include "these dark young men—so proud of their plumes and their black and silver cloaks" [*Letters* II, p. 318].)

[2]*Letters* II, p. 343. Mansfield's response to Joyce was not always as negative as the letter to Lady Ottoline suggests. Her opinions vacillated between disgust and admiration. For example, see the following letter, written to Sydney Schiff more than two years later: "One word I must say about Joyce. Having re-read the *Portrait* it seems to me on the whole awfully *good*. We are going to buy *Ulysses*. But Joyce is (if only Pound didn't think so too) immensely important. Sometime ago I found something so repellent in his work that it was difficult to read it—It shocks me to come upon words, expressions and so on that I'd shrink from in life. But now it seems to me the *new novel*, the seeking after Truth is so by far and away the most important thing that one must conquer all minor aversions. They are unworthy."

# Conclusion

In a letter to her friend Sydney Schiff on March 12, 1921, Mansfield discusses Lawrence: "When he gets on to the subject of *maleness* I lose all patience. What nonsense it all is—and he must know it is. His style changes he can no longer write. He *begs the question.* I can't forgive him for that—it's a sin."[3] Her annoyance with Lawrence's exaggerated insistence on sexual difference was of long duration.[4] As I mentioned in relation to her process of writing "Prelude" in 1915, her friendship with Lawrence had long been caught up in a dialogue around differences in gender. Her return to the same subject of disagreement five years later is strong evidence of its continuing power. A few months before the letter to Sydney Schiff she had complained to Murry about Lawrence's *The Lost Girl*: "Take the scene where the hero throws her in the kitchen, possesses her, and she returns singing to the washing-up. It's a *disgrace.*"[5] She soon follows up her complaint with: "Oh, don't forget where Alvina feels '*a trill in her bowels*' and discovers herself with child. A TRILL—what does that mean? And why is it so peculiarly offensive from a man? Because it is *not on this plane* that the emotions of others are conveyed to our imagination. It's a kind of sinning against art."[6]

Mansfield's impatience with Lawrencian sexual politics must have intensified during the last stage of her writing career, as these letters give evidence. Just two months after her letter to Sydney Schiff, she had begun writing "At the Bay," a story completed by September

---

This and several other letters referring to Joyce are quoted by Clare Hanson in *The Critical Writings of Katherine Mansfield*, pp. 123–25.

[3]"Forty-Six Letters by Katherine Mansfield," *Adam International Review*, no. 300 (1965), p. 112.

[4]In a letter to Beatrice Campbell in May 1916, Mansfield had complained about Lawrence's sexual obsessiveness: "And I shall *never* see sex in trees, sex in the running brooks, sex in stones & sex in everything. The number of things that are really phallic from fountain pen fillers onwards! But I shall have my revenge one of these days—I suggested to Lawrence that he should call his cottage The Phallus & Frieda thought it was a very good idea" (*Letters* I, pp. 261–62). It is not hard to imagine her reaction to Lawrence's advice to her in a letter of November 1918: "I do think a woman must yield some sort of precedence to a man, and he must take this precedence. I do think men must go ahead absolutely in front of their women, without turning round to ask for permission or approval from their women. Consequently the women must follow as it were unquestioningly. I can't help it, I believe this. Frieda doesn't. Hence our fight." *The Collected Letters of D. H. Lawrence*, ed. Harry Moore (New York: Viking, 1962), p. 565.

[5]*Letters to John Middleton Murry*, p. 620.

[6]Ibid., p. 621.

10, 1921. Antony Alpers notes a reemergence of concern about Lawrence during that same period. Murry had received *Women in Love* for review at the end of July, and undoubtedly both Murry and Mansfield must have read it shortly afterward. Since it was surely clear to both of them that Lawrence had patterned Gerald and Gudran after themselves as a critique of their own relationship, their response to his novel must have been defensive, to say the least.[7] Alpers attributes Mansfield's focus on "family love" in "At the Bay" to her reaction to Lawrence's fevered sexual passion in *Women in Love*. She recognized the power of Lawrence's writing, however, even though she disagreed with his constant fixation. As she wrote to Dorothy Brett on August 29, 1921: "What makes Lawrence a *real* writer is his passion. Without passion one writes in the air or on the sand of the seashore. But L. has got it all wrong, I believe. He is right, I imagine or how shall I put it...? Its my belief too, that nothing will save the world but Love. But his tortured, satanic demon lover I think is all wrong."[8]

Nearly a year later, Mansfield described Lawrence to Koteliansky as "the only writer living whom I really profoundly care for." She could say that in spite of her disagreements with him, in spite of her disgust for many of his opinions. His uniqueness for her was his desperate vitality, his awed absorption in the smallest details of natural life:

> When he mentions gooseberries these are real red, ripe gooseberries that the gardener is rolling on a tray. When he bites into an apple it is a sharp, sweet, fresh apple from the growing tree. Why has one this longing that people shall be rooted in life? Nearly all people swing in with the tide and out with the tide again like a heavy seaweed. And they seem to take a kind of pride in denying life. But why? I cannot understand.[9]

Despite her violent disagreements with Lawrence, she did not consider him one of the "dark young men" who epitomized the male modernists for her: Eliot, Joyce, Pound, Wyndham Lewis. Lawrence's "passion" was worlds apart from Eliot's diffidence. She

[7]See Alpers, *Life,* pp. 339–41.
[8]*Selected Letters*, p. 222.
[9]*Letters of Katherine Mansfield*, pp. 477–78.

could never say of Lawrence as she had of Eliot (in the letter quoted earlier to Woolf): "How one could write so absolutely without emotion—perhaps thats an achievement" (*Letters* II, p. 318). The exclusion of Lawrence from such a canon results from her recognition of his status as outsider, as outlaw, as a man of feeling. Yet his difference from the other modernists made her even more impatient with his more blatantly sexual form of "male arrogance."[10]

Mansfield's later fiction continues to reflect her concern with gender differences and the ways they reproduce familiar patterns of isolation and self-enclosure in heterosexual relationships. Kate Fullbrook has noted that in Mansfield's late fiction her "analysis of gender remains the central instance of her presentation of corruption."[11] This later fiction is much more focused on the psychological—even metaphysical—differences than was her early work, which depicted physical violence and overtly sexual power struggles, such as an attempted rape by a stranger in "The Swing of the Pendulum" (1911), the uncovering of the murder of an abusive husband in "The Woman at the Store" (1912), and the lecherous seduction attempt by the old man in "The Little Governess" (1915). In the later stories difference is conveyed through momentary insights, gestures, clusters of metaphorical associations, sentence rhythms. The dominance of the tyrannical father in "The Daughters of the Late Colonel" (1921) is conveyed by the fear expressed by his now-middle-aged daughters, Josephine and Constantia, after arranging for his funeral, that they "had done this thing without asking his permission" (p. 469). Within the consciousness of Josephine remains the sound of "his stick thumping." In "The Stranger" (1921), the quality of a man's possessive love for his wife

---

[10]The subject of Mansfield and Lawrence's relationship and its literary consequences is a large and important one that I only touch upon here. One of the most enlightening studies of this relationship which I have read is that of Lydia Blanchard, "The Savage Pilgrimage of D. H. Lawrence and Katherine Mansfield: A Study in Literary Influence, Anxiety, and Subversion," *Modern Language Quarterly* 47 (March 1986), 48–65. Applying a Bloomian analysis to this relationship, Blanchard finds that "Lawrence's revision of Mansfield followed a pattern—one of correction and antithesis—that was significantly different from that of Mansfield's revision of him, which was a response less to Lawrence's reading of her fiction than to his reading of *her*. While Lawrence directly challenged Mansfield, taking her stories and altering them, Mansfield undercut Lawrence's message by subverting his ideas and plots" (p. 49).

[11]Fullbrook, *Katherine Mansfield*, p. 88.

is conveyed by his jealousy over her wish to read letters from her children: "And now those letters from the children rustled in her blouse. He could have chucked them into the fire" (p. 455).

Mansfield's late, great story about the Burnell family, "At the Bay" (1921), usually appears after "Prelude" in collected editions of the fiction, mainly because Murry decided it should be linked this way even if he had to break Mansfield's chronology of composition to do so. Although Mansfield indicated in her journal that she was planning a novel, *Karori* (*Journal*, p. 262), and Murry in an editorial note on the same page remarked that "Prelude" and "At the Bay" were "to have formed parts" of this novel, we shall never know whether she really would have gathered these and other New Zealand stories and shaped them to form a novel, perhaps of the type of Sherwood Anderson's *Winesburg, Ohio* or other collections that aspire to a novelistic coherence. Or, whether she might have used the stories as material for a novel of a new kind, as Woolf did later with *Mrs. Dalloway*, incorporating earlier short stories into a seamless whole.[12]

Clare Hanson and Andrew Gurr see "At the Bay" as "concerned with acceptance of the cycles of life and death, in contrast with the earlier *Prelude* where the dominant theme is one of discovery and opening out."[13] But it is still possible to discern the maintenance of gender roles as a subtext of "At the Bay," even if it may not seem the predominant theme of the story as a whole. The evidence for that subtext is in Stanley's assertion of "masculine" behavior in contrast to Jonathan Trout's deviance from the conventional role; in the Burnell women's sense of relief and relaxation when Stanley goes off to work; in Beryl's growing recognition of her entrapment as an unmarried, dependent woman in her brother-in-law's home; and in Linda Burnell's reversal of feeling for her little son.

In contrast to the anger that marks Linda Burnell's realization of "her real grudge against life," the societal dictum that "it was the

---

[12]*Undiscovered Country*, Ian Gordon's collection of Mansfield's complete oeuvre of New Zealand stories and sketches, is one attempt to put this large body of work into perspective. But since he includes anything she wrote which was set in New Zealand—much of that material being quite diverse: "The Woman at the Store," "Milly," and so on—it cannot convey what a novel about the Burnells might have turned out to be like.

[13]Hanson and Gurr, *Katherine Mansfield*, p. 100.

common lot of women to bear children" (p. 279), is the calmness that accompanies that reversal of feeling. When she looks at this infant—after she says to herself "I don't like babies"—the boy seems to her to be rejecting her negativity: "'Don't like *me*?' . . . He didn't believe a word she said" (p. 280). Consequently, "Linda was so astonished at the confidence of this little creature" (p. 280) that her resistance is overcome. Her belief in the ultimate power of transcendence of the male gives this boy-child the love she had denied to her girl-children. (In Freudian terms, it is the woman's final acceptance of her "feminine" role, her resolution of her "penis envy" by having a son of her own.) It is, however, important to notice that Mansfield recognizes that the confidence Linda perceives in her infant son is not really in the infant himself (after all, the same behavior must have been displayed by her infant daughters at one time) but in Linda's projection of it to him. Thus, the confidence she sees in him will free this infant to grow up undivided, not infected by the self-hate that the girls absorb through their mother's rejection. It is this difficult knowledge that Mansfield, the daughter of such a mother, conveys obliquely through this story. For after all, as we know, this same male infant will grow up adored—by the sisters he outshone in his mother's affections, by the mother who did not love her children, by the father who alternately demanded obedience and affection—yet he will be the one to die just at the point of adulthood.

As the letters to Garnet Trowell prefigure Mansfield's modernism, so "At the Bay" demonstrates its most sophisticated development. Its origins are only recoverable through its many levels of influence and obsession. For they all seem to be there: Mansfield's interest in gender differentiation, her dissection of the family structure and its inherent conflicts, her Freudian/Lawrencian interpretation of the oedipal romance, as well as her predilections for psychologically associative symbolic patterns, narrative disjunction, free indirect style, and cinematic spatial structuring. The story's richness of imagery, its moods and indeterminacies, its attention to transience and the illuminating moment are vestiges of Paterian aestheticism, shorn of their late-Victorian diction.[14]

[14]A regular critical industry seems to have grown up around the analysis of symbolic images in Mansfield's later work. The meanings of the little lamp in "The

Even Wilde survives in the intrusions of Mr. and Mrs. Harry
Kember. Mrs. Kember, who behaves seductively with Beryl, prais-
ing her beauty and encouraging her to have "a good time," insinu-
ates into the story the secret Wilde embodied for Mansfield. Although Beryl feels "she was being poisoned by this cold woman,"
she seems drawn to the woman's call to experience. When Harry
Kember appears in her garden later that evening and tries to seduce
her, Beryl is again both drawn and revulsed. While Harry is "so
incredibly handsome that he looked like a mask," his wife is
"parched, withered, cold," a woman who could never get enough
of the sun. Yet when Beryl watches Mrs. Kember swim out and
back, "she looked, in her black waterproof bathing-cap with her
sleepy face lifted above the water, just her chin touching, like a
horrible caricature of her husband" (p. 277). The Kembers, in their
roles as doubles, ironically seem to hark back to *The Picture of Dorian
Gray*; in this case, Mrs. Kember seems to be the picture on which
the sins of her husband are inscribed:

> Harry Kember was like a man walking in his sleep. . . . Of course
> there were stories, but such stories! They simply couldn't be told. The
> women he'd been seen with, the places he'd been seen in... but noth-
> ing was ever certain, nothing definite. Some of the women at the Bay
> privately thought he'd commit a murder one day. Yes, even while
> they talked to Mrs. Kember and took in the awful concoction she was
> wearing, they saw her, stretched as she lay on the beach; but cold,
> bloody, and still with a cigarette stuck in the corner of her mouth. (P.
> 276)

The implications of lesbianism in "At the Bay" have long since lost
their earlier associations with beauty and adventure, as in "Summer

---

Doll's House," the destruction of the fly in the inkwell by the "Boss" in "The Fly,"
the aloe in "Prelude," the pear tree in "Bliss" have all been the subject of innumerable critical studies. "At the Bay," in particular, has lent itself to studies of symbolism. Critics have considered its complex patterns of light and dark, ocean and land,
feminine and masculine. See Hankin, *Katherine Mansfield and Her Confessional Stories,*
pp. 222–34, for a particularly detailed and evocative study of such patterns. Recent
critics, such as Hankin, Hanson and Gurr (pp. 99–106), and Fullbrook (pp. 106–
14), give considerable attention to the significance of gender differences in Mansfield's use of symbols; earlier critics were more apt to concentrate on images related
to time and cycles of life and death (for example, see Berkman, *Katherine Mansfield:
A Critical Study,* pp. 168–69).

Idylle," where the plunge into the sea is both feared and desired, in which the sea suggests an erotic potentiality. It is noteworthy then that Beryl does *not* plunge; "the waves just reached her breast." Rather, "Beryl stood, her arms outstretched, gazing out, and as each wave came she gave the slightest little jump, so that it seemed it was the wave which lifted her so gently" (p. 277). And, although Mrs. Harry Kember swims quickly, "like a rat," her face remains "lifted above the water."

Instead of experimentation, Mansfield's late fiction gives a sense of consolidation. Instead of a self-conscious performance of modernistic technique, it reveals now a sureness of gesture and an absorption into the lives of her characters which confirm a statement she had made in a letter to Sydney and Violet Schiff on May 2, 1920: "Delicate perception is not enough; one must find the exact way in which to convey the delicate perception. One must inhabit the other mind and know more of the other mind and your secret knowledge is the light in which all is steeped."[15]

Mansfield's reference to "secret knowledge" is yet another example of her insistence on ineffability as a necessary component of the modernist aesthetic gesture. If "secret knowledge" is added to her description of "a hidden country" in the letter to Ottoline Morrell, cited above, it tends to suggest an implicitly female discourse as well. If we consider modernism as Katherine Mansfield tried to shape it, we find a modernism stripped of its tendency toward objectification, stripped of either its apotheosis or its debasing of the feminine. It is a modernism full of doubts, questionings, and terrors, but it is also a modernism that leaps beyond both the despair of the "waste land" and the hierarchical, traditional escapes from it posed by many of her male contemporaries. Instead, Mansfield refuses systems or rituals. She remains infused in the paradox expressed in "At the Bay" (p. 293) by Linda Burnell's brother-in-law, Jonathan Trout (the anti-archetypal male): "The shortness of life! I've only one night or one day, and there's this vast dangerous garden, waiting out there, undiscovered, unexplored."

[15]*Letters of Katherine Mansfield*, p. 312.

# Selected Bibliography

Alpers, Antony. *Katherine Mansfield: A Biography*. New York: Knopf, 1954.
——. *The Life of Katherine Mansfield*. New York: Viking, 1980.
Baldeshwiller, Eileen. "Katherine Mansfield's Theory of Fiction." *Studies in Short Fiction* 7 (Summer 1970), 421–32.
Beauchamp, Sir Harold. *Reminiscences and Recollections*. New Plymouth, N.Z.: Thomas Avery & Sons, 1937.
Beauchamp, Kathleen. "The Pine-tree, the Sparrows, and You and I," *The Queen's College Magazine* 22 (December 1903), 74–76.
Benstock, Shari. *Women of the Left Bank: Paris, 1900–1940*. Austin: University of Texas Press, 1986.
Berkman, Sylvia. *Katherine Mansfield: A Critical Study*. New Haven: Yale University Press, 1951.
Blanchard, Lydia. "The Savage Pilgrimage of D. H. Lawrence and Katherine Mansfield: A Study in Literary Influence, Anxiety, and Subversion." *Modern Language Quarterly* 47 (March 1986), 48–65.
Bradbury, Malcolm, and James McFarlane, eds., *Modernism: 1890–1930*. New York: Penguin, 1976.
Brett, The Hon. Dorothy, and John Manchester. "Reminiscences of Katherine." *Adam International Review* 38, nos. 370–75 (1972–73), 84–92.
Brophy, Brigid. *Don't Never Forget*. London: Jonathan Cape, 1966.
Burgan, Mary. "Childbirth Trauma in Katherine Mansfield's Early Stories." *Modern Fiction Studies* 24 (Autumn 1978), 395–412.
Carswell, John. *Lives and Letters: A. R. Orage, Katherine Mansfield, Beatrice Hastings, John Middleton Murry, S. S. Koteliansky, 1906–1957*. New York: New Directions, 1978.
Cather, Willa. "Katherine Mansfield." *Not under Forty*. New York: Knopf, 1936. Pp. 123–47.
Daly, Saralyn R. *Katherine Mansfield*. New York: Twayne, 1965.

# Selected Bibliography

DeSalvo, Louise A. "Katherine Mansfield and Virginia Woolf's Revisions of *The Voyage Out*." *Virginia Woolf Miscellany* 11 (Fall 1978), 5–6.

DuPlessis, Rachel Blau. *Writing beyond the Ending: Narrative Strategies of Twentieth-Century Women Writers*. Bloomington: Indiana University Press, 1985.

Eliot, T. S. *After Strange Gods*. New York: Harcourt, Brace, 1934.

Else, Anne. "From Little Monkey to Neurotic Invalid: Limitation, Selection, and Assumption in Antony Alpers' *Life of Katherine Mansfield*." *Women's Studies International Forum* 8, no. 5 (1985), 497–505.

Eustace, Cecil Johnson. *An Infinity of Questions: A Study of the Religion of Art, and of the Art of Religion in the Lives of Five Women*. Freeport, N.Y.: Books for Libraries Press, 1969 [repr. from 1946 ed.].

Fullbrook, Kate. *Katherine Mansfield*. Bloomington: Indiana University Press, 1986.

Garlington, Jack. "Katherine Mansfield: The Critical Trend." *Twentieth Century Literature* 2 (July 1956), 51–62.

Gilbert, Sandra M., and Susan Gubar. *No Man's Land: The Place of the Woman Writer in the Twentieth Century. Vol. I: The War of the Words. Vol. II: Sexchanges*. New Haven: Yale University Press, 1988, 1989.

Glenavy, Beatrice Campbell, Lady. *Today We Will Only Gossip*. London: Constable, 1964.

Gordon, Ian A. *Katherine Mansfield*. British Writers and Their Work no. 3. Lincoln: University of Nebraska Press, 1964.

Gubar, Susan. "The Birth of the Artist as Heroine: (Re)production, the *Künstlerroman* Tradition, and the Fiction of Katherine Mansfield." In *The Representation of Women in Fiction*. Selected Papers from the English Institute, 1981, new series, no. 7. Ed. Carolyn G. Heilbrun and Margaret R. Higonnet. Baltimore: Johns Hopkins University Press, 1983. Pp. 19–59.

Gurr, Andrew. *Writers in Exile: The Identity of Home in Modern Literature*. Atlantic Highlands, N.J.: Humanities Press, 1981.

Hankin, C. A. *Katherine Mansfield and Her Confessional Stories*. London: Macmillan, 1983.

Hankin, Cherry. "Fantasy and the Sense of an Ending in the Work of Katherine Mansfield." *Modern Fiction Studies* 24 (Autumn 1978), 465–74.

Hanson, Clare. *Short Stories and Short Fictions, 1880–1980*. London: Macmillan, 1985.

Hanson, Clare, and Andrew Gurr. *Katherine Mansfield*. London: Macmillan, 1981.

Humanities Research Center. *Katherine Mansfield: An Exhibition*. Austin: University of Texas Press, 1973.

Justus, James H. "Katherine Mansfield: The Triumph of Egoism." *Mosaic* 6 (1973), 13–22.

Kirkpatrick, B. J. *A Bibliography of Katherine Mansfield*. Oxford: Clarendon, 1989.

# Selected Bibliography

Lea, F. A. *The Life of John Middleton Murry*. London: Methuen, 1959.

Levenson, Michael. *A Genealogy of Modernism: A Study of English Literary Doctrine 1908–1922*. Cambridge: Cambridge University Press, 1984.

"L.M." (Ida Constance Baker). *Katherine Mansfield: The Memories of L.M.* New York: Taplinger, 1972.

McLaughlin, Ann L. "The Same Job: Notes on the Relationship between Virginia Woolf and Katherine Mansfield." *Virginia Woolf Miscellany* 9 (Winter 1977), 11–12.

———. "The Same Job: The Shared Writing Aims of Katherine Mansfield and Virginia Woolf." *Modern Fiction Studies* 24 (Autumn 1978), 369–82.

Magalaner, Marvin. *The Fiction of Katherine Mansfield*. Carbondale: Southern Illinois University Press, 1971.

Mansfield, Katherine. *The Aloe*. Ed. J. Middleton Murry. New York: Knopf, 1930.

———. *The Aloe: With Prelude*. Ed. Vincent O'Sullivan. Wellington, N.Z.: Port Nicolson, 1982.

———. *The Collected Letters of Katherine Mansfield*. Vols. I–II. Ed. Vincent O'Sullivan and Margaret Scott. Oxford: Clarendon, 1984, 1987.

———. *The Critical Writings of Katherine Mansfield*. Ed. Clare Hanson. New York: St. Martin's, 1987.

———. "Fifteen Letters from Katherine Mansfield to Virginia Woolf." *Adam International Review* nos. 370–75 (1972–73), 19–24.

———. "Forty-Six Letters by Katherine Mansfield." *Adam International Review* no. 300 (1965), 88–118.

———. *Journal of Katherine Mansfield*. Ed. John Middleton Murry. London: Constable, 1954.

———. "Katherine Mansfield and S. S. Koteliansky: Some Unpublished Letters." Ed. John W. Dickinson. *Revue de Litterature Comparée* 45 (January–March 1971), 79–99.

———. *Katherine Mansfield's Letters to John Middleton Murry 1913–1922*. Ed. J. Middleton Murry. New York: Knopf, 1951.

———. *The Letters of Katherine Mansfield*. Ed. John Middleton Murry. New York: Knopf, 1929.

———. *Novels and Novelists*. New York: Knopf, 1930.

———. *Poems of Katherine Mansfield*. Ed. Vincent O'Sullivan. Auckland, N.Z.: Oxford University Press, 1988.

———. *The Scrapbook of Katherine Mansfield*. Ed. John Middleton Murry. New York: Knopf, 1940.

———. *Selected Letters*. Ed. Vincent O'Sullivan. Oxford: Clarendon, 1989.

———. *The Short Stories of Katherine Mansfield*. New York: Knopf, 1937.

———. "The Unpublished Manuscripts of Katherine Mansfield." Transcribed and edited by Margaret Scott. *The Turnbull Library Record* (n.s.): 3 (March 1970), 4–28; 3 (November 1970), 128–33; 4 (May 1971), 4–20; 5 (May 1972), 19–25; 6 (October 1973), 4–8; 6 (May 1974), 4–14; 12 (May 1979), 11–28.

# Selected Bibliography

——. *The Urewera Notebook*. Edited with an Introduction by Ian A. Gordon. New York: Oxford University Press, 1978.

Mantz, Ruth Elvish. *The Critical Bibliography of Katherine Mansfield*. New York: Roy Lang & Richard Smith, 1931.

Mantz, Ruth Elvish, and J. Middleton Murry. *The Life of Katherine Mansfield*. London: Constable, 1933.

Martin, Wallace. *Recent Theories of Narrative*. Ithaca: Cornell University Press, 1986.

Maurois, André. *Prophets and Poets*. Trans. Hamish Miles. New York: Harper & Bros., 1935.

Meyers, Jeffrey. *Katherine Mansfield: A Biography*. New York: New Directions, 1978.

——. "Murry's Cult of Mansfield." *Journal of Modern Literature* 7 (February 1979), 15–38.

Moore, James. *Gurdjieff and Mansfield*. London: Routledge & Kegan Paul, 1980.

Mortelier, Christiane. "The Genesis and Development of the Katherine Mansfield Legend in France." *Journal of the Australasian Universities Language and Literature Association* 34 (November 1970), 252–63.

Murry, John Middleton. *Aspects of Literature*. New York: Knopf, 1920.

——. *Between Two Worlds: The Autobiography of John Middleton Murry*. New York: Julian Messner, 1936.

——. *The Letters of John Middleton Murry to Katherine Mansfield*. Ed. C. A. Hankin. London: Constable, 1983.

Nathan, Rhoda B. *Katherine Mansfield*. New York: Continuum, 1988.

Nebeker, Helen E. "The Pear Tree: Sexual Implications in K.M.'s 'Bliss.'" *Modern Fiction Studies* 18 (Winter 1972–73), 545–51.

O'Connor, Frank. "An Author in Search of a Subject." *The Lonely Voice: A Study of the Short Story*. Cleveland: World, 1963. Pp. 128–42.

Orage, A. R. "Talks with Katherine Mansfield." *Selected Essays and Critical Writings*. London: Stanley Nott, 1935. Pp. 125–32.

O'Sullivan, Vincent. "The Magnetic Chain: Notes and Approaches to K.M." *Landfall* 114 (June 1975), 95–131.

Porter, Katherine Anne. "The Art of Katherine Mansfield" (1937). In *The Days Before*. New York: Harcourt, Brace, 1952. Pp. 82–87.

Pritchett, V. S. "Katherine Mansfield." *The New Yorker,* October 26, 1981, pp. 196–200.

Rawlings, Marjorie Kinnan. "Introduction." In Katherine Mansfield, *Stories: A Selection Made by J. Middleton Murry*. Cleveland: World, 1946.

Rice, Anne Estelle. "Memories of Katherine Mansfield." *Adam International Review* no. 300 (1965), pp. 76–85.

Scholefield, Guy H. "Katherine Mansfield." In Sir Harold Beauchamp, *Reminiscences and Recollections*. New Plymouth, New Zealand: Thomas Avery & Sons, 1937.

# Selected Bibliography

Showalter, Elaine. *A Literature of Their Own: British Women Novelists from Brontë to Lessing*. Princeton: Princeton University Press, 1977.

Stead, C. K., ed. *The Letters and Journals of Katherine Mansfield*. London: Penguin, 1977.

Tomalin, Claire. *Katherine Mansfield: A Secret Life*. New York: Knopf, 1988.

Waldron, Philip. "Katherine Mansfield's *Journal*." *Twentieth Century Literature* 20 (January 1974), 11–18.

Wilde, Oscar. *The Picture of Dorian Gray*. Ed. Isobel Murray. London: Oxford University Press, 1974.

Woolf, Virginia. *The Common Reader, First Series*. New York: Harcourt, Brace & World, 1925.

——. *Contemporary Writers*. New York: Harcourt Brace Jovanovich, 1965.

——. *The Diary of Virginia Woolf, Vols. I–III*. Ed. Anne Olivier Bell. New York: Harcourt Brace Jovanovich, 1977, 1978, 1980.

——. *The Letters of Virginia Woolf. Vol. II*. Ed. Nigel Nicolson and Joanne Trautmann. New York: Harcourt Brace Jovanovich, 1976.

——. *Mrs. Dalloway*. New York: Harcourt, Brace & World, 1925.

# Index

# Index

# Index

# Index

# Index

Martin, Wallace, 12, 93n19, 142n28
Mask, theory of, 175
Masochism, 40, 206
Maternal role, 113–17, 135, 139, 157
Maurois, André, 159
Meisel, Perry, 60–61, 179
Meyers, Jeffrey, 4, 21n4, 46n17, 125–26, 195n10
"Milly," 122n5, 216n12
"Miss Brill," 75, 123, 188–89, 192
Modernism, 1–3, 6–9, 38, 47, 190, 219
  critique of, 138–39, 183–87, 211–12
  and impersonality, 178–81
  and the "waste land," 75, 79, 190–91, 208, 210–11, 219
  see also Eliot, T. S.: The Waste Land;
    Women: and modernism
Modernist fiction, 1, 17
Modernist sentence, 186
"Modern Soul, The," 138
Monroe, Jonathan, 47–48
Morrell, Lady Ottoline, 34, 75, 76n12, 77, 141, 146, 153n15
  Mansfield's letters to, 191, 211–12
Mortelier, Christiane, 3n6
Multiplicity, 30, 37, 39, 169–70, 177–79, 183, 188
Murry, Isobel, 23n10, 30n25
Murry, John Middleton, 13, 79n20, 109–10, 180, 192, 195–96, 214
  depiction of Mansfield, 3–4, 104, 195
  editing of Mansfield's work, 3, 27n22, 103n1, 171–72, 177n15, 216
  editorship of journals, 13, 97, 99, 109, 161, 204
  friendship with D. H. Lawrence, 13, 43, 97, 106n7, 112
  Mansfield's letters to, quoted, 33–34, 77n17, 78, 84, 97, 108, 143–44, 150n14, 175, 190–91, 213
  relationship with Mansfield, 2n2, 3–5, 13, 33, 43, 79, 97, 104–7, 157, 193–94
  Woolf's opinion of, 143n31, 145
Murry, Richard, 35n31, 203–4

Narrative conventions, 82–87, 92, 98–102, 118, 163–64
Natural, the, 55–58, 65–67, 70, 135. See also Artificial
Nature, 55, 61, 66, 91–92, 170, 172
New Age, The, 5, 10, 12, 75, 100n25, 128, 136, 140–43
New Critics, 3

"New Dresses," 106
New Zealand, 4–5, 13–14, 71, 76, 89, 96, 104, 149
  Mansfield's writing about, 53, 57, 80–81, 102, 110, 216
Nietzsche, Friedrich, 132, 142
Novel, 83–87, 97, 100–103, 149, 216
Novels and Novelists, 150–51, 162–63, 165, 175, 205

O'Connor, Frank, 189n2
Orage, A. R., 12, 140–43
Organicism, 167, 178, 180–81
Orton, William, 27n22
Ostriker, Alicia, 201n25
O'Sullivan, Vincent, 19–20, 33, 40–41, 53n2, 67n1, 76n12, 82n1, 103n1, 109, 112

Pater, Walter, 8, 19, 53–56, 58–62, 64, 85, 153, 179, 207
  "The Child in the House," 53–54, 59, 61–62
  The Renaissance, 54–56, 58, 62, 103
Payne, Sylvia, 130, 140, 176
Pearlman, Daniel, 6n13
Phallocentric criticism, 145, 197–98
Phelps, Gilbert, 192n6, 197–98
"Pictures," 71, 73–75
Plagiarism, accusations of, 199, 202
Poems of Katherine Mansfield, 48, 56–57, 67–68
Poststructuralism, 179–80
Pound, Ezra, 7, 142n28, 143n31, 181, 190–91, 212, 214
Pratt, Annis, 92n18
Pregnancy, 28, 73, 109–10, 129, 206
  in Mansfield's writing, 90, 92, 110, 114–15, 137
  see also Childbearing
"Prelude," 8, 14–15, 102–17, 119–20, 147, 153n16, 167, 192, 202, 213, 216, 218n14
Pritchett, V. S., 20n4
Prose poem, 47–48, 54, 56–57, 67–69, 83–84, 90–91
Prose style, 59–62, 68–69, 90–96, 151–52, 155–57, 207–12
"Psychology," 153–55

Queen's College, 5, 14, 33, 58, 68, 71, 88
  and education of governesses, 123

*231*

# Index

Library of Congress Cataloging-in-Publication Data

Kaplan, Sydney Janet
  Katherine Mansfield and the origins of modernist fiction / Sydney Janet Kaplan.
    p.  cm.
  Includes bibliographical references and index.
  ISBN 0-8014-2328-7 (alk. paper). — 0-8014-9915-1 (pbk. : alk. paper)
   1. Mansfield, Katherine, 1888–1923—Criticism and interpretation.   2. Feminism
and literature—Great Britain—History—20th century.   3. Modernism (Literature)—
Great Britain.   I. Title.
PR9639.3.M258Z73   1991
823'.912—dc20
                                                  90–45880

# DATE DUE